YANIS V

In 2015, Yanis Varoufakis became the world's most prominent opponent of austerity when, as finance minister of Greece, he refused to accept the terms of the loan agreement dictated to his bankrupt country by the eurozone's leaders. Since resigning his post he has become the figurehead of an international grassroots movement, speaking to audiences of thousands across Britain, France, Germany, Portugal, Spain, Ireland, Italy, Singapore and Russia. Born in Athens in 1961, for many years he was a professor of economics in Britain, Australia and the USA before he entered government. He is currently Professor of Economics at the University of Athens. His next two books, *Adults in the Room* and *Talking to My Daughter About the Economy*, are forthcoming from The Bodley Head in 2017.

yanisvaroufakis.eu / @yanisvaroufakis

ALSO BY YANIS VAROUFAKIS

The Global Minotaur

YANIS VAROUFAKIS

And The Weak Suffer What They Must?

Europe, Austerity and the Threat to
Global Stability

VINTAGE

5 7 9 10 8 6 4

Vintage
20 Vauxhall Bridge Road,
London SW1V 2SA

Vintage is part of the Penguin Random House group of companies
whose addresses can be found at global.penguinrandomhouse.com.

Penguin
Random House
UK

First published by Vintage in 2017
First published by The Bodley Head in 2016

penguin.co.uk/vintage

A CIP catalogue record for this book is
available from the British Library

ISBN 9781784704117

Printed and bound by Clays Ltd, St Ives plc

Penguin Random House is committed to a sustainable future
for our business, our readers and our planet. This book is made
from Forest Stewardship Council® certified paper.

MIX
Paper from
responsible sources
FSC
www.fsc.org
FSC® C018179

For my mother, Eleni,
who would have savaged with the greatest elegance
and compassion anyone contemplating the notion
that the weak suffer what they must

CONTENTS

Foreword to the Paperback Edition

Writing a book should be a life-changing experience for its author. This book was no exception: it was as if, halfway through writing it, the subject matter jumped off the page and demanded a real-life response. I soon found myself in the belly of the beast I had been writing about.

I started researching and writing this book in response to a series of questions. Why is the European Union disintegrating (Brexit being the first symptom of its malaise)? Why is Europe so clearly failing to emulate the United States, which also began life as a loose confederacy of fractious states before consolidating magnificently in response to its various existential crises?[1]

While researching these questions my own country, Greece, was already becoming the sacrificial canary in the coal mine. This was an early warning that the European Union was incapable of turning the 2008 financial crisis into a programme of consolidation, opting instead for a self-defeating mixture of authoritarianism and incompetence.

Soon after I finished the book's sixth chapter, which tells the story of how countries like Greece were being marched off the cliff

---

1 The nineteenth-century stock exchange collapses and the 1907 financial disaster led to the establishment of the Federal Reserve. The crash of 1929 and the ensuing 'grapes of wrath' gave Americans the New Deal institutions that serve them well to this day, including social security, the use of US treasuries for public investment projects and the federal deposit insurance scheme. The social tensions of the 1960s, especially the race riots and the civil liberties movement, engendered Lyndon B. Johnson's Great Society policies, which reduced poverty and helped stabilise the United States' social economy after Wall Street's 2008 implosion. In short, despite its many demerits, with every crisis that has come its way the United States has become more united, more cohesive.

propelled by self-defeating austerity policies, accelerating the European Union's fragmentation, all of a sudden duty called. On New Year's Day 2015 I had to stop writing and throw myself into a short election campaign that would see me installed as Greece's finance minister. My book's subject matter had indeed jumped out of my laptop and demanded that I put, so to speak, my money where my mouth was.

During the six months I spent in government I strove to strike a deal that would be mutually beneficial for Greece and the European Union – an agreement that would begin the healing process of a Europe already at an advanced stage of disintegration. Brussels, Berlin and Frankfurt responded with indescribable brutality, as if intent on quickening the break-up of the European Union.

By the summer of 2015 the writing was on the wall: Greece would be locked into a debtor's prison and I, refusing to sign the surrender documents, resigned my ministry. The European Union would again pretend that it had solved a crisis by throwing new debt into the bottomless pit of unpayable older debts. And the peoples of Europe would lose what little confidence they had left in the EU's institutions.

Within weeks of Greece's fresh humiliation, countless refugees were being washed up on our shores, and before long the European Union had disgraced itself by signing a scandalous deal with Turkey which effectively bribed an increasingly authoritarian Turkish president, enabling European governments to violate international law concerning the rights and protection of refugees.

Freed from ministerial duties, I returned to my book convinced that my initial questions had become infinitely more urgent and that I could now bring a wealth of new insights to the subject. The book was completed during the summer of 2015, after the European Union had lost its integrity by crushing Greece and while it was in the process of forfeiting its soul by abrogating its responsibilities to refugees.

When my manuscript was complete, I feared that British readers might find the book too distant from their daily concerns. David Cameron promptly put my mind to rest, however, by scheduling the EU referendum for June 2016. The British media was suddenly abuzz with parallels between Grexit and Brexit. Debates on the merits and future of the European Union were raging. My book had unexpectedly found a mass British audience.

Within weeks I was traversing Britain campaigning against Brexit. Audiences were puzzled: 'How can you, given the way the EU treated you and your country, tell us that we should *remain*?' The confusion was not eased by Michael Gove and other Brexiteers, who heaped praise on my book, mischievously presenting it as the best argument for Britain to *leave* the EU.

The reason I remain convinced that the European Union must be confronted from *within*, rather than through a series of exits, is explained painstakingly in the following pages. Suffice to say that those who think that Brexit will bring about closer links between the UK, the United States and the rest of the world misunderstand the origins of the EU, the role of the US in piecing it together (see Chapters 1–3) and the negative effects the EU's fragmentation is already having on the rest of the world.

My British friends on the Remain side of the referendum campaign seemed vexed by the alleged causes of Brexit, lamenting voters' xenophobia and their fixation with immigration. This book digs deeper in search of the true causes of the EU's structural instability, going back to the mid-1940s, taking in developments in the 1960s, stopping to scrutinise a decisive announcement on 15 August 1971, before examining more recent events.

As the book's narrative approaches the 1990s and beyond, the reader should be able to discern the causes of Brexit, why exits of this kind cannot be the answer to the challenges we face simultaneously in continental Europe and in the UK and how our fates as Europeans are closely intertwined. I also hope to convince the reader that what some of us are attempting in Britain and on the Continent is not totally daft: putting together DiEM25 (the Democracy in Europe Movement), a pan-European political movement that reaches out across borders and political party affiliations in order to stem the slide into a post-modern 1930s.

On a personal note, pressured to define myself, I once came up with the self-characterisation 'erratic Marxist'. Why erratic? Well, in November 2011 I addressed crowds at Occupy Wall Street and a gathering of Wall Street bankers on the very same day. This was not a one-off. More recently, in April 2016, I spoke at the Nuit debout in

Paris, addressing left-wing demonstrators in support of their campaign against the labour market policies of Minister Emmanuel Macron, but also visited Monsieur Macron in his ministry to discuss Europe and the very labour market policies that helped create Nuit debout. And on the political-cum-personal level, I work with comrades-in-arms Caroline Lucas and John McDonnell, but I also think of Norman Lamont as a friend. How is this possible?

The reason it *is* possible is quite startling and indicative of the times we live in: I can say the *same* things to Norman Lamont or to Wall Street bankers that I tell the crowds at Occupy Wall Street or Nuit debout or to friends amongst the Corbynistas or the Greens, and elicit the *same* agreement! This is powerful evidence of the depth of the crisis we are in. When capitalism's crisis deepens, as happened in the 1930s and as is happening again today, people from opposite ends of the political spectrum find common ground.

The prerequisite for this precious common ground is a willingness to look for it and build alliances that confront the monsters that have a habit of crawling out of the fault lines in the crisis: the Le Pens, the Golden Dawns, the AfDs, the BNPs, the UKIPs and indeed the bureaucrats, politicians and opinion-formers that insist on business as usual when it is business as usual that is tearing our societies apart. If one must appear 'erratic' to the more politically correct, so be it. I am prepared to wear the adjective with pride.

What about the left-wing Marxist part of my character and my tendency to appreciate the insights of a political enemy like Margaret Thatcher (see Chapter 4)? At the risk of blaming my sins on my parents, I think there is a clear thread linking my Marxist disposition to the milieu my parents grew up in. My father was born and raised in Cairo within a large Greek community embedded in a mini-version of Europe comprising French, Italian and British expats, alongside cosmopolitan Jews, Armenians and Arabs. French was spoken at home, courtesy of my French-educated grandmother, Greek at his school, English at work, Arabic on the street and Italian at his sports club.

At the age of twenty my father left Egypt to study chemistry at the University of Athens. It was 1946 and the first Greek civil war had just subsided, with the Left and the Right attempting a form of détente.

He arrived during this lull and, as an outsider acceptable to all political factions, was invited to take on the leadership of the students' union. Soon after, as the civil war clouds gathered again, he was arrested by the secret police for appealing to the university's authorities against an increase in fees at a time when students were increasingly impoverished and malnourished. And so a young man raised on a diet of Voltaire, Rousseau and Montesquieu ended up in a prison camp for communists. Refusing to sign a denunciation of communism on the grounds that it was no business of the state to persecute individuals for their private beliefs, he was interned for three years on barren islands. Surrounded by barbed wire and armed guards, he read physics from a book smuggled into the camp, made friends with left-wing intellectuals and, naturally, joined the communist party.

Meanwhile my mother, whom my father had not yet met, was abducted at the age of sixteen by left-wing partisans who mistook her for a Nazi collaborator's daughter. Her loathing of communists was thus established at an early age. When she subsequently enrolled at the University of Athens, a fascist organisation called X recruited her on the strength of her anti-communist feelings. Her first – and last – mission was to follow a fellow chemistry student who had just been released from a prison camp. So, in a nutshell, that's how I came about.

The reason I am bothering you with this story is to illustrate that from the outset I have always been a living, breathing contradiction. From my parents' stories I have come to believe that the truth does not reside exclusively on one's own political side. My father reinforced this one day when he told me something that has remained etched in my mind ever since. 'When I was in the prison camp,' he said, 'I knew in my bones that, even if our side had won the civil war, I would still be in the camp, only the guards would have been different.'

My father's words made me appreciate the capacity of both the Left and the Right for authoritarianism and misanthropy. This does not mean that I refuse to take sides or to pretend that the left–right, capital–labour, profits–wages divide is meaningless or outdated. What it does mean is that I strive to find common ground when this is possible without betraying my opposition to the hideous dictum, 'And the weak suffer what they must.'

Journalists have described me as an academic who unexpectedly abandoned the ivory tower to enter politics. They are wrong. At the age of twelve I was arrested for the first time during the last few months of the Greek military dictatorship for distributing anti-regime leaflets. This was in 1973. Thankfully the police only locked me up overnight. Upon returning home at the crack of dawn, I was told by my despairing parents in no uncertain terms, 'You're not staying in Greece. As soon as you finish high school, we are packing you off to England. We don't care what you study. Anything from anthropology to zoology.'

Happy to make my own way in the world, I landed in Britain during Jim Callaghan's Winter of Discontent in good time to prepare for Mrs Thatcher's Britain. The country's violent transition from industrial nation to a post-modern consumerist haven, fed by the twin bubbles of finance and housing, was the environment in which I cut my political and intellectual teeth. Daily life was dominated by picket lines, from Wapping to the various battlefields of the 1984 miners' strike, and by delving into mathematical economics models. It was these very models that became the handmaidens of policies that brought down the world of finance in 2008, precipitating the crisis that is pulling the European Union apart today. Looking back, I see that this combination of models and picket lines provided excellent training for the eventual writing of this book

Yanis Varoufakis
September 2016

Preface:
The Red Blanket

One of my enduring childhood memories is the crackling sound of a wireless hidden under a red blanket in the middle of our living room. Every night, at around nine I think, Mum and Dad would huddle together under it, their ears straining, bursting with anticipation. Upon hearing the muffled jingle, followed by a German announcer's voice, my six-year-old boy's imagination would travel from our home in Athens to Central Europe, a mythical place I had not visited yet except for the tantalizing glimpses offered by an illustrated Brothers Grimm book I had in my bedroom.

My family's strange red blanket ritual began in 1967, the inaugural year of Greece's military dictatorship. Deutsche Welle, the German international radio station that my parents were listening to, became our most precious ally against the crushing power of state propaganda at home: a window looking out to faraway democratic Europe. At the end of each of its hour-long special broadcasts on Greece, my parents and I would sit around the dining table while they mulled over the latest news. Not understanding fully what they were talking about neither bored nor upset me. For I was gripped by a sense of excitement at the strangeness of our predicament: that, to find out what was happening in our very own Athens, we had to travel, through the airwaves – veiled by a red blanket – to a place called Germany.

The reason for the red blanket was a grumpy old neighbour called Gregoris. Gregoris was known for his connections with the secret police and his penchant for spying on my parents, in particular my dad, whose left-wing past made him an excellent target for an ambitious if lowly snitch. After the *coup d'état* of 21 April 1967 brought the neo-fascist colonels to power, tuning in to Deutsche Welle broadcasts became one of a long list of activities punishable by anything from harassment to torture. Having noticed Gregoris snooping around in our backyard, my parents took no risks. And so it was that the red blanket became our defence from Gregoris's prying ears.

During the summers my parents would use up their annual leave to escape the colonels' Greece for a whole month. We would load up our black Morris and head to Austria and southern Germany, where, as my father kept saying during the interminable drive, 'Democrats can breathe.' Willy Brandt, the German chancellor, and a little later Bruno Kreisky, his Austrian counterpart, were discussed as if they were family friends who also happened to be great champions of isolating 'our' colonels and supporting Greek democrats.

The demeanour of the locals we encountered while holidaying in these German-speaking lands, away from the kitsch neo-fascist aesthetic of the colonels' propaganda, was consistent with our conviction that we, as Greeks abroad, were being bathed in genuine solidarity. And when our Morris sadly puttered back into Greece, through border crossings replete with photographs of our mad dictator and symbols of his crazy reign, the red blanket beckoned as our only refuge.

A hand shunned

Almost fifty years later, in February 2015, I made my first official visit to Berlin as Greece's finance minister. The Greek economy had collapsed beneath a mountain of debt, and Germany was its main creditor. I was there to discuss what to do about it. My first port of call was, of course, the Federal Ministry of Finance, to meet its incumbent leader, the legendary Dr Wolfgang Schäuble. To him and his minions I was a nuisance. Our left-wing government had just been elected, defeating Dr Schäuble and Chancellor Angela Merkel's allies in Greece, the New Democracy Party. Our electoral platform was, to say the least, an inconvenience for Germany's Christian Democratic administration and its plans for keeping the eurozone in order.

The lift door opened onto a long cold corridor at the end of which waited the great man in his famous wheelchair. As I approached, my extended hand was refused. Instead of a handshake, he rushed me purposefully into his office.

While my relations with Dr Schäuble warmed in the months that followed, the shunned hand symbolized a great deal that was wrong with Europe. It was symbolic proof that in the half-century separating my nights under the red blanket and that first meeting in Berlin, Europe had changed profoundly. How could my host even begin to imagine that I had arrived in his city with my head full of childhood memories in which Germany featured as my security blanket?

By 1974 the Greeks, with moral and political support from Germany, Austria, Sweden, Belgium, Holland and France, had overthrown totalitarianism. Six years after that Greece joined the democratic union of European nations, to the delight of my parents, who could at last fold up the red blanket and put it away in the cupboard. Less than a decade later the cold war ended and Germany was reuniting in the hope of losing itself, in important ways, within a uniting Europe. Central to this project of embedding the new united Germany into a new united Europe was an ambitious programme of monetary union that would put the same money, the same banknotes and even the same coins (one side of which would be identical, no matter where they were issued) into every European's pocket. 'Make them use the same money,' an Athenian taxi driver told me once in the early 1990s, 'and, before they know it, a United States of Europe will creep up on them.'

By 2001 the two countries brought together beneath our family's red blanket in the bygone era of my childhood – Greece and Germany – shared the same money, along with more than a dozen other nations. It was an audacious project redolent with an ambition that no European of my generation could resist.

Beacon on the hill

In fact, this process of European integration had begun long before I was even born, in the late 1940s under the tutelage of the United States. It was foreshadowed by the so-called Speech of Hope delivered by US Secretary of State James F. Byrnes in Stuttgart in 1946, in which he promised the people of Germany, for the first time since their defeat, 'the opportunity, if they will but seize it, to apply their great energies and abilities to the works of peace . . . the opportunity to show themselves worthy of the respect and friendship of peace-loving nations, and in time, to take an honourable place among members of the United Nations'.

Soon after, Greeks and Germans, together with other Europeans, started to meet and discuss the possibility of joining together in what would later become the European Union. We would unite despite different languages, diverse cultures, distinctive temperaments, and in the process of coming together, we would discover, with great joy, that there were fewer differences between our nations than the differences observed within our nations. And when one nation faced a challenge, as Greece did in 1967 with the military takeover, the rest came together to assist. It took half a century for Europe to heal its war wounds through solidarity and to turn into a beacon on humanity's proverbial hill, but it did.

Unifying hitherto warring nations on the basis of popular mandates founded on the promise of shared prosperity, the erection of common institutions, the tearing-down of ludicrous borders that previously scarred the continent – this was always a tall order, an enchanting dream. Happily, by the end of the twentieth century, it was an emergent reality. The European Union could even pose as a blueprint that the rest of the world might draw courage and inspiration from so as to eradicate divisions and establish peaceful coexistence across the planet.

Suddenly the world could imagine, realistically, that diverse nations rather than an authoritarian empire might create a common land. We could forge bonds relying not on kin, language, ethnicity or a common enemy, but on common values and humanist principles. A commonwealth became feasible where reason, democracy, respect for human rights and a decent social safety net would provide its multinational, multilingual, multicultured citizens with the stage on which to become the women and men that their talents deserved.

'When can I have my money back?'

Then came Wall Street's implosion in 2008 and the ensuing global financial disaster. Nothing would be the same again.

Once the universe of Western finance outgrew planet Earth, its imploding banks and the subsequent credit crunch took their toll on

European nations, in particular those relying on the euro. Britain's Northern Rock was the first European bank to buckle, Greece the first state. A death embrace between insolvent banks and bankrupt states ensued throughout Europe. However, there was a great difference between Britain and countries like Greece: while Gordon Brown could rely on the Bank of England to pump out the cash needed to save the City of London, eurozone governments had a central bank whose charter did not allow it to do the same. Instead, the burden of saving the inane bankers fell on the weakest citizens.

By late 2009 the Greek state's bankruptcy was threatening French and German banks with the fate of Lehman Brothers. Meanwhile the Irish banks' annihilation brought down the Irish state, magnifying the woes of France's and Germany's banks. Panic-ridden politicians rushed in with gargantuan taxpayer-funded bailouts that burdened the poorest taxpayers, as Google, Facebook and Greece's oligarchs enjoyed tax immunity. Incredibly, the bailout loans were given under conditions of income-sapping austerity which further attacked the debilitated taxpayers on whom the whole edifice depended. As nothing spreads faster than justifiable panic, Portugal, Spain, Italy and Cyprus were the next dominoes to tumble. Lacking a credible response to the euro's inevitable crisis, Europe's governments turned against one another, pointing accusatory fingers everywhere, falling prey to the beggar-thy-neighbour attitude last seen in Europe in the 1930s. By 2010 European solidarity had been eaten up from within, leaving nothing but the wretched shell of a once-solid camaraderie.

What caused the euro crisis? News media and politicians love simple explanations, and from 2010 onwards the story doing the rounds throughout Germany and Protestant north-east Europe went something like this.

The Greek grasshoppers did not do their homework and their debt-fuelled summer ended abruptly one day. The Calvinist ants were then called upon to bail them out, together with various other grasshoppers from around Europe. Now, the ants were being told, the Greek grasshoppers did not want to repay their debt; they wanted another bout of loose living, more fun in the sun and another bailout so that they could finance it. They even elected a cabal of socialists and radical lefties to bite the hand that fed them. These grasshoppers had to be taught a lesson, otherwise other Europeans, made of lesser stuff than the ants, would be encouraged to adopt loose living.

It is a powerful story, a story that justifies the tough stance that many advocate against the Greeks, against the government I served in.

'When am I getting my money back?' a German junior minister asked me playfully, but with a hint of despondent aggression, on the sidelines of that first meeting with Dr Schäuble. I bit my tongue and smiled politely.

Grasshoppers everywhere

As I hope to demonstrate with this book, Aesop's fable about the grasshopper and the ant, or any narrative of this type, is terribly misleading as a description of the causes of our current crisis.

For a start, it fails to acknowledge that every nation, including Germany and other surplus nations, has powerful grasshoppers. It neglects to mention that these grasshoppers, of the north and the south, have a habit of forging commanding international alliances against the interests of the good ants that work tirelessly not only in places like Germany but also in places like Greece, Ireland and Portugal. More importantly though, the real cause of the eurozone crisis is nothing to do with the behaviour of grasshoppers or ants or any such thing. It is to do with the eurozone itself and, specifically, with the invention of the euro. Indeed, this book is about a paradox: European peoples, which had hitherto been uniting so splendidly, have ended up increasingly divided by a common currency.

The paradox of a divisive common currency is a central theme of this book. To make sense of this paradox and thus to understand the real reasons why the narrative of grasshoppers and ants, of bailouts and austerity, is so wrong, we will need first to examine the historical roots of the euro in the postwar settlement of Europe, with the Bretton Woods conference of July 1944, in which the economic structure of Europe was forged, and in the collapse of that structure with the so-called Nixon Shock in 1971. It is a story in which the USA played the critical role, and it occupies the first two chapters of this book.

Europe and America: the book in three events

In fact, this book began life as a sequel to my previous one, *The Global Minotaur*, in which I outlined my take on the causes and nature of the 2008 global crash. Unlike *The Global Minotaur*, in which America took the lead role, this book casts Europe as its main player. But even though Europe is the protagonist, America provides the air our protagonist breathes, the nutrients that it feeds on, the global context in which it evolves, and also features as a potential victim of our protagonist's avoidable failures. In this book I turn the spotlight on three historical events that bind together, and at once push apart, Europe and America's fortunes.

The first occurred in 1971 when, in a bid to preserve its global economic dominance, America expelled Europe from the dollar zone (an equivalent to the eurozone) instituted at Bretton Woods. The influence of this event can be felt to this day throughout Europe and, indeed, feeds back into America itself (see Chapters 1 and 2). The second event was lengthier and came when an unhinged Europe tried repeatedly to make amends for its expulsion from the dollar zone by bundling together its many different currencies into a monetary union of sorts – first into the European Monetary System, then into its very own currency zone (see Chapters 3, 4 and 5). Much of the book is devoted to showing how Europe's monetary union came about and, importantly, the manner in which its evolution was guided, often unseen, by economic decisions, past and present, made in Washington, DC.

The third event once more begins in the United States with Wall Street's 2008 implosion. This set off a chain reaction that Europe's flimsy monetary union was never designed to survive (see Chapters 6 and 7). The book then turns to the root causes of Europe's failure to deal with its crisis rationally and efficiently, to the ghastly effects of this failure on the peoples of Europe, and to the detrimental impact of this failure on America's efforts to recover from the never-ending crisis that the 2008 event occasioned (see Chapters 7 and 8).

In short, I see this book as an account of Europe's crisis in the context of its historic connection to America's attempts to regulate global capitalism and, crucially, as a warning that the euro crisis is too important for the United States to leave to the Europeans, let alone ignore. Indeed, the euro crisis, the final chapter warns, is weighing down the United States in a manner detrimental to everyone's future.

Our 1929

Judging by the way it sometimes repeats itself, history has a flair for tragic farce. The cold war began not in Berlin but actually in December 1944 on the streets of Athens – as this book will recount. The euro crisis also started in Athens, in 2010, triggered by Greece's debt woes. Greece was, by a twist of fate, the birthplace of both the cold war and the euro crisis. For a small nation to be the epicentre of one global disaster is bad luck. To spark off two within living memory is a tragedy.

There is another reason to look to the past as we contemplate Europe's future. Following the tumult of Europe's expulsion from the dollar zone in 1971 (the subject of Chapter 1), European nations attempted to huddle together, like sheep in a storm. But as the solidarity of the 1970s evolved into a badly designed common currency, toxic bailouts produced psychological fault lines along the Alps and up the Rhine. An irrepressible evil is crawling out of these fault lines (see Chapters 7 and 8) with the power to devastate the European project and, moreover, to destabilize the world at large. These new divisions remind us that it would be foolhardy to forget how Europe has managed, twice in the past century, to become so unhinged as to inflict stupendous damage upon itself and the world.

The moment monetary union between different nations begins to fragment, and as the fault lines expand inexorably, only serious dialogue and a readiness to return to the drawing board can mend the fences on which peace and shared prosperity must rely. The lack of such a dialogue in the 1930s led to the disintegration of that era's common currency: the gold standard. Eighty years later, it is happening all over again in a Europe that ought to know better. Europeans have taken far too long to understand that 2008 is our version of 1929. Wall Street was the epicentre on both occasions and, once finance melted, credit evaporated and paper assets went up in smoke, the common currency began to unravel. Before long the working class in one nation turned against the working classes of all other nations, looking to protectionism for succour. In 1929 protectionism took the form of devaluing one's currency vis-à-vis others. As we shall see, in 2010 it took the form of devaluing one's labour vis-à-vis others. In a depressingly similar chain of events, it was not long before underpaid German workers hated the Greeks and underemployed Greek workers hated the Germans. With the eurozone buffeted by a massive economic downturn, the whole world watched eagerly to see how this postmodern version of the 1930s would pan out. They are still watching.

Debt and guilt

'A debt is a debt is a debt!' was what another high-ranking official of the Federal Republic of Germany told me during that first official visit to Berlin. Upon hearing this, it was impossible not to be reminded of something Manolis Glezos, Greece's symbol of resistance against the Nazis, wrote in a book in 2012 entitled *Even If It Were a Single Deutsche Mark*.[1] This carried an equivalent message to the German official's pronouncement: every Deutsche Mark of war reparations owed to Greece must be paid. Even one Deutsche Mark paid could help undo a gross injustice. Just as in Germany, once the euro crisis erupted and it was considered self-evident that the Greeks were insufferable debtors, so too in Greece, Germany's unpaid wartime debts may remain for ever unforgiven.

The last thing I needed, as I was attempting to establish common ground with Germany's Ministry of Finance, was this clash of moralizing narratives. Ethical issues are central to bringing peoples together. Closure must be achieved so as to heal festering wounds, as South Africa's Truth and Reconciliation Commission so vividly demonstrated. But when it comes to managing modern finance and a complicated, ill-designed monetary union, biblical economics is an insidious enemy. A debt may be a debt, but an unpayable debt does not get paid unless it is sensibly restructured. Neither German teenagers in 1953 – when the United States convened a conference in London to 'write down' (to reduce without payment) Germany's public debt to, among other nations, Greece – nor Greek teenagers in 2010 deserved a life of misery because of unpayable debts amassed by a previous generation.

Upon hearing this statement I thought, *Yikes! Using these meetings to bring about a rapprochement will not be easy*. A tale of two debts was turning into a morality play with no end. Europe is an ancient continent, and our debts to each other stretch decades, centuries and millennia into the past. Counting them vindictively and pointing moralizing fingers at each other was precisely what we did not need in the midst of an economic crisis in which large new debt piled upon mountains of legacy liabilities was a mere by-product.

Capitalism, lest we forget, flourished only after debt was de-moralized. Debt prisons had to be replaced by limited liability, and finance had to ride roughshod over any guilty feelings debtors had been encumbered with before 'the rapid improvement of all instruments of production . . . [and] the immensely facilitated means of communication' could draw 'all, even the most barbarian, nations into civilization' – to quote from none other than Karl Marx.[2]

My response in Berlin was that restructuring Greece's public debt was essential for creating the growth spurt necessary to help us repay our debts; otherwise Greece would have nothing with which to pay. The proposal went down like a lead balloon.

Ghosts of a common past

On the day our government was sworn in in late January 2015, Prime Minister Alexis Tsipras laid a wreath at a memorial commemorating the execution of Greek patriots by the Nazis. The international press considered this a symbolic gesture of defiance towards Berlin and insinuated that we were attempting to draw parallels between the Third Reich and a German-led eurozone imposing a new iron rule on Greece. This didn't help my job of making friends in Berlin, especially in the ultra-austere Federal Ministry of Finance.

Convinced that it was essential to emphasize that our government was not drawing any parallels between Nazi Germany and today's Federal Republic, I scripted the following text, which became part of my statement in the joint press conference with Dr Schäuble. It was meant as an olive branch.

> As finance minister, in a government facing emergency circumstances caused by a savage debt-deflationary crisis, I feel that the German nation is the one that can understand us Greeks better than anyone else. No one understands better than the people of this land how a severely depressed economy, combined with ritual national humiliation and unending hopelessness, can hatch the serpent's egg within one's society. When I return home tonight, I shall find myself in a parliament in which the third-largest party is a Nazi one.
>
> When our prime minister laid a wreath at an iconic memorial site in Athens immediately after his swearing-in, that was an act of defiance against the resurgence of Nazism. Germany can be proud of the fact that Nazism has been eradicated here. But it is one of history's cruel ironies that Nazism is rearing its ugly head in Greece, a country that put up such a fine struggle against it.
>
> We need the people of Germany to help us in the struggle against misanthropy. We need our friends in this country to remain steadfast in Europe's postwar project; that is, never again to allow a 1930s-like depression to divide proud European nations. We shall do our duty in this regard. And I am convinced that so will our European partners.

Call it naivety, but I confess I expected a positive response to my short speech. Instead there was a deafening silence. The next day the German press was lambasting me for daring to mention the Nazis in the Federal Ministry of Finance, while much of the Greek press was celebrating me for having called Dr Schäuble a Nazi. Reading these divergent reactions back in Athens, I allowed myself a brief moment of despair.

Incensed by Europe's introversion and the ease with which we turned against each other, and in a bid to let off some steam, I decided to blame it all on another Greek: Aesop. For his simplistic fable was evidently casting a long shadow over the truth, turning one proud European nation against another. Under his influence, partners became foes, almost every European risked ending up a loser, and the only winners were the racists lurking in the shadows and those who had never made their peace with European democracy. This book provides another narrative in the hope that it can do the opposite.

It's not too late. We still have everything to lose.

1

And the Weak Suffer What They Must

My philosophy is that all foreigners are out to screw us and it's our job to screw them first.

John Connally[1]

It was midsummer at Camp David, the president of the USA's country retreat, when Richard Nixon's treasury secretary and former governor of Texas John Connally convinced his president to unleash the infamous Nixon Shock upon Europe's unsuspecting political leaders. At the end of a crucial weekend of consultations with key advisers, President Nixon decided to make a startling announcement on live television: the global monetary system, which America had designed and been nurturing since the end of the war, was to be dismantled in one fell swoop.[2] The calendar read Sunday, 15 August 1971.

A few hours after the president's televised address, exactly at the stroke of midnight, a military transport plane took off from Andrews Air Force Base heading for Europe. On board, Paul Volcker, Connally's under-secretary, was intent on confronting European finance ministers already on the verge of a collective nervous breakdown.[3] Meanwhile, Connally himself was preparing an address to the nation before flying to Europe to tell a gathering of uppity European prime ministers, chancellors and presidents that it was game over. Washington was intent on pulling the plug from the global financial system it had engineered in 1944 and had been protecting lovingly ever since.

While Volcker dealt with European finance ministers and bankers in London and in Paris, trying to steady their nerves, Connally was conveying, up close and personally, a blunter message to their bosses. In effect, what he was saying was: Gentlemen, for years you have been disparaging our stewardship of the postwar global financial system – the one we created to help you rise from ashes of your own making. You felt at liberty to violate its spirit and its rules. You assumed we would continue, Atlas-like, to prop it up whatever the cost and despite your insults and acts of sabotage. But you were wrong! On Sunday President Nixon severed the lifeline between our dollar and your currencies.[4] Let's see how this will work for you! My hunch is that your currencies will resemble lifeboats jettisoned from the good ship USS *Dollar*, buffeted by high seas they were never designed for, crashing into each other and generally failing to chart their own course.[5]

And in a sentence still resonating across Europe today, Connally summed it all up succinctly, painfully, brutally: 'Gentlemen, the dollar is our currency. And from now on, it is your problem!'[6]

Europe's leaders realized immediately the gravity of their situation but responded with a sequence of knee-jerk reactions that led them from one error to the next, culminating forty years later in Europe's current circumstances. In 2010 Europe came face to face with the consequences of these forty years of accumulated mistakes (see Chapters 2, 3 and 4). The crisis of its common currency was due to failures traceable to the events of 1971, when Europe was jettisoned from the so-called dollar zone by Nixon, Connally and Volcker.[7] The comedy of errors with which European leaders responded to the post-2010 euro crisis (see Chapters 5 and 6) is also attributable to Europe's clumsy reaction to the Nixon Shock.

It is this critical event in history that will occupy this chapter.

A long time coming

Nixon had not acceded to Connally's crude philosophy lightly. Nor was Connally's philosophy as crude as he loved to make it sound. The postwar global financial system that Nixon's midsummer announcement assigned to the dustbin of history had been creaking like a doomed hull whose inevitable sinking threatened to bring down with it America's postwar hegemony.

Lyndon B. Johnson, Nixon's immediate predecessor in the White House, and Connally's fellow Texan and political mentor, had also understood that the American-designed postwar financial system could not continue.[8] In a discussion he had in 1966 with Francis Bator, his deputy national security adviser, President Johnson was adamant that he was ready to end it by severing the link between the dollar and the value of gold, on which that global system depended: 'I will not deflate the American economy, screw up my foreign policy by gutting aid or pulling troops out, or go protectionist just so we can continue to pay out gold to the French at $35 an ounce.'[9] Distracted, however, by his Great Society programmes, his intensification of the Vietnam War and his reluctance to destroy a global system that President Franklin Roosevelt's administration (the so-called New Dealers) had put together two decades earlier, Johnson allowed it to chug along.[10]

Nixon too, once in the White House, tried to delay the inevitable. Even though his squabbling team of policymakers were increasingly coming to the view that the global monetary system was broken, their warnings alone would not have sufficed to convince Nixon to unleash his shock (and John Connally) upon the befuddled Europeans. In fact, as we shall see, it took several aggressive moves by the French, the Germans and the British between 1968 and the summer of 1971 to free Nixon's hand. These were foolhardy challenges to America's management of global capitalism that gave Connally and 'that goddam Volcker'[11] the opportunity to impress upon the president that there was no alternative: he had to ditch the international monetary system known as Bretton Woods and he had to dump Europe along with it.

Could things have turned out differently? By 1971 everyone knew that the Bretton Woods postwar global financial system had been undermined by powerful economic forces beyond the control of either the United States or Europe. But instead of seeking to reform a faltering system by negotiation, Europe's leaders overplayed a weak hand against a bold hegemon. They would now have to suffer the consequences. And suffer them Europe did. In fact, Europe is still suffering them from Dublin to Athens and from Lisbon to Helsinki.

A simple idea for a stricken Europe

The financial system that President Nixon terminated in 1971 was born in July 1944 in the conference rooms of the Mount Washington Hotel in the New Hampshire town of Bretton Woods. The pristine setting could not have been more at odds with developments forged of blood and steel in Europe and the Pacific.

D-Day had preceded the Bretton Woods conference by only three weeks, its dreadful toll not yet digested by thousands of grieving families, the majority of them American. During the conference itself the Red Army liberated Minsk at great human cost, the US Air Force bombed Tokyo heavily for the first time since 1942, Siena fell to Algerian troops under General Charles de Gaulle's command and V-1 rockets pounded London mercilessly. On 20 July, the day before the conference was successfully completed, Claus von Stauffenberg led the conspiracy to assassinate Adolf Hitler at his bunker in Rastenburg. Even though the conspirators failed, the writing was on the wall. July 1944 was undoubtedly the right time for the Allies to begin planning the postwar order of things.

With their heads full of the conflict and considerable uncertainty about their own positions in that postwar order, the delegates from the forty Allied nations attending the conference hammered out an impressive financial deal in the space of three weeks. In anticipation of the guns falling silent in Europe, and before the Soviet Union had emerged as the dragon to be slain, the New Dealers in power in the USA understood that America was about to inherit the historic role of remaking global capitalism in its own image.

At the conference's opening ceremony, on 1 July 1944, President Roosevelt declared his administration's abandonment of any remnants of American isolationism. 'The economic health of every country,' he announced, 'is a proper matter of concern to all its neighbours, near and far.' Clearly, the United States, the only country that came out of the war (save perhaps for inconsequential Switzerland) with its monetary system intact, its industry booming and with a healthy trade surplus, was intent on taking a war-torn world under its wing.

One of the casualties of the European war was money. Nazi-affiliated regimes in occupied countries had printed so much of the local currencies to support the Axis war effort that the money in Europeans' pockets was not even worth the paper it had been printed on. And even in countries that had escaped occupation, such as Britain, the cost of the war and the collapse of trade had led to a combination of government indebtedness and value destruction that rendered the currency worthless – at least in the arena of international trade. In short, the greenback was the only currency left standing and capable of lubricating world trade.

Washington understood that its first task, once the German armies had been defeated, was to remonetize Europe. This was of course easier said than done. With Europe's gold either spent or stolen, its factories and infrastructure in ruins, hordes of refugees roaming its highways and byways, the concentration camps still reeking with the stench of humanity's unspeakable cruelty, Europe needed much more than freshly minted paper money. Something had to give value to the new notes. It was not perhaps surprising that the 'something' the New Dealers came up with was none other than their own dollar. America was about to share its greenback with the European countries sheltering, at war's end, under its geopolitical umbrella. In practice this entailed new European currencies backed by dollars at a fixed rate, meaning that a certain number of Deutsche Marks, French francs, British pounds, even Greek drachmas, would be worth a prespecified, constant number of dollars. It was this dollar guarantee that would instantly impart global value to Europe's new money.

Would this not risk debasing the dollar? If the dollar was to be the anchor for the new European currencies, what would underpin the dollar's own value? Tapping into a long tradition of tying paper money to precious metals that no alchemist could fake, the answer was that America would guarantee a fixed exchange rate, and full convertibility, between the dollar and the gold that it held in a bunker under the New York Federal Reserve building, as well as in Fort Knox.

It was a simple idea for a simpler world. The holder of a given number of dollars (thirty-five was the figure finally chosen) was to be offered the unqualified claim to an ounce of gold owned by the United States, regardless of the holder's nationality or location on the planet. Equally, the holder of another amount of each of Europe's new currencies would be guaranteed a given amount of dollars, which would in turn guarantee access to America's gold. In essence, gold-backed greenbacks became the guarantors of the currencies within a new global financial structure that has gone down in history as the Bretton Woods system.

A disciple to trump the master

In the Bretton Woods negotiations President Franklin D. Roosevelt was represented by Harry Dexter White, an economist who had entered public service on the coat-tails of Roosevelt's New Deal.[12] New Dealers like White had cut their teeth in the 1930s, following the collapse of unfettered financial markets in 1929 and the ensuing Great Depression. Their ambition was to counter deprivation and hopelessness by beefing up the federal government's existing institutions and creating new ones that would make another 1929 impossible. Bretton Woods offered White the opportunity to project the New Deal onto a global canvas. His brief for the conference was nothing less than to design from scratch a stable, viable, worldwide financial system for the postwar era, at the same time staving off those Europeans whom Washington was expecting to attempt to skew the new system in their favour.

White's economics had been influenced heavily in the 1930s by the writings of Cambridge economist John Maynard Keynes. In a delicious twist of fate, the one European he had to face down at Bretton Woods was none other than John Maynard Keynes himself, dispatched to Bretton Woods by Winston Churchill's wartime national unity government to represent Europe's last, and fading, empire.[13]

Keynes had it all planned well before he even arrived in America. He brought with him a razor-sharp perception of global capitalism's ways, a unique grasp of the economic forces that had caused the Great Depression, a splendid plan to refashion global finance and, last but not least, a poet's way with words and a novelist's talent for narrative.[14] The only person at the Bretton Woods conference who could deny him the crowning glory of putting his stamp on the new global system was his American disciple Harry Dexter White. And this is precisely what White did.

Keynes's proposal was brimming with intellectual power; White was overflowing with the power vested in him by America's economic and military might. Keynes advocated a global system that could stabilize capitalism for a fabulously long time; White's brief was to push through a system consistent with the United States' new-found strength but viable only as long as America remained the surplus nation extraordinaire. It was surely inevitable that the two men would clash and that White would prevail, even if Keynes succeeded in persuading his adversary on every theoretical point.

And so it was that, in July 1944, with D-Day fresh in the background, with Allied troops advancing in both Europe and the Pacific and with the rest of the world in America's debt, Keynes returned to London a defeated man, refusing to discuss in any detail either the agreement that had ultimately been imposed by the American side or his own plan, which White had trashed in the Mount Washington Hotel. Shortly afterwards Keynes put his remaining energies into another negotiation with Washington's New Dealers, at a conference in Savannah, Georgia, this time in a bid to convince them to write down Britain's gargantuan wartime loans. It did not go well. During the negotiation, which Keynes described as 'hell', he had his first heart attack. Soon after his return to England, at the age of sixty-two, another heart attack ended his life.

The Melians' reply

Forty years later, in 1988, while looking through Keynes's papers and books at King's College, Cambridge, I noticed a copy of Thucydides' *Peloponnesian War* in the original ancient Greek. I took it out and quickly browsed through its pages. There it was, underlined in pencil, the famous passage in which the powerful Athenian generals explained to the helpless Melians why 'rights' are only pertinent 'between equals in power' and, for this reason, they were about 'to do as they pleased with them'. It was because 'the strong actually do what they can and the weak suffer what they must'.[15]

These words were ringing in my head during the spring of 2015 as I faced Greece's lenders and their unwavering commitment to crush our government. Keynes's head, I am certain, must also have been ringing with these words at Bretton Woods. I wonder, however, if he was tempted, as I was, to address his adversaries with a version of a line from the Melians, who in a bid to save themselves attempted to appeal to the Athenians' self-interest:

> Then in our view (since you force us to base our arguments on self-interest, rather than on what is proper) it is useful that you should not destroy a principle that is to the general good – namely that those who find themselves in the clutches of misfortune should . . . be allowed to thrive beyond the limits set by the precise calculation of their power. And this is a principle which does not affect you less, *since your own fall would be visited by the most terrible vengeance, watched by the whole world.*[16]

In the case of the arrogant Athenians, these words surely resonated years later when their mortal enemies the Spartans scaled the walls of Athens intent on destruction. After the Great War, Keynes had used a logic similar to the Melians' argument to warn the victorious Allies that the vengeful terms they had imposed on Germany at Versailles were a boomerang that would come back to strike at the foundation of their own interests[17] – which is of course what happened after the Versailles Treaty engendered an economic crisis in Germany that brought Adolf Hitler to power. Perhaps the Melians' words also reflect how the surviving New Dealers felt in the mid-1960s when the Bretton Woods system that White had forced through against Keynes's better judgement began to unravel. But by then it was too late to do much about it. Bretton Woods was at the end of its tether, and the Nixon Shock simply demonstrates the ruthless efficiency with which American officials come to terms with new unpleasant realities, in sharp contrast to their European counterparts, who will hang on to failed projects for as long as possible.

When it came, the Nixon Shock saw to it that America, unlike Athens, would continue to enjoy the trappings of uncontested hegemony – at least till 2008. That was in essence what John Connally had proposed to his president: screw them before they screw us!

Europe and Japan were consequently badly screwed,[18] but so was the political project of the New Dealers, who had pushed aside Keynes's proposals in 1944. Indeed, after 1965 the New Dealers and their successors lost every domestic battle they fought against the resurgent Republicans. Their abject failure to revive the spirit of the New Deal, even under Democrat presidents who may have wanted to resuscitate it (such as Jimmy Carter, Bill Clinton and Barack Obama), can arguably be traced to their dismissal of Keynes's proposals back in 1944.[19]

Fair-weather recycling

Keynes's proposal was internationalist and multilateral to the core. It was historically informed (by the Wall Street crash of 1929) and theoretically buttressed by a thought obvious to everyone except most professional economists: global capitalism differs fundamentally from Robinson Crusoe's solitary economy.

What this means is that a closed, autarkic (meaning self-sufficient) economy, like that of Robinson Crusoe in literature or perhaps North Korea today, may be poor, solitary and undemocratic, but at least it is free of problems caused by other economies, by external deficits or surpluses.[20] In contrast, all modern economies have relations with others and can expect that these relations will almost all be asymmetrical. Think Greece in relation to Germany, Arizona in relation to neighbouring California, northern England and Wales in relation to the Greater London area or indeed the United States in relation to China – all imbalances with impressive staying power. Imbalances, in short, are the norm, never the exception.

In 1944 Keynes conceded that, in view of Europe's frightful state, there was no alternative to a regime of fixed exchange rates relying extensively on the dollar. However, while dollarizing Europe would solve one problem, a dollar-backed fixed-exchange-rate system would, he predicted, cause trade imbalances to grow with ultimately terrible effects first upon the deficit countries and then upon everyone else. His logic as to why fixed exchange rates would beget instability in a world of persistent surpluses and deficits was rooted directly in the events leading to the Great Depression, which the New Dealers under-stood so well, and it went as follows.

Just as one person's debt is another's asset, one nation's deficit is another's surplus. In an asymmetrical world the money that surplus economies amass from selling more stuff to deficit economies than they buy from them accumulates in their banks, but these banks are then tempted to lend much of it back to the deficit countries or regions, where interest rates are always higher because money is so much scarcer. In this way, banks help maintain some semblance of balance during the good times. If an exchange rate seems likely to remain stable or even the same, banks will tend to lend more to the deficit country in question, unworried by the prospect of a devaluation further down the line that might make it hard for debtors in the deficit country to repay them. Bankers, in this sense, are fair-weather surplus recyclers. They profit from taking a chunk of the surplus money from the surplus nations and recycling it in the deficit nations.

But if the exchange rate is fixed, the banks go berserk, transferring mountains of money to the deficit regions as long as the storm clouds are absent, the skies are blue and the financial waters calm. Their credit line allows those in deficit to keep buying more and more stuff from the surplus economies, which thrive on a spree of exports. Import-export businesses grow fatter everywhere, incomes boom in surplus and deficit countries alike, confidence in the financial system swells, the surpluses get larger and the deficits deeper.

As long as the fair financial weather continues, fair-weather surplus recycling endures. But it cannot endure for ever. With the certainty and abruptness that a pile of sand will collapse once the critical grain is added on top of it, vendor-financed trade will always go into sudden, violent spasm. No one can predict when but only fools doubt that it must. The equivalent of the critical grain of sand is one container full of imported goodies that goes unclaimed by an insolvent importer, or one loan that is defaulted upon by some over-leveraged real estate developer. It takes just one such bankruptcy in a deficit country to start a whirlpool of panic among surplus nations' banks.

Suddenly, confident globetrotting bankers turn into jelly. Lax lending turns to no lending at all. In the deficit regions importers, developers, governments and city councils which have grown dependent on the banks are hung out to dry. House prices collapse, public works are abandoned, office buildings turn into ghostly towers, shops are boarded up, incomes disappear and governments announce austerity. In no time bankers are left holding 'nonperforming loans' the size of the Himalayas. Panic reaches a deafening climax and Keynes's inimitable words resonate once more: 'As soon as a storm rises,' bankers behave like a 'fair-weather sailor' who 'abandons the boat which might carry him to safety by his haste to push his neighbour off and himself in'.[21]

It is the destiny of fair-weather surplus recycling to prompt a crash and occasion a complete halt to all recycling. This is what happened in 1929. It is also what has been happening since 2008 in Europe.

Political surplus recycling, or barbarism

By contrast, when the value of a nation's money is flexible, it operates like a shock absorber, soaking up the jolt caused by a banking crisis occasioned by unsustainable trade and money flows. When unsustainable banking practices caused Iceland to collapse in 2008, its currency slumped, the fish the island exports to Canada and the United States became dirt cheap, revenues picked up and, crucially, debts denominated in the local currency shrank (at least in terms of dollars, euros and pounds). This is why Iceland recovered so quickly after a terrible shock.

But when a deficit nation's currency is exchanged in unchanging proportions with the currencies of its surplus trading partners, its international value is fixed. This sounds great if you live in such a country and possess a lot of its money. Except it is a terrible thing for the vast majority of its people who hold little of it. Once the sequence of bankruptcies has begun, incomes are destined to fall while private and public debts to foreign banks remain the same. The price of a fixed exchange rate is a bankrupt state in a death embrace with impecunious citizens and an insolvent private sector. A doom loop, a hideous vortex, leads the majority to debt bondage, the country to stagnation and the nation to ignominy.

John Maynard Keynes knew this too well.[22] And so did Harry Dexter White, who had lived through the desolation of the 1930s, which gave him first-hand experience of what happens when the burden of adjustment falls crushingly upon the weakest of shoulders: on the debtors languishing in the deficit regions, where incomes are squeezed, investment disappears, and the only thing looming increasingly larger is the black hole of debt and banking losses. White understood all this perfectly well, just as the Greeks, the Irish, the Spaniards and assorted Europeans do today.

It was because White appreciated this problem that he agreed with Keynes on one crucial point: some alternative shock-absorbing mechanism had to be introduced into the global system they were designing. One that the gold standard lacked in the 1920s and which, tragically, Europe is desperately missing today. A mechanism that can kick in the moment the bankers' fair-weather surplus recycling disappears, so as to prevent the doom loop from taking hold and plunging first the deficit countries, and then global capitalism, into another spiral of depression and barbarous conflict. What was this mechanism to be? The answer was a set of political institutions that step in and recycle surpluses once fair-weather surplus recycling runs aground.

The New Dealers, whom White represented at Bretton Woods, had already tackled this problem at home. They had created federal institutions whose role was, at times of crisis, to recycle surpluses automatically to where they were most needed. Political surplus recycling, in short. The very point of the New Deal, which had preceded the Bretton Woods conference by a decade, was precisely that: social security, a federal deposit insurance scheme run by the Federal Deposit Insurance Corporation for all banks in all states, Medicare, food stamps and the military budget were institutions geared towards political surplus recycling so as to combat the Great Depression and to prevent a future one.[23]

The therapeutic impact of this political surplus recycling mechanism can still be felt in America today. When Wall Street imploded in 2008, Nevada was one of the states where the pain was felt most intensely. As unemployment, bankruptcies and foreclosures shot up in Las Vegas and its suburbs, the extra cost of unemployment benefits and the funds necessary for refloating Nevada's banks were found not by Nevadan taxpayers but by the federal government and Washington's monetary authorities, the Federal Bank (the Fed) and the FDIC.[24]

This was not an act of solidarity with the state of Nevada on the part of the rest of the United States; it was rather an automated mechanism that kicked in so as to stop the Nevadan malaise from spreading further afield. Through social security, the FDIC's intervention, Medicare and other mechanisms, surpluses from states like California, New York and Texas were automatically redirected towards Nevada's desert plains to stop the rot. Many Americans take this political surplus-recycling mechanism for granted and forget that it was first put in place under the Roosevelt administration a few short years before the same men hosted the Bretton Woods conference.[25]

Keynes thus had good reason to hope that he could appeal to a New Dealer like White to augment Europe's dollarization with the creation of a political mechanism for recycling surpluses on a global scale. For if the dollar zone were to be stretched to include Europe, and later Japan, surely political surplus recycling had to be spread out as far and as wide as the Bretton Woods jurisdiction reached.

'Our surpluses, our recycling mechanism'

Keynes's blueprint for the surplus recycling that was required by the Bretton Woods system was wonderfully grandiose. It included the creation of a new world currency, a system of fixed exchange rates between this world currency and the national currencies, and a world central bank that would run the whole system.

The purpose of this system would be to maintain monetary stability everywhere, to keep both surpluses and deficits in check throughout the Western world and, at the first sign of a crisis in a troubled nation, speedily recycle surpluses into it so as to prevent the crisis spreading. An international fund would be created to play the role of the world's central bank and issue its currency – the bancor, as Keynes provisionally named it. The bancor would not be printed, just as the digital crypto-currency bitcoin does not exist in material form today, only as numbers on some spreadsheet or digital device. But it would function as the world's currency nevertheless. Every country would have a bancor account with the International Monetary Fund (IMF), from which to draw when it bought goods from other countries, and into which other nations would deposit bancors when their citizens or corporations bought goods and services from it. All international trade would thus be denominated in the global currency, with the national currencies continuing to oil the cogs of the national economies.

Crucial to this system was a fixed exchange rate between each national currency and the bancor, and thus between all participating national currencies. The board of the IMF, on which all nations would be represented, would decide these rates centrally and by negotiation. They would be adjusted whenever necessary, so that countries with stubborn surpluses would see their currencies buying increasingly more bancors (to make their exports more expensive and their imports cheaper), and vice versa for nations in persistent deficit.

Even more radically, Keynes's IMF, recognizing that one nation's deficit is another's surplus, would levy a tax on a nation's bancor account if its imports and exports diverged too much. The idea was to penalize both types of imbalance (excessive surpluses as well as excessive deficits; the Germanys of the world as well as the Greeces) and in the process build up a war chest of bancors at the IMF so that, when some crisis hit, deficit nations in trouble could be propped up and prevented from falling into a black hole of debt and recession that might spread throughout the Bretton Woods system.

White certainly understood the importance of political surplus recycling within the global system they were setting up, but Keynes's proposals sounded ludicrous to his American ears. Is this wily Englishman, he might have asked, seriously proposing that the Europeans have a majority say in how our surpluses are recycled? Is he for real?

As a good Keynesian, White agreed that Bretton Woods should do more than merely dollarize the Western world. He recognized the need for a politically administered (extra-market) surplus recycling mechanism, which of course meant the recycling of America's surpluses to Europe. Nevertheless, the idea that bankrupt Europeans who had put the world through the wringer of two world wars in less than three decades and still yearned for the reconstitution of their repulsive empires would now control America's surplus was anathema to an anti-imperialist patriotic New Dealer like White. Quite under-standably, he was going to have none of it. America was the only surplus nation, and America alone would decide how, when and to whom it would recycle it.

White listened respectfully while Keynes presented his grandiose scheme but then immediately rejected two of its key features. First on the chopping block was the idea of a new shadow global currency (the bancor) to be managed by an IMF governing committee in which the United States would be one of many. The second idea White vetoed was that of taxing the surplus nations – namely the United States. For White, the die had already been cast: Europe was to be dollarized and the dollar would be the world currency. The bancor was a great idea in a multilateral world but a joke in one where the dollar had already been crowned king and queen. Moreover, the idea that the IMF's governing committee, with the Europeans in the majority, would tax America's surpluses seemed to him too ludicrous for words. America owned its surpluses and would recycle them herself, without petitioning a group of bankrupt Europeans for their permission to do so.

Defence of the realm

By the end of the Bretton Woods conference, White had cherry-picked Keynes's proposal so eclectically that its multilaterist spirit had vanished. Yes, the IMF would be created, but its purpose would not be to issue a new world currency.[26] The loss of the bancor and the official elevation of the dollar to world currency status meant that the IMF could not function as the world's central bank. That role was now assigned de facto to America's central bank, the Fed.

Deprived of its central bank function, the IMF was to resemble the monetary council of a mini-United Nations, where representatives of national governments, some of them more equal than others, constantly haggled over the exchange rate of every currency with the dollar. As for pegging the dollar to gold at $35 per ounce, this went against Keynes's conviction that tying the new system to precious metals, gold in this case, was a dangerous throwback to a dismal past. This global architecture put the Fed in a tight spot: it was being asked to issue the world's money without having a direct say on its exchange rates with the Deutsche Mark, the French franc, sterling and every other European currency involved.

Europe's central banks faced a related challenge: the politicians would negotiate their currencies' exchange rates (under the IMF's auspices), but the defence of these rates, primarily from speculators, would be left to the central bankers.[27] Typically, politicians loathe devaluing their nation's currency, even if they know that devaluation is going to be beneficial – as was the case in Italy prior to the euro: every devaluation of the lira diminished the price of Italian exports in Germany and elsewhere while also reducing the Deutsche Mark or dollar value of loans previously taken out by Italians in lira. Devaluation is associated in the public mind with failure, weakness, national humiliation even. Breaking news stories dominated by graphs depicting the decline of the pound or the dollar are not good for the chancellor of the exchequer or the treasury secretary's popularity ratings. Moreover, if it becomes widely accepted that a further devaluation is likely, currency speculators will take out loans in the weakening currency and use them to buy a stronger foreign currency in the expectation that when another devaluation takes place they will be able to use the strong currency to buy back more of the now-weaker currency than they borrowed, pay off the loan and pocket the difference. Markets being what they are, the effect of this is to turn the expected devaluation into a reality: the more of the weaker currency speculators sell (exchange it for the stronger one), the greater its availability and thus the lower its price (and thereby its value).

Therefore, given the chance to 'defend' an exchange rate, politicians will usually take it. This entails taking the precise opposite of the speculators' course: using whatever stock they have of the stronger currency in the vaults of their central bank to buy their own currency and reverse the trend. A tension thus builds up between politicians and their central bank: seeing that such measures will not fix the underlying problem but simply delay the inevitable, central bankers usually prefer not to waste their foreign currency reserves fighting a losing battle on behalf of politicians, especially since the higher exchange rate this fight is trying to preserve works against the nation's exporters. In other words, by vesting in politicians the power to set exchange rates it was as if the Bretton Woods system was designed to pit central bankers against governments, a conflict that would become all too apparent once the system began to falter, as it did towards the end of the 1960s. At times global finance felt like a vehicle with many opinionated drivers, with some yanking the steering wheel and others taking turns on the brake and accelerator pedals.

Keynes's idea of a single planetary central bank might have seemed utopian in 1944, but by the early 1960s the system as actually implemented was proving even more far-fetched. The reason for this was that defending exchange rates was itself not a simple technical task to be delegated to technocratic central bankers but required enthusiastic and permanent coordination between central bankers from many nations in defence of rates that they had not chosen and with which they often had issues. Such enlightened cooperation became increasingly decisive (and decreasingly forthcoming) as the system was destabilized by trade imbalances and the resulting bank-mediated fair-weather surplus recycling that Keynes had been so worried about. The most important of these imbalances was between Germany and France.

With every additional Volkswagen Beetle that a French family bought, unreciprocated by German purchases of Renaults or extra cases of French wine, France's trade deficit grew. If this continued, somewhere down the line the IMF board would have to decide to devalue the French franc (in relation to the Deutsche Mark and by extension to the dollar) in a bid to cheapen French wine in Germany, make Volkswagens dearer in France and thus redress the balance. Even the whiff of such a devaluation was enough to blow inauspicious winds into the speculators' sails, giving them the cue to take out bets that the franc would fall. What did these bets look like? Given that no sensible bookmaker would give odds on currency movements, the speculators placed their bets as follows: they took out loans in Paris in French francs and used them to buy Deutsche Marks at the current exchange rate. They then waited for the franc to devalue against the mark. If it did devalue, they would use their stash of marks to buy a lot more francs than they had borrowed in the first place (courtesy of the lower franc value), repay these debts in francs and keep the handsome difference.

The critical problem, though, was that unlike bets on the weather or sporting events, which do not make the predicted event more likely just because they are placed, bets that the franc would fall made it more likely that it would do so. With every franc that the speculators borrowed in Paris to buy marks, expectations of a devaluation increased, thus pushing the franc's real value down a little in the market for tourist currency, in informal dealings between foreign corporations and so on. Suddenly a fault line between the franc's official and unofficial values developed. To defend the official exchange rate, the central bank of France, the Banque de France, had to use whatever marks it kept in its vaults to buy francs in order to defend the franc–mark rate. A game of chicken was now on. Who would blink first? The speculators? Or the Banque de France?

Without assistance and left to fight the speculators alone, the Banque de France's pile of marks and other foreign currency would eventually run out. At that juncture the French central bank could prolong the agony a little by increasing interest rates, making the return on the franc higher and thus encouraging people to buy it so as to attract foreign money into France, which could then be used as further ammunition against the speculators. However, higher interest rates meant that French businesses would pay more to invest, leading to a domestic slump – not quite what the stuttering French economy needed.

Alternatively, the Banque de France could bite the bullet and ring the French finance minister with the terrible news: 'We cannot defend the franc as long as our compatriots keep buying so many Volkswagens. Time to call the IMF and arrange for its devaluation against the Deutsche Mark and the dollar.' At which point speculators would boost sales of the best French champagne, eager to celebrate in style their lucrative victory over the franc.

But there was one thing standing in the way of the speculators' route to riches and glory, and that was the central bank of Germany, the at-once dreaded and esteemed Bundesbank. Were it willing to print Deutsche Marks (which, naturally, the Banque de France could not do) to buy francs, the speculators would be burnt. The reason is simple. The speculators believed that by selling the francs they had borrowed in Paris to trade for Deutsche Marks they were precipitating the franc's devaluation – on the assumption that other speculators would be doing the same. Indeed, a torrent of offers to sell francs would ensure that many more traders wanted to part with francs than to buy them. Just like in a farmers' market, when a bumper supply of potatoes overwhelms demand and the price of potatoes crashes, currency speculators predicted that at the end of the day the Deutsche Mark would buy them more francs than it had been able to earlier in the day. A 10 per cent devaluation, for example, would mean they would need to convert back into francs only 90 per cent of their new stock of Deutsche Marks in order to repay in full the French banks from which they had borrowed francs in the first place, resulting in a 10 per cent profit (minus the cost of the interest on the loan).

Here is where the Bundesbank might come in. For if the German central bank were to print extra Deutsche Marks, give them anonymously to selected money traders and instruct them to buy francs on its behalf, the imbalance between sellers and buyers of francs would vanish and the franc's value would not decline. This would be a catastrophe for the speculators since they would not be able to repay their loans in Paris and retain a profit, by converting their new pile of marks back into francs.[28] If the Bundesbank intervened in this manner until the speculators gave up, the system would prevail despite the increasing French trade deficit in relation to Germany. That the Bundesbank had the capacity to do this there was never any doubt, as it owned the Deutsche Mark printing press. The question was its willingness.

On the one hand, the Bundesbank had a duty – to the Bretton Woods system, to defend the realm of Germany – to see the speculators off and hold the line. On the other hand, the Bundesbank intensely disliked printing Deutsche Marks in defence of exchange rates it had not chosen and in quantities it despised because these marks threatened to flood back into Germany later, causing domestic prices to rise and bringing back memories of the hyperinflation of the early 1920s.

Would the Bundesbank and the central banks of other surplus nations do what was necessary to support the central banks of the deficit nations, as they were meant to under the rules of the Bretton Woods system? Yes, however reluctantly, they would, as long as they felt that the Bretton Woods system was sound. And the system was sound as long as America was in surplus with the rest of the world.

America's deficit, Germany's qualms, France's conceit

American surpluses were everything. Unlike Europe today, where German surpluses play no stabilizing role,[29] the postwar global order depended on America's surpluses entirely, as did Europe's stability. They sustained the necessary dollar recycling process between the United States and Europe and secured the future of the Bretton Woods system. As long as America sold enough stuff to Europeans, the dollars that America was sending to Europe (as aid, to purchase European goods or even to fund US military bases on the continent) were steadily repatriated. Every plane that Boeing sold to the Europeans and every John Deere excavator transported across the Atlantic soaked up the greenbacks sloshing around Europe (which came to be known as euro-dollars) and brought them home. These returning dollars supported the currency against the German, French and Italian currencies. Thus the Fed could step in and use its infinite dollar pile to buy as many francs, pounds or lire as necessary to defend their official fixed exchange rates against the Deutsche Mark. American surpluses, in this sense, begat stability within Europe and afforded the Europeans good cause to think of the recycled dollars as 'paper gold'.

Things began to go awry, as Keynes had predicted they would, when America began to spend consistently more money on European and Japanese goods than foreigners were spending on wares made in America.[30] At that moment, when American surplus turned into deficit, the net stream of dollars reversed its flow, feeding into an ever-expanding euro-dollar lake. By the late 1960s, that stream had turned into a torrent; the euro-dollar lake was larger than the Caspian Sea, and the Bretton Woods system came under siege.

It was now the case that the total quantity of dollars in Europe far exceeded the dollar value of America's stockpile of gold.[31] Which meant that if the Europeans were to ask the United States to swap even a fraction of their euro-dollars for the precious metal – as Bretton Woods allowed them to – the United States would run out of gold in minutes. Convinced that the American government would prefer to dismantle Bretton Woods rather than sit idly by while its stock of gold withered, speculators predicted that, at some point, Washington would drop its commitment to selling gold at $35 per ounce, thus formally allowing its price to rise and rise.

Nothing motivates speculators more than foreseeing a price rise in a precious commodity, especially if they think that others like them will cotton on to this expectation, thus increasing greatly the rate at which the price appreciates. Just as the speculators betting on the fall of the French franc and the rise of the Deutsche Mark financed their bets by borrowing francs to buy marks, so the speculators betting on gold's rising dollar price borrowed dollars to purchase gold in the belief and hope that it would go up. And as they did, the price of gold strained at its Bretton Woods leash with the ferocity of a crazed pit bull.

The speculators' plan was to amass a stock of gold using borrowed dollars, wait until its dollar value rose above some threshold and then cash in by selling the gold for many more dollars than they had borrowed – courtesy of the rise in the dollar value of gold – repay the dollars that they had borrowed to place the bets and keep the difference. Crucially, this difference would be all the greater if they cashed in following the formal collapse of Bretton Woods,[32] which is what the Nixon Shock represented. Bretton Woods and the speculators' plans were thus deeply incompatible. One of the two had to give.

To hold the Bretton Woods system together, the Americans had to rely on the kindness of strangers.[33] To defend the price of gold at $35 per ounce, Europe's central banks were required to join the Fed in selling gold at the official low price.[34] They were also obliged to keep printing more of their money in order to continue buying up the dollars flooding Europe from America. But European solidarity with Washington was undermined not only by widespread pessimism regarding the system's long-term chances but also by the fault lines that were developing, quite naturally, between European nations whose money was on the way up (surplus countries such as Germany and the Netherlands) and those whose money was losing value (countries nursing a growing deficit, such as France).

From as early as 1961 the Bundesbank began to baulk at the prospect of either increasing the Deutsche Mark's value against the dollar at the IMF or printing as many marks as was necessary to defend its current value. Revaluing the mark would penalize German exporters, whose goods would become relatively more expensive on the international market. Printing more marks smacked of inflation. Doing neither, as was the Bundesbank's preference, would damage Bretton Woods and infuriate Washington.

Meanwhile, politicians in deficit European states like France and Italy had reason to be cross with America too. As their nations' currencies were squeezed by the mark, they felt the earth shifting under their feet. It was one thing for Paris or Rome to request a devaluation vis-à-vis the dollar; it was quite another constantly to lose ground in relation to the Deutsche Mark, whose value was being buoyed by Germany's trade surplus. With the Fed incapable of defending the franc or the lira now that America was in deficit, the burden fell increasingly on the Bundesbank to prop up the franc and the lira against its own currency, as well as the dollar against gold and the Deutsche Mark. France and Italy thus began to recognize that they were running the risk of becoming, financially speaking, German vassal states, an unwelcome prospect fifteen short years after the end of the Second World War.

None of this gave German policymakers much joy either. The dollar glut in Europe, and the simultaneous slide of the franc, the lira and the pound, meant that the Bundesbank had to crank up its printing presses ad nauseam on behalf of almost everyone else. German policymakers suddenly found themselves in a ruthless dilemma that divided them bitterly: print marks in defence of Bretton Woods at the risk of inflation, or risk bringing down an international financial system which in their eyes was the economic foundation of the Pax Americana (which kept the Soviets at bay) and of the European Union (which offered Germany perhaps its only chance to become a 'normal' European state)?

Meanwhile, President de Gaulle of France was growing angrier with a global system that was diminishing French influence. Reflecting his unhappiness with Washington's stewardship of global capitalism, France's monetary authorities not only refused to sell gold in support of the dollar's gold value but in fact did the opposite: they followed the cue of speculators and actually bought gold from the US at $35 per ounce. Of course, unlike the speculators, de Gaulle's aim was to send a message of discontent to Washington, rather than profit from buying gold cheaply and selling it at a higher dollar price.

In late 1967 de Gaulle's government attempted to harden the franc by embarking upon a harsh austerity drive. Alas, the result was a slump, with rising unemployment followed by great social unrest culminating in the world-famous May 1968 insurrection. As students and workers poured onto the Parisian streets, the proud president – a soldier who had been a prisoner of war in the German town of Ingolstadt, before becoming France's Second World War hero two decades later – lost control of downtown Paris and suffered the ignominy of having to flee to, of all places, Germany. Although his army restored him to power, and he won another landslide election, a year later he resigned the presidency, despondent amid renewed pressure on the franc.

Meanwhile, Britain was feeling the pinch too. With its empire almost gone, its industry losing customers both abroad and at home, and with de Gaulle having vetoed its entry into the European Union (partly as a signal to Washington that France was unhappy and unwilling to accommodate its European lackey),[35] the United Kingdom was looking to America to stabilize its trade balance. But America was preparing to do the opposite: to jettison the whole lot of them.

From the early 1960s America had been losing its surpluses but throughout the decade remained understandably unwilling to tighten its belt, crush its own economy and lose its global hegemony in order to preserve Bretton Woods. Under the delusion that the United States could be counted on come hell or high water to maintain 'its' global financial system, assorted European officials took liberties with Washington's nerves. The Bundesbank, struggling to retain its independence from German politicians (whom it considered susceptible to France's influence), repeatedly refused to meet its commitments to help stabilize gold's dollar value and the franc. Paris, fully dependent on the Bundesbank to defend the franc, lost no opportunity to insult the Americans verbally and symbolically, as when a French naval vessel was ordered to New Jersey packed with greenbacks to be exchanged for American gold. London too, feeling vulnerable as its empire disappeared and de Gaulle kept Britain out of the European Union, also began to test America's resolve.[36] Put in a manner reflecting John

Connally and Paul Volcker's 1971 mindset, the global ship was listing, and various European rodents were testing the water. It was at that point that Connally and Volcker finally prevailed upon President Nixon to screw the foreigners.

Thus in 1971 Europe was jettisoned from the dollar zone by a United States intent on preserving its hegemony and unwilling to turn to austerity to save Bretton Woods. Europe's response, as we shall see over the coming chapters, was to create its own kind of Bretton Woods, culminating, after countless trials and tribulations, in a common currency, the euro. Disastrously, those who built the European version of Bretton Woods were no Harry Dexter White or John Maynard Keynes. Innocent of the macroeconomic problems monetary unions throw up, they created a system that removed all shock absorbers and at the same time unwittingly ensured that when the shock came, as it did in 2008, it would be gigantic, causing Europe to turn in on itself.

On 18 October 2008, in the midst of our generation's version of 1929 and just before boarding a plane to Washington, where he was to meet President George W. Bush for talks on how to respond to the collapsing global financial system that had taken Bretton Woods's place, French president Nicolas Sarkozy told journalists in his usual emphatic manner, 'Europe wants it. Europe demands it. Europe will get it.' What exactly was it that Europe demanded and would get, according to Monsieur Sarkozy? The answer, as provided by Manuel Barroso, president of the European Commission at the time, was a 'new global financial order'.[37]

Of course Nicolas Sarkozy did not get what he travelled to America to demand in 2008, just as his predecessor Georges Pompidou failed during the latter part of 1971 to convince the United States to rescind the Nixon Shock and to reconstitute Bretton Woods, albeit with fresh exchange rates.[38] Still, President Sarkozy's boisterous words confirm that, eight years after Europe's common currency was created, France and the European Commission were still hankering after a global system along the lines of that which Nixon, Connally and Volcker had torn down on that August day.

Europe's unhinging occurred in 1971 but is still haunting the continent decades later, despite (in fact because of) the creation of a common currency infused with none of the lessons that the designers of Bretton Woods learned from the interwar gold standard. John Connally would no doubt have chuckled at his enduring capacity to haunt European leaders, only his amusement would be spoiled by an acute awareness of the clear and present danger an unhinged Europe poses to a tricky post-2008 world.

2

An Indecent Proposal

Kurt Schmücker was not a man to give in to strong emotions.[1] But on the morning of 23 March 1964 he could hardly trust his ears and only barely managed to contain his astonishment.

As Germany's Minister for the Economy, Herr Schmücker was used to meeting regularly his French counterpart, Valéry Giscard d'Estaing, President Charles de Gaulle's finance minister and the man who would ten years later become president of France himself. So when Giscard dropped in at his Bonn office for a two-hour chat, Minister Schmücker was relaxed, anticipating another anodyne meeting like all the previous ones – an effort to put on a show of European unity between two erstwhile foes shouldering the burden of constructing a union at the early stages of its development. The European Economic Community (EEC), as the European Union was then known, comprised Germany, France, the Netherlands, Luxembourg, Belgium and Italy, the original six founding members and signatories of the Treaty of Rome, signed on 25 March 1957.[2]

Schmücker and Giscard normally exchanged polite views on how each saw the economic policies of the other, on how the two countries dealt with movements of money across their borders, on interest rates and trade balances, on their attitudes towards taxing business and, of course, on their joint efforts at cementing a European Union still in its infancy. Occasionally they would also swap tales of woe concerning tense relations with their central bankers, the Bundesbank and the Banque de France. Nothing, in other words, that might have prepared Herr Schmücker for what he was about to hear. But, that morning, once the obligatory niceties had been dispensed with, Giscard came out with a shocking proposal: France and Germany should create a common currency, inviting the other four European Union members to join in when and if they were ready.

No one can know what thoughts crossed Schmücker's mind at that moment, but his surprise must have bordered on bewilderment. What on earth was the aristocratic Frenchman saying? That Germany and France ought to share the same banknotes, the same coins, the same central bank? Which one? The Bundesbank? For heaven's sake!

Outwardly, Schmücker pretended not to have been taken aback. Indeed, the record shows that he responded as if he had not heard the earth-shattering proposition. Why not be more modest? he countered. Why don't we just try to stabilize our exchange rates through our central banks and on the basis of (a conservative German's strategy of last resort) 'strict discipline' and 'contractual rules'?[3]

Giscard was having none of this. 'Why choose this system, which works only as long as everybody gets along?'[4] he riposted energetically, adding that his proposal was coming from the very top – from President Charles de Gaulle himself. Flabbergasted, Schmücker tried to alert France's minister of finance to the deeper meaning of what de Gaulle was proposing: France was proposing to forfeit its national sovereignty! Was Paris serious about that? Giscard neither conceded nor repudiated Schmücker's obvious point. He bypassed it by urging that a common Franco-German currency be created forthwith, leaving it open to other European Union members to join in.

Schmücker knew that this was not an issue he had any authority to get seriously involved in, so he dutifully passed de Gaulle's proposal on to Ludwig Erhard, his chancellor. Upon reading Schmücker's brief, Dr Erhard smelled a rat. France could not possibly be suggesting so lightly giving up its power to set taxes, to spend public funds, to set interest rates, to pursue its beloved *planification*.[5] *De Gaulle must be up to something again*, thought Erhard. After all, the only reason Ludwig Erhard had risen to the highest office in Germany, a few short months earlier, was because of his role in frustrating President de Gaulle's designs.[6] This outrageous common currency proposal, thought Erhard, could only be made sense of as a continuation of those same designs.

Unwilling to enter into an official public confrontation with France, Chancellor Erhard 'misplaced' Schmücker's brief and pretended never to have received it. And so it was that a common European currency was first tabled, briefly discussed and spectacularly ignored. Nevertheless, when in 1966 he was forced out of the chancellery, among the very few papers that Erhard took with him into retirement was that brief – a memento of the euro's first official appearance.[7]

A French embrace twice shunned

Giscard d'Estaing was never de Gaulle's stooge. Indeed, de Gaulle fired him in 1966, and Giscard had to wait for three years until a new president, Georges Pompidou, entered the Elysée Palace to reclaim the Ministry of Finance – from where, in 1974, he rose to the presidency of the French Republic. Of course, back in 1964 Giscard strove loyally to serve de Gaulle, often against his better judgement regarding some of the former soldier's fixations, whether in the realm of economic policy[8] or in the French president's determination to wreck America's geopolitical dominance of Europe. However, on 23 March 1964 the 'indecent proposal' he brought to Bonn was fully in tune with his own thinking.

Giscard shared with de Gaulle one crucial judgement. They agreed that the hegemon was reaching for the moon. Literally and metaphorically. The Americans were starting wars in Indochina. They were announcing grand, expensive social programmes at home. Their corporations bought up venerable European companies and treated them disgracefully.[9] And how did they pay for all this? By printing dollars which flooded Europe's economies, forcing the Europeans, particularly the French, to finance America's profligacy through higher inflation. The fact that France was more susceptible than other countries to these inflationary forces also weighed heavily upon de Gaulle and Giscard's thinking.

From Giscard's own perspective, the Americans were forcing the Europeans to lend them the money with which they bought up Europe and destabilized global finance. Giscard encapsulated this verdict famously in a two-word phrase – exorbitant privilege – the inordinate advantage enjoyed by the United States, and its currency, which America squandered. He believed it was an advantage that ought to be done away with before world capitalism was destabilized for good and the opponents of the ruling bourgeoisie, especially in France, gained the upper hand.

'Exorbitant privilege' became a signifier of American financial might when Giscard coined it, and remains so to this day.[10] But what could be done to curb it? From Giscard's 1964 perspective it was possible to imagine that the only way of ending America's imprudent monetary supremacy was for France and Germany, Europe's dominant nations, to get together to forge a common currency and thus overcome their monetary dependence on a wayward United States. But would that not jeopardize, as Schmücker warned, France's sovereignty? Of course it would, but it was a price that Giscard, a firm believer in a United States of Europe, did not mind paying.

Giscard may not have minded the loss of French national sovereignty, but his boss, President de Gaulle, certainly did. Europe was important for de Gaulle, as it was for Giscard. It had to be won. But not at any price, as far as de Gaulle was concerned. And certainly not at the price of losing France in the process. So why did de Gaulle send his finance minister to Berlin with a proposal that, if accepted, would have dismantled Paris's economic power? A common currency with Germany would rob Paris of control over France's economy. But a proposal for a common currency was not the same thing as an actual common currency.

De Gaulle was, lest we forget, a military tactician. Proposals for treaties and common currencies, just like manoeuvres on a battlefield, were packed with diversionary intent. A united Europe began to appeal to de Gaulle quite late in the piece (around 1958) and only when he started seeing it as a new source of grandeur for France's nation-state; in sharp contrast to Germany's first two chancellors, Konrad Adenauer and Ludwig Erhard, for whom the European Union was an escape route from their nation-state.

January 1963 was a month of political fire and brimstone, with Paris at its centre. On 14 January President de Gaulle gave a press conference that amounted to a declaration of hostilities against the Anglosphere. Against Washington's express wishes, he announced that France was vetoing Britain's entry into the European Union. And as if that were not enough, almost in the same breath he turned down an American offer for nuclear cooperation within a multilateral force.

Eight days later the German chancellor, Konrad Adenauer, went to Paris. In the splendour of the Elysée Palace, amid considerable pomp and ceremony, Adenauer and de Gaulle put their signatures on the Elysée Treaty, an agreement that was presented to the world as the cornerstone of French–German rapprochement, testimony to the permanent cessation of hostilities between Europe's dominant nations and the beginning of a beautiful friendship. Washington was incensed. George Ball, undersecretary in the State Department, later wrote, 'I can hardly overestimate the shock produced in Washington by this action or the speculation that followed, particularly in the intelligence community.'[11]

Washington's ire had nothing to do with opposition to France and Germany burying the hatchet, getting closer and reinforcing European unity. The United States government fretted that de Gaulle was up to something aimed at America's military dominance in Western Europe and its control of the capitalist global order. More precisely, they were concerned that de Gaulle was attempting to lure Adenauer into a strategic alliance with a twofold aim: at the level of international finance, to undermine the dollar-centred Bretton Woods system, and, at the level of geopolitics, to bypass NATO in offering Moscow a non-aggression pact, cutting the United States out of the deal. Washington's fears were heightened by the fact that the German chancellor was a Catholic Anglophobe with a long history of seeking unity with France.[12]

De Gaulle's strongest hand was his grand vision of a Europe from the Atlantic to the Urals. This appealed to a plurality of Europeans keen to remove the nuclear threat that hovered over their continent – especially after the Cuban Missile Crisis of the previous October – and hopeful of raising the Iron Curtain, which bisected it so brutally. For the Germans a Europe from the Atlantic to the Urals had added significance, as it hinted at German reunification.

The day before the Elysée Treaty was signed, an American diplomat[13] enlisted the only member of Adenauer's cabinet with the power to, and an interest in, opposing Adenauer's drift into de Gaulle's embrace, Ludwig Erhard. Adenauer's respected Minister for Economics, Erhard had overseen Germany's *Wirtschaftswunder*, the economic miracle that had transformed Germany from 1949 to that day. This had relied on investment-led ultra-rapid growth aided by America giving Germany massive debt relief,[14] encouraging Wall Street and US multinationals to invest in the Federal Republic and making possible (through the Bretton Woods system) stable prices and copious markets for German exports.

Erhard did not act rashly. He bided his time before coming firmly down on the side of Washington and against Adenauer's plan to join forces with de Gaulle. When Adenauer convened the German federal cabinet in Bonn on 25 January to discuss the Elysée Treaty, Erhard kept quiet. Four days later, however, he gave a forceful speech critical of French foreign policy, taking the unprecedented step of predicting that the Elysée Treaty would never be implemented. At the following cabinet meeting, in Bonn on 30 January, Erhard went further, speaking against 'de Gaulle's French dictatorship',[15] even comparing the French president with Hitler. In an article published in Die Zeit on 5 February Erhard warned his compatriots that Germany 'cannot run with the hare and hunt with the hounds', signalling clearly his allegiance to Washington and challenging Adenauer for having become too close to de Gaulle. On that same day President Kennedy signalled that Germany had a clear 'choice between working with the French or working for us'.[16]

By April 1963 Erhard's interventions had diminished Adenauer's position within the ruling Christian Democrats and he had emerged as the party's sole candidate for replacing the ageing chancellor. On 16 May, after a great deal of backroom dealing, Erhard and his allies succeeded in getting through the federal parliament an amendment to the Elysée Treaty in the form of a preamble that ended de Gaulle's dream of a Franco-German alliance in opposition to America.[17] Meanwhile, secure in the belief that de Gaulle had been seen off, the US State Department recalibrated its European strategy, avoiding further confrontations with de Gaulle and focusing instead on cultivating stronger ties with Bonn. In October 1963 Ludwig Erhard moved to the chancellery, bequeathing the economics ministry to Kurt Schmücker.

The second embrace

Having his embrace shunned so spectacularly, it was quite remarkable that President de Gaulle bore no grudge against Germany's new chancellor. Even being compared with Hitler washed over him like water off a duck's back. When Erhard was made chancellor, he made a point of visiting Paris immediately to reaffirm the 'great new friendship between the two nations'[18] and their leaders. President de Gaulle welcomed him with open arms, as he would a long-lost friend, and six months later dispatched his finance minister, the charming Valéry Giscard d'Estaing, to Bonn to astound Herr Schmücker with his proposal for an instant Franco-German monetary union.

Was de Gaulle just not getting it – that Germany was averse to another of his asphyxiating embraces? Whatever else was going on in the general's mind, one thing is for sure: he was under no illusions. The notion that de Gaulle expected Erhard to agree to a Franco-German common currency is as absurd as the alternative notion, namely that de Gaulle wanted such a currency. The shared money proposal had two tactical features that attracted France's strategizing president: the element of surprise and the capacity (even if the proposal were ignored or rejected) to rope Germany into a sufficiently close relationship with France to afford de Gaulle more freedom in his opposition to the United States.

The element of surprise was undoubtedly achieved. Erhard and Schmücker had every reason to expect that, after Adenauer's departure, de Gaulle would have left them alone. A common currency proposal was the last thing they anticipated. As Schmücker told Giscard, nothing in Paris's demeanour signalled a willingness to forfeit national sovereignty or even to refer important decisions on France's economy to supranational institutions. He was right. France, and in particular de Gaulle, was guarding her economic levers jealously and had no interest in letting go of them. For well over a decade[19] de Gaulle had stood alone among conservative European politicians in dogged opposition to the new French–German economic relationship that America's New Dealers were keen to turn into the emergent European Union's backbone.[20]

Unlike many of his compatriots, who took great pride in the European integration project and waxed lyrical about it as a great achievement of the European spirit, de Gaulle had seen the European Union project as an American design that privileged German industry in order to cement American global dominance. The common European market and the process of European integration was, in his eyes, part of an American global plan that de Gaulle deemed ill founded, unsustainable and therefore detrimental to both France and Europe.[21] Eventually de Gaulle softened his opposition to the European Union, after repeated American pledges in the 1950s that France would remain Europe's administrative centre. But he would only embrace it as long as, in his own words to a visiting journalist, the European Union resembled 'a horse and carriage: Germany [being] the horse and France . . . the coachman'.[22]

Alas, by 1963 it was clear that the horse was developing a mind of its own and the coachman was losing his grip. France's accelerating trade deficit with Germany meant that Paris would be forced into a perpetual Sophie's choice. Regularly go cap in hand to the IMF for permission to devalue the franc, admitting to permanent national weakness, or rely for ever on the Bundesbank to print Deutsche Marks with which to buy francs, admitting to an unending dependency upon the old enemy. Either way, France's aspirations for political and diplomatic domination of the European Union were unravelling.

It was a nightmare for de Gaulle but also for the French establishment, which saw in the general a fearless champion of its interests and ambitions, domestically as well as across Europe. De Gaulle's brashness sometimes clashed with polite society's sense of decorum, but when it came to addressing German politicians, American officials and Anglo-Saxon financiers, the French elites liked the president's inherent suspiciousness, his readiness to speak out, as well as his commitment to hard money – to a stable non-inflationary currency that would revive France's image, bolster its banking sector and, importantly, weaken the recalcitrant French trade unions.[23]

De Gaulle was always cagey about closer union with Germany. He saw unity across the Rhine as a fine sentiment fraught with danger, whatever its merits for France. Even after 1958, when he embraced the idea of a European Union erected along the Franco-German axis, de Gaulle remained guarded about it. When Henry Kissinger asked him how France would prevent German dominance of the European Union, the French president replied, *'Par la guerre!'*[24] France's war hero was not joking. Indeed, his indecent proposal for a common currency with Germany which Giscard conveyed to a gob-smacked Schmücker was a form of war by other means. De Gaulle used the common

currency proposal as a troubled boxer employs a strategic embrace –
as a ploy to catch his breath before launching an uppercut.

Chancellor Erhard knew this. He immediately recognized de
Gaulle's common currency proposal as a ploy to smother his country,
neuter the Bundesbank, enhance France's standing at the expense of
Germany and drive a wedge between Bonn and Washington.[25] He
could also see that, whatever his response, he was on the losing side.
If he accepted de Gaulle's offer, he ran the risk of surrendering the
Bundesbank to Paris or, at the very least, incurring the Bundesbank's
undying wrath. If he dithered for a while, de Gaulle would have
bought precious time (as the speculators would cease betting against
the franc until the dust settled) and Erhard would have looked inde-
cisive. If he rejected the offer outright and publicly, his own European
unionist credentials would suffer and de Gaulle's would strengthen.

But Erhard had undermined Adenauer and risked everything to
help his country wriggle out of de Gaulle's first embrace; he was not
going to submit to this second one. Unwilling publicly to push de
Gaulle away for the second time in a year, and fearful that any public
response to the common currency proposal would damage his government, the German chancellor pretended never to have received
Schmücker's note.

And so it was that, in early March 1964, the idea of the euro lit up
Europe's skies, but ever so briefly and unseen by most Europeans. It
was only when Europe was fully jettisoned from the dollar zone that
it resurfaced.

War by other means

Unperturbed by Bonn's silent rebuff, de Gaulle decided to go it alone.
On 4 January 1965 he called a news conference. With superb lyricism
he countered his compatriots' fear of national decline with an open
attack on America's exorbitant privilege, aiming to restore the glory
of France by demonstrating it was the only Western power able and
willing to stand up to the hegemon. With his slings and arrows trained
on the dollar and America's alleged failure to manage global finance
properly, de Gaulle called for a new global currency.

And what would he replace the dollar with? His mischievous answer was to call for the restoration of gold to its rightful throne:[26] 'We . . . consider it necessary that the system of international exchanges be re-established . . . on an indisputable monetary base which bears the mark of no country in particular. What base? *Eh! Oui.* Gold, which does not change its nature . . . which has no nationality, which is held eternally and universally as the inalterable fiduciary value par excellence.'[27] Behind the evocative rhetoric, the French president was only talking gold up, and the dollar down, because he felt, quite astutely, that a fraying Bretton Woods was no longer consistent with his ambition for a France that dominated Europe.[28]

It is tempting to dismiss de Gaulle's interventions as the whims of a man embittered by his struggle to get the British and the Americans to recognize a defeated France, and himself personally, as one of the Allies that beat Germany into submission. De Gaulle never forgave the Americans for having denied France a place at the victors' table in the closing stages of the Second World War, especially at the Yalta meetings between Franklin D. Roosevelt, Winston Churchill and Joseph Stalin. But to imagine that this was the reason for his 1965 attack on the dollar and Bretton Woods is to underestimate de Gaulle's legitimate intellectual concerns regarding the propensity of superpowers to grow arrogant and eventually destabilize themselves.[29]

De Gaulle's objections to America's postwar global design went back at least to 1946. To 6 September 1946, to be precise, when James F. Byrnes, the US secretary of state, travelled to Stuttgart to deliver his Speech of Hope – a significant restatement of America's policy on Germany. Until then the Allies had been united in their commitment to convert 'Germany into a country primarily agricultural and pastoral in character'.[30] Byrnes's speech was the first postwar sign the German people were given of an end to the revanchist deindustrialization drive that, by the end of the 1940s, had destroyed 706 industrial plants. Byrnes heralded a major policy reversal with the statement that 'the German people [should] not . . . be denied to use . . . [such] savings as they might be able to accumulate by hard work and frugal living to build up their industries for peaceful purposes'.[31]

Of course, one person's hope is another's nightmare. De Gaulle for one had been exasperated, for he knew that, in the context of a financial system pegged on the dollar, a reindustrialized net-exporting Germany would render France financially dependent on the Anglosphere, on America, even on Britain – heaven forbid!

General de Gaulle was the embodiment of the French army's obsession with Prussian military and industrial prowess. He feared and admired German resolve and efficiency in equal measure. In the 1930s he had opposed the building of the defensive Maginot Line, accusing France's Ministry of Defence of trying to fight the Great War all over again. De Gaulle's vision of the oncoming Second World War was precisely how the Nazi high command was planning it: highly mobile, based on tank columns moving rapidly and liberated from snail-like infantry divisions, who were to follow later in trucks and lorries. When the war broke out, de Gaulle's tank units were the only ones to cover themselves in some glory, while the Maginot Line's static defences proved a national embarrassment. De Gaulle's disgust at his country's failure was replete with respect for how German tactics and industry had combined to humiliate France, occupy as much of it as Berlin wanted, create a vassal Nazi state with the town of Vichy as its capital and start another French civil war (pitting Vichy supporters and collaborators against the Resistance), which lasted, at the rhetorical level, well into the 1980s.

It is a mark of ancient societies that contemporary tribulations reinvent old fears. De Gaulle was born and bred in a cloud of national disgrace. Twenty-eight years before his birth, in 1862, Prussia's chancellor, Otto von Bismarck, had delivered his Blood and Iron Speech, in which he presciently declared that Prussia would settle the 'great questions of the day' not 'through speeches and majority decisions . . . but by iron and blood'. The prospect of a reindustrializing Germany cranking up its steel output in the 1950s could never appeal to a man whose life, from a tender age, had been shaped by images of German iron liberally spilling French blood.

Even worse, de Gaulle was burdened by the capacity of the French to spill their own blood while German smelters and Bessemer converters were spewing out high-quality steel. In 1871, as Bismarck was proclaiming German unification and crowning the Prussian king emperor of the German empire, France's government army was entering the French capital to commence a pitiless battle against the revolutionaries of the Paris Commune, killing tens of thousands in the process. For de Gaulle, the first half of the twentieth century had been nothing more than a recapitulation of that sorry contrast: French impotence juxtaposed against German success which made France dependent on the Anglo-Saxons.

Fierce French resistance to the reversal Secretary Byrnes had fore-shadowed with the Speech of Hope slowed down the process of rehabilitating Germany. However, once Washington had decided, for its own reasons, that Germany was to play a crucial role within America's plan for the postwar world, it was only a matter of time before Germany was indeed rehabilitated and its industrial base not only spared but bolstered as well. A speech on 18 March 1947 made by Herbert Hoover, President Roosevelt's predecessor, flagged up America's new policy on Europe. 'There is an illusion,' Hoover said, 'that the New Germany . . . can be reduced to a pastoral state. It cannot be done unless we exterminate or remove 25 million people out of it.'[32]

It was then that General de Gaulle, and the majority of France's policymakers, understood they had a new fight on their hands requiring a fresh strategy. The strategy de Gaulle chose to contain the new Germany was odd though not illogical: an asphyxiating embrace with which France would attempt to stifle its revived neighbour. The Elysée Treaty in January 1963 and Giscard's indecent proposal in March 1964 were early manifestations of that strategy. Many more were to follow.

America's global plan[33]

It was not for humanitarian motives that Washington decided to spare Germany a return to a bucolic past.[34] Nor was America's change of heart caused exclusively by the gathering clouds of the cold war and the real imperative to contain the Soviet Union. While the geopolitical incentive was clear and present, New Dealers like James Byrnes, James Forrestal,[35] George Marshall[36] and Dean Acheson[37] had another excel-lent reason for allowing Germany to retake its place among the indus-trialized nations.

The Bretton Woods system, already set out in 1944,[38] posited the dollar as the sole linchpin holding together the edifice of global trade and finance. If for any reason the American economy were to experience a slump, the dollar might function like a superconductor for recessionary waves, which would immediately travel unimpeded to the far corners of global capitalism. Even small American recessions could pick up speed and ferocity reaching Europe, Japan and the rest of Asia, where they might cause a great deal more damage than in Chicago or Ohio. Shock absorbers were urgently needed to prevent this.

In a global system of fixed exchange rates, shock absorbers take the form of strong regional currencies, issued by potent central banks, to act as secondary pillars in support of the system's main currency. There was need for at least one such currency in Europe and another in Asia. Of course strong regional currencies cannot be created; heavy industry powerhouses must underpin them. But here is the tricky part: industrial powerhouses produce more manufacturing goods than their domestic economies can absorb – think China today. To keep going, powerhouse economies need markets – surrounding states in permanent deficit with them so that they can remain in surplus.[39]

So the first question was: which would the powerhouse economies in Europe and Asia be? In Europe the United Kingdom was an early candidate. Only, like most early front-runners, Britain went by the wayside. Its elites were determined to retain their grip on an empire that, in Washington's eyes, was both repugnant and unsustainable. Its returning soldiers, having shed their blood for king and country, were determined not to return to their prewar pitiful wages and abject living conditions. This was why Winston Churchill, the nation's wartime tower of strength, was swept away in a 1945 electoral landslide that ushered in a radical-sounding (especially to American ears) Labour government. A year later a fiscal crisis ended sterling's convertibility and further tarnished Britain's candidacy as the European pillar of America's global plan. These developments gave Washington second thoughts multiplied by the British establishment's delusion that it had won the war and thus deserved to dictate the terms of peace.

Looking at the Far East, the American administration saw that the only nation capable of playing the necessary shock-absorbing role there was Japan: a mighty industrial power whose factories were largely unharmed except in Hiroshima and Nagasaki, whose workforce was highly skilled and impressively disciplined, whose constitution the United States had had the opportunity to script and, last but certainly not least, a country ruled by America's armed forces. Once their gaze turned back towards Europe, the puzzle dissolved: West Germany was the obvious equivalent and a splendid candidate for the role of the global plan's European shock-absorbing pillar.

Why not France? For three excellent reasons. First, German industry was far more advanced than France's. In 1945, despite the hammering it had received from the Allies in the final stages of the war, German factories produced more than twice as much as France's. Secondly, the defeated Germans, fearing a pastoral future, would breathe a sigh of relief if the United States were to patronize their economy, invest in it and generally take it under their wing. In contrast, General de Gaulle and the vast majority of the French would be incensed by any hint of similar intervention, let alone a takeoever. Thirdly, just as in the case of Japan, America had written the constitution of the Federal Republic of Germany and even created the Bundesbank from scratch. The fact that American forces controlled West Germany's land, sea and airspace did not harm the notion either.

The second question now remained: who would provide the deficit hinterland for Germany's and Japan's powerhouse economies?

De Gaulle's insight

In 1945, to take their plan from conception to implementation, Washington needed to overcome de Gaulle in particular and French opposition generally. General de Gaulle could see a world evolving in which France would be reduced to a third-rate power, bringing back painful memories of his nation's wartime humiliation. However, his opposition to this prospect hit the shoals of a postwar Central European conservative consensus that was enthusiastic about Europe's dollarization. On 20 January 1946 high inflation and broad dissatisfaction with de Gaulle's austere conservatism caused his removal as leader of France's provisional government. The interesting question is: why did de Gaulle not attempt a comeback soon after? Why did he volunteer to go into the wilderness and stay there until 1958?[40]

De Gaulle could sense that the French elites were not keen to share his deep misgivings about America's global plan and thus risk losing the perks that America was offering them for going along with it. Nevertheless he strove to warn them against the idea of a global dollar standard in which the Deutsche Mark would be the greenback's supportive currency within Europe. He could see that, to play this role, the mark required substantial German heavy industry, which in turn necessitated neighbouring nations being in perpetual trade deficit to Germany. Only thus could the demand for German industrial exports be generated. Could his people not see this? They could. Except that Washington played a smart game, making French officials and bankers an offer they could not refuse.

France's advantage has always been the quality of its administrators. Every year the *grandes écoles* produce a steady stream of men, and more recently some women, with a predilection for public service, of remarkable erudition, superior numeracy and the capacity to run multinational bureaucracies efficiently and with panache. This was a lasting legacy, a gift to the French nation, of Napoleon Bonaparte. Additionally, French banks were far more sophisticated than Germany's. Cognizant of this, the New Dealers offered the French establishment a powerful incentive to acquiesce in Germany's reindustrialization: at the price of accepting German industrial might and the inevitable power of the Deutsche Mark, French administrators would run a unified Central Europe (from Paris and from Brussels), while French banks would handle the flow of capital and German profits both within and outside this entity.

De Gaulle was perhaps one of the very few establishment figures in France who refused to be lured by this tempting offer. Jean Monnet (one of the fathers of the European Union), Jacques Rueff (an influential economist) and Robert Marjolin (who was to lead the Marshall Plan administration, which evolved into today's OECD) understood that de Gaulle would have none of it. Unlike them, he suspected that, despite Washington's promises, France would languish if America's global plan were implemented.

The fact of the matter was, and this is where de Gaulle was right, that a reindustrialized export-oriented Germany would always result in a weak French franc within a global monetary system of fixed exchange rates relying on the dollar. France would then depend on Washington's support to keep its currency at a par with Germany's money. But such transatlantic support for France could only be provided if America continued to generate surpluses. De Gaulle's premonition was that the United States would squander its surpluses, and at that point Paris would become dependent on the kindness of the Bundesbank. Which is exactly as things panned out.

The Greek trigger

There was one other crucial factor that lay behind the USA's commitment to Germany: the cold war. What most people forget is that my tiny nation had been the harbinger of this larger drama too. The first clash between East and West occurred in the streets of Athens in the aftermath of the Nazis' April 1944 withdrawal, and it involved right-wingers supported by Britain and left-wing partisans supported by the USSR. These clashes reached a peak in December 1944 and led to Greece's sordid 1946–9 civil war, which left every Greek family I know indelibly marked. It was also the prelude for an East–West confrontation that furnished the United States Treasury and State Department with the opportunity and congressional clout to implement an audacious experiment in Europe: the bringing together of France and Germany into a European Union that was part and parcel of a global economic design.

The reversal of the plan to demolish Germany's heavy industry was facilitated by the increasing tensions which first erupted in Athens. American diplomat George Kennan's so-called Long Telegram from Moscow, warning of the Soviets' expansionist ambitions, imbued Washington with the urgency to contain the USSR and coincided with the escalation of Greece's civil war. Byrnes's Speech of Hope, foreshadowing Germany's steady rehabilitation, came after the Greeks had been plunged into a hideous fratricidal conflict that was the original proxy confrontation between the emerging cold war superpowers.[41]

The Truman Doctrine, announced by President Truman on 12 March 1947, focused on winning Greece for the West[42] but, more importantly, constituted the president's unofficial declaration of the cold war.[43] It shaped America's Europe. From that moment onwards, and beginning with Greece, the United States would make the containment of Soviet influence its top priority.

At the very sound of Truman's declaration, Paris shuddered. French leaders, with de Gaulle first and foremost, understood that the new American emphasis on Soviet containment translated into a German industrial revival. Germany's reindustrialization happened only because the United States chose to make it happen. Equally, the European Union was formed because Washington understood that a strong Deutsche Mark needed successful German heavy industry, which needed neighbouring markets for its wares, which necessitated an American-brokered deal with Paris – a deal that the French establishment reluctantly accepted but which pushed General de Gaulle out of politics for more than a decade.

Some years later, in 1953, Hermann Josef Abs, a Nazi-era director of Deutsche Bank,[44] led a German government delegation to Britain. The occasion was a conference convened by the Americans to reach the so-called London Debt Agreement. In essence, the United States leaned on Britain, France, Greece, Italy, Spain, Sweden, Yugoslavia, Norway, Switzerland and many other countries to write off the greatest part of Germany's prewar debt to them. The British government protested, arguing that Germany had both the capacity and the moral duty to pay. Washington ignored London and, leading by example, instantly wrote off the loans that it had made to Bonn after 1945. Nations and private creditors owed money by the German state and by German corporations were persuaded to write off more than 70 per cent of the money they were due.[45]

Debt relief is essential for any person, company or nation that has fallen into the unforgiving clasp of insolvency. Without it, individuals languish in debtors' prison and nations wither until either their inhabitants migrate or rise against the creditors and their quislings. If capitalism went from strength to strength in the nineteenth century it is because prisons were replaced by limited liability. If General Motors is alive and kicking today, it is because in 2009 President Obama's administration wrote off 90 per cent of its debt. If Germany rose in the 1950s to become an economic superpower, it did so because the United States strong-armed other Europeans to give it substantial debt relief.

The villain of the war, Germany, thus emerged from its ashes, while Greece – the first country to have pushed back Axis forces[46] – was having a disastrous postwar experience: first it burned in the flames of its civil war and then, after that sorry episode ended in 1949, was almost emptied of its people, who took the long road of economic emigration. During the early 1950s, while the Greeks were migrating to the United States, Canada, Australia, Belgium and, ironically, Germany (as highly productive *Gastarbeiter* – guest workers), the Greek government was bowing to pressure to write off the substantial sums owed to it by Germany. Meanwhile, though their postwar fate was nowhere near as tragic as Greece's, France and Britain, supposedly the war's victors, braced themselves for interesting economic times ahead.

Ironically, if Greece today remains in a deep economic depression, it is because since 2010 Germany has been refusing point-blank to grant Athens debt relief, and no one, including the United States, is willing or able to strong-arm Berlin to do for Greece what America did for Germany in 1953. The result is not just a predictable depression but also the rise of the Golden Dawn Nazis.

During my first official visit to Berlin, on 5 February 2015, I invoked the spectre of the Greek Nazis and the debt-fuelled depression that had propelled them into parliament as Greece's third-largest party.[47] The combination of annoyance and rejection with which my plea for debt relief was met confirmed my – and the rest of Europe's – worst fears: the German establishment had either erased all memory of America's act of mercy or believed that the German state had deserved, immediately after the end of a terrible war that it had started, special treatment that other European states now do not.

Dollarized cartel

To establish the European pillar of its global plan, Washington had to make a significant concession. The economic union that it coveted as the Deutsche Mark's hinterland would have to be built around a cartel of heavy industry enjoying a degree of market power that the New Dealers were allergic to. But they had no other option. The only two unifying European movements they could draw support from, and work with, were the internationalist Marxist Left and a time-honoured conservative Central European tradition associated with catchwords such as *Mitteleuropa* or *Paneuropa*. There was no contest.

At its most wholesome, *Mitteleuropa* evoked a multinational multi-cultural intellectual ideal for a united Central Europe that the non-chauvinistic section of its conservative elites were rather fond of. However, *Mitteleuropa* was also the title of an influential book by Friedrich Naumann, authored in the midst of the Great War, which advocated an economically and politically integrated Central Europe run on German principles and with the 'minor' states placed under German rule.[48] A great deal more liberal than *Mitteleuropa*, *Paneuropa* was the brainchild of Count Coudenhove-Kalergi, an Austrian–Japanese intellectual who conducted a lifelong campaign to bring about a pan-European political and economic union.[49]

Despite their differences, *Mitteleuropa* and *Paneuropa* were aimed at protecting Europe's centre from the geopolitical and economic encroachments of Russia from the east and the Anglosphere from the west. They also shared a view that European unity would have to be overlaid on Central Europe's existing national institutions and, indeed, on its prevailing corporate power structures. A European union consistent with *Mitteleuropa* and *Paneuropa* visions would have to operate by limiting competition between corporations, between nations and between capital and labour. In short, Central Europe would resemble one gigantic corporation structured hierarchically and governed by technocrats, whose job would be to depoliticize everything and minimize all conflicts.

Needless to say, the *Mitteleuropa–Paneuropa* vision enthused German industrialists. Walter Rathenau, chairman of AEG (Allgemeine Elektricitäts-Gesellschaft) and later Germany's foreign minister, went as far as to suggest that a Central European economic union would be 'civilization's greatest conquest'.[50] The idea appealed greatly not only to corporations like AEG, Krupp and Siemens, but also to the Roman Catholic Church and politicians like Robert Schuman, another of the European Union's fathers, who was born in Germany but ended up French, courtesy of a shifting border.

In September 1947, as the New Dealers were contemplating a European union consistent with their global plan, Count Coudenhove-Kalergi was giving a speech at the European Parliamentary Union Conference, which he had convened in a bid to bring together Central European parliamentarians. The theme of his talk was the urgent need to bring about a united Europe by building a large Central European market with a stable currency. What he neglected to say was that this 'market' would by necessity be dominated by several large corporations at liberty to coordinate their prices so as to avert any real competition among themselves, from upstarts and, importantly, from the Anglosphere.

These were the people – men like the good Count Coudenhove-Kalergi, Robert Schuman and Jean Monnet – that the Americans had to do business with.

The process of building *Mitteleuropa–Paneuropa*, once begun, was inexorable. In January 1946, at the behest of the US Mission to France, the Planning Commission (Commissariat général du Plan) was established in Paris. A few months after the Truman Doctrine was made public, George Marshall, Truman's secretary of state, addressed a Harvard audience with a speech that marked the beginning of the Marshall Plan: a massive aid package, amounting to more than 2 per cent of US national income, that kicked off Europe's dollarization.[51]

Within weeks, the Commissariat général du Plan was distributing one third of all Marshall aid to Europe, setting growth targets across Europe and employing no fewer than 3,000 employees in Paris to do so. On 3 April 1948 President Truman established the Economic Cooperation Administration, and thirteen days later the United States and its European allies created the Organization for European Economic Cooperation (OEEC), with a remit to work out where to channel the funding, under what conditions and to what purpose. In 1961 the OEEC changed its name to what we know today as the OECD, the Organization for Economic Cooperation and Development.

While France's elite was being placated with plush administrative roles and oodles of money, the real game was being played in the realm of heavy industry. In 1950 the European Union was officially born in the form of a German-dominated coal and steel cartel, run of course by a cross-border French-dominated administration located in Brussels. Its name? The European Coal and Steel Community. It was a remarkable departure from American principles of governance, which since President Theodore Roosevelt had included a healthy dose of cartel busting. However, America's global plan could not fly in Europe unless it made its peace with the *Mitteleuropa–Paneuropa* ideology intimately associated with Central Europe's cartels.

Making their peace with Central European corporatism, American policymakers had to swallow not only the idea of building the new Europe on a cartel of big business but also the unsavoury political agenda that went with it. Corporatists like Robert Schuman and Jean Monnet were bent on constructing the Brussels-based bureaucracy as a democracy-free zone. Count Coudenhove-Kalergi put it succinctly in one of his speeches when he declared his ambition for Europe to 'supersede democracy' and for it to be replaced by a 'social aristocracy of the spirit'.[52] As always happens when a technocracy harbouring a deep Platonic contempt for democracy attains inordinate power, we end up with an antisocial, dispirited, mindless autocracy.

Europeans recognize this in today's Brussels-based bureaucracy. Every survey of European public opinion finds large majorities with no trust in the EU's institutions. While it is true that citizens around the world – for example in Britain, the United States or India – are highly critical of their state's institutions, the discontent with Brussels is qualitatively different. Take Britain for instance. The British state evolved as a set of institutions whose function was to regulate the struggle between different social groups and classes. The tussle between the king and the barons gave rise to Magna Carta, a deal the essence of which was to limit the king's powers. After the merchant class acquired economic power disproportionate to its social and political rank, the state evolved further to accommodate its interests with those of the aristocracy, especially after the 1688 Glorious Revolution. The Industrial Revolution brought new social strata into the mix (industrialists, trade unions, local communities made up of former peasants), extending the franchise and refining the state's apparatus.

Meanwhile, on the other side of the Atlantic a similar process was spawning the American constitution. The United States government and bureaucracy also emerged at a time of intense conflict between vested interests and social classes. Slave-owning landowners, mainly in the South, clashed with East Coast traders and manufacturers in Illinois, Boston and Wisconsin. The Louisiana Purchase triggered a variety of new tussles between multiple interest groups. A brutal civil war proved impossible to avert and facilitated America's consolidation. Later on, the rise of the labour unions and the military-industrial complex signalled fresh rivalries. To bring the nation together and to homogenize its institutions so as to deal with the political, social and financial crises that these tensions threw up, Congress had to play a central equilibrating role. Indeed, no authority in the United States can defy Congress or ignore it. Whatever demerits American democracy may have, there can be no doubt that the democratic process is essential in keeping the union together.

In contrast, the European Union's institutions did not evolve in response to social conflicts. National parliaments and institutions did all the heavy lifting in terms of ameliorating social conflicts while the Brussels bureaucracy was devised for the purpose of managing the affairs of an industrial cartel made up of Central European heavy industry. Lacking a Demos – a 'We the people . . .' – to keep them in line, and indeed to legitimize their activities, Brussels bureaucrats both disdained democracy and were shielded from its checks and balances. While the cartel they administered was doing well under the auspices of the American-designed global financial system, the European Union's institutions enjoyed widespread acceptance. However, unlike America's Congress-centric system, the European Union lacked the democratic process necessary to fall back on in times of trouble.

From the viewpoint of its official ideology, the European Union sounded very similar to the United States, even to liberal Britain. Free-market liberalism seemed to be the order of the day, and a single market free of state patronage the union's objective. And yet, remarkably, the European Union began life as a cartel of coal and steel producers which, openly and legally, controlled prices and output by means of a multinational bureaucracy vested with legal and political powers superseding national parliaments and democratic processes. Indeed, the inaugural task of the Brussels bureaucracy was to fix the price of steel and coal products and remove all restrictions on their movement and trading among the cartel's member states. Curiously perhaps, this made perfect sense: what would be the point of a cross-border cartel if its products were stopped at the borders, taxed and generally impeded by national government officials? The equivalent in the United States would have been a Washington bureaucracy, operating without a Senate or a House of Representatives to keep the bureaucrats in check, able to overrule state governments on almost anything and bent on fixing prices at levels higher than the market would have selected.

The next step was obvious too: once tariffs on coal and steel were removed, it made sense to remove all tariffs. Except that French farmers, who always exerted exceptional influence on France's political system, did not like the idea of untrammelled competition from imported milk, cheese and wine. So to co-opt French farmers, the so-called Common Agricultural Policy was established. Its purpose? To secure the farmers' consent to a European free trade zone by handing over to them a chunk of the cartel's monopoly profits.

By the end of the 1950s a fully fledged European Union (then known as the European Economic Community, which had evolved from the European Coal and Steel Community[53]) had sprung from the multinational heavy industry cartel and its political incarnation in Brussels. Dollarized by the United States, it soon began to create large surpluses, which funded postwar Central European prosperity in the stable world environment provided by the Bretton Woods system, which was itself constantly stabilized by a United States ready and willing to recycle to Europe a large chunk of America's surpluses. A golden age dawned, brimming with high growth, non-existent unemployment and low inflation, spawning a new Europe of shared prosperity. It was an American triumph that Europe's elites were determined to portray as their own.

Tumult across the Rhine

Europe's golden age began to frazzle as soon as America's surpluses withered. The rise of German and Japanese manufacturing exports – which the United States had variously supported – led its two protégés to build up their own surpluses. And since one economy's surplus is another's deficit, German and Japanese surpluses came at the expense of a United States more concerned with the continued stabilization of the world economy than the preservation of its own surpluses. So, even while it was becoming obvious that America was turning from a creditor to a debtor nation, from an economy that enjoyed a trade surplus to one nursing an increasing trade deficit, Washington officials knew that tightening the nation's belt – reducing government expenditure, increasing taxes and printing fewer dollars – in order to reign in the emerging deficits would destabilize a global order reliant on American largesse. And so the Fed continued to print as many dollars as necessary to prevent a sharp recession throughout global capitalism. As a result, the United States government and private sector got deeper into the red, becoming net debtors towards Europe and Japan. But as long as America maintained its monopoly over the world's single currency, the dollar, exploiting what Giscard had referred to as its exorbitant privilege, there was still some life left in the Bretton Woods system.

Meanwhile, America's Europe began to turn in on itself. President de Gaulle's twin attempts in 1963 and 1964 to lure Germany into an asphyxiating embrace were a reflection of his anxiety at the sight of the American global plan fraying at the edges and threatening France's political predominance within the European Union.

When Chancellor Erhard snubbed his proposal for an immediate currency union, de Gaulle responded by upping the ante against the United States and Bretton Woods. Convinced that America had more power than was good for it but less than it often realized, a few months after his provocative January 1965 press conference, at which he had called for a return to the gold standard, the French president ordered the removal of 25,900 bars of gold, weighing more than 350 tons, from the basement under the New York Federal Reserve and their immediate transportation to Paris.[54] No one can deny that, when it comes to semiology, the French are unbeatable.

The news led several European companies, and various European central banks, to demand from the American authorities gold in exchange for their stockpiled euro-dollars. As we saw in the last chapter, speculators sniffing blood joined in, borrowing oodles of dollars to buy gold, and the unofficial price of gold rose to more than $70 per ounce when America was still legally bound to sell gold at only $35 an ounce. To add injury to insult, de Gaulle also pulled France's military forces out of NATO, demanding the removal at once of all NATO facilities from French soil.[55]

In Germany a parallel drama was unfolding. The Bundesbank's reluctance to support Bretton Woods was mounting at a time when the bank's cooperation was proving of the essence. Supporting Bretton Woods meant in practice that the Bundesbank was printing more and more Deutsche Marks with which to soak up the dollars and francs that speculators were borrowing from commercial banks in order to buy them – betting, as was their wont, on a rise in the value of the German currency. As long as the Bundesbank did this, the speculators were kept at bay. The moment, however, the Bundesbank slowed down its printing presses, the dollar's and franc's official (Bretton Woods) values would become untenable. At such moments of Bundesbank reluctance, either the politicians needed to get together at the IMF's Washington offices to agree to a politically poisonous revaluation of the exchange rates or the whole system would perish.[56] It is not far-fetched to say that, by the mid-1960s, the future of America's postwar design depended on the Bundesbank's readiness to print marks.

Irritated German central bankers saw Chancellor Ludwig Erhard as a loathsome figure. They considered him Washington's man, a politician who cared more about helping America stabilize Bretton Woods (and fending off de Gaulle's overtures) than the Bundesbank's crusade to keep the lid on German prices, which they feared would escalate if they were forced to print more money. Harbouring long memories and packing sharp knives, they had never forgiven Erhard for having, while economics minister in 1961, overruled their objections to an American request that the mark be revalued.[57]

So what did the Bundesbank men do? In a move more reminiscent of a banana republic than a European democracy, Germany's central bank engineered a sharp recession to oust the government. How did the Bundesbank do that? Simple. It curtailed the capacity of commercial banks to issue business and household loans. This cap on liquidity reduced economic activity and tightened the labour market, causing a short recession that the electorate blamed on Erhard's government.

And how do we know this? We know because the Bundesbank's president, Karl Blessing, admitted to it years later. Without a smidgeon of embarassment or regret he said, '[W]e had to use brute force to put things in order.'[58] By 'order' Herr Blessing meant the accession to the chancellery of Georg Kiesinger, another former member of the Nazi Party, who led a grand Right–Left coalition government that granted the Bundesbank, courtesy of the new administration's weakness, a great deal more freedom to drag its feet in defence of the Bretton Woods system.

In the three-year period that followed the Bundesbank's putsch a dual monarchy reigned in West Germany. Christian Democrats (the Right) and Social Democrats (the Left) ruled together in a national effort to overcome a recession that their central bank had caused in its successful bid to oust Erhard and usher them in.[59] With this in mind, they came up with the so-called Stability and Growth Pact, a blueprint for recovery based on a simple logic: wage restraint to keep German inflation lower than France's, Britain's and America's and a push to export more. Within a year, the Stability and Growth Pact had borne fruit. Germany recovered as its exports flooded France, Britain and the United States at the expense of everyone else, further destabilizing the Bretton Woods system.[60]

Meanwhile, west of the Rhine, France was at boiling point. De Gaulle knew that his grip over organized labour was weak compared to that of the German elites, which had incorporated trade unions not only into government (courtesy of the Social Democrats' participation) but also placed them in boardrooms, where unionists sat next to company directors, delivering wage restraint in return for power. De Gaulle imagined that adopting hard money – either the gold standard or the Deutsche Mark – would bolster the French state and weaken the leftist riff-raff. However, as Germany had refused his overtures and a return to the gold standard was just rhetoric, de Gaulle was stuck in a morass of uncontrolled inflation and rising discontent. In a last stand against the tide, he ordered Giscard d'Estaing to tighten the monetary reins in a bid to make the franc stronger, more Deutsche Mark-like.[61]

The result was the worst of both worlds: employment in France shrank, prices continued to rise, the French–German trade balance went deeper into the red, and speculators kept borrowing francs to buy Deutsche Marks in anticipation of one more Waterloo for the franc. As we've seen, in May 1968 French students led an uprising that was to mark a generation and cause de Gaulle the greatest embarrassment possible, as the French strongman had to seek refuge in Germany. Even though, with army support, he managed to hold on to the presidency, a year later he resigned, passing the baton to his deputy, Georges Pompidou. In one of President Pompidou's first interviews, when asked to comment on France's economic weakness relative to Germany, his disturbing answer was, 'The Germans have their Deutsche Mark and we have our little bomb,' meaning the French nuclear capability.[62] Clearly, the French establishment had bowed to a German financial dominance that was, to them, as inescapable as it was abominable, looking to counter it with France's nuclear weapons.

A few months later, in September 1969, Germany was to have a general election. Speculators sensed that the next government would have to revalue the Deutsche Mark in order to restore a modicum of balance in European trade, so they borrowed from anyone who would lend them dollars, francs, liras or even gold to buy marks. A mass of money invaded Germany, threatening the inflation-phobic nation with rising prices. The Right–Left administration shut down the stock exchange and the financial system for four days, hoping to stem the tide.

The election result was mixed. While the Christian Democrats won most votes, Willy Brandt's Social Democrats increased their vote more than any other party and would go on to stake a claim to government in alliance with the small Free Democratic Party. While this deal was being hammered out, the caretaker Kiesinger government had to figure out what to do with the money markets. The Social Democrats in the cabinet surprised everyone by suggesting that the government should bite the bullet and revalue the mark handsomely. This was the equivalent of a British Labour Party leader today advocating more austerity than the Tories or an American Democrat promising greater reductions in social security than the Tea Party! The Social Democrats were known for their reluctance to harm the export industries on which their largest constituency (the industrial working class) relied, and yet on this occasion they were proposing a major revaluation of the German currency.

Kiesinger baulked, worried that German industrialists and exporters would turn against him. During the stand-off the vice president of the Bundesbank, Otmar Emminger, came up with an intriguing compromise: 'Do nothing. Just relieve us, silently, from the obligation to defend the dollar's value.' Exhausted, the politicians gave the Bundesbank the go-ahead: Bretton Woods would be set aside, even if only temporarily; the Bundesbank would be allowed to give the Deutsche Mark printing presses a rest, while the mark would float into uncharted waters.[63]

When the markets reopened, the mark duly began to rise, while the Bundesbank, in gross violation of its Bretton Woods obligations, sat on its hands. For a whole month, until the new Brandt administration was in place, the Bundesbank allowed the German currency to rise in relation to the dollar but intervened to restrain any rise against the franc so as to sustain German exports into France. Paris was furious while Washington remained nonchalant. Giscard d'Estaing sent fiery missives to Bonn and to Frankfurt, accusing the Germans of tearing up the postwar monetary order and jeopardizing the European Union.

Washington's initial reluctance to scold Bonn resulted from a certain relief occasioned by a temporary lull in the pressure to defend the dollar. As the mark rose, stemming the flow of dollars into Germany and limiting American purchases of Mercedes-Benz cars, the Fed could relax a little. Soon, however, the Nixon administration came to see the Bundesbank's unilateral move as an aggressive act. Even though Bonn was eager to explain that the flotation was temporary and that the Deutsche Mark would only be allowed to float gently for a while until it was locked back (at a higher value) into its proper Bretton Woods value, it was clear that putting the genie back into the bottle would be very hard indeed.

Britain and France were on their knees. The mark's rise was not fast enough to rebalance their trade with Germany. Volkswagens and Siemens washing machines were now dearer in London and Lyon but not sufficiently so to make a significant dent in Germany's trade surplus. However, the impressive rise of the Deutsche Mark, and the realization that the authorities had not intervened to stop its ascent for the first time since the 1940s, led rich people with money to spare to predict that the Deutsche Mark would rise further. Seeking to take advantage of this new situation, they sent their cash to Germany, causing an exodus of money from Paris and London to Frankfurt.

Faced with an increasingly impossible situation, Giscard d'Estaing remembered his 1964 trip to Bonn and issued fresh calls for a common currency, only this time (freed from General de Gaulle) he wanted to include other European nations in the deliberations. Bonn repeated its sensible argument that a common currency would have to be preceded by political integration, which France would not countenance.

This pattern was to repeat itself again and again – in the 1970s, the 1980s, the 1990s, indeed to this day: Paris would call for a monetary union and the German government would agree on condition of a political union that would allow it to control French government expenditure. Even after the monetary union was implemented, and especially once the euro began to feel the heat of its own crisis, the same disagreement continued. I have first-hand experience, circa 2015, of heated arguments between top French and German officials along precisely these lines. Indeed, it is clear to me as a result of these encounters that the euro crisis is persisting because Paris will not agree to accept supervision of its national budget. (For more on this, see Chapter 4.)

Returning to March 1971, the world of finance woke up one morning to unbelievable news: the Federal Republic of Germany now held more foreign reserves – in dollars, yen, etc. – than the US government. Merely two and a half decades after Secretary Byrnes's Speech of Hope marking America's decision to allow Germany to bounce back, Germany had overtaken its much larger and richer benefactor in the amount of foreign money, including dollars, it possessed. The news startled the world, elevated Germany's economic power to mythical status and played a significant role in speeding up capital flight to Germany. The expectation that America would have to give up its pledge to sell each ounce of its gold for a pitiful $35 grew even stronger, convincing speculators that gold's dollar price was about to explode. Dollars were swapped for gold in droves. And when traders could not find enough gold to buy, convinced that the dollar was doomed, they even started swapping their dollars for francs and pounds. Paris and London found themselves with new stocks of dollars, even though their currencies were continuing to lose ground to Germany.

On 9 May 1971 Chancellor Brandt attempted to steady President Pompidou's nerves with a handwritten letter restating his unwavering personal commitment to 'the establishment of [European] economic and monetary union'. Pompidou was not convinced.[64] At the same time as Brandt was reassuring him, Pompidou had it on good authority the Bundesbank was preparing to refloat the mark, as it had done in 1969. The consequences of this would be seriously destabilizing for both France and Britain. As the summer approached, Paris asked the Americans if its new-found dollars could be swapped for gold. Washington was livid. So, when on 11 August 1971, London joined in, requesting that $3 billion of its own euro-dollars be swapped for American gold, Paul Volcker told John Connally, who immediately agreed, that it was time to persuade President Nixon to throw the book at the Europeans. On 15 August the Europeans heard the news: it was game over.[65]

A close friend of mine once told me that, upon informing her father she was getting married, he responded by asking, 'Against whom?' This is exactly in the spirit of de Gaulle's 1964 monetary marriage proposal to the Federal Republic of Germany. Lacking the economic might to subdue German industry and the Bundesbank in a straight tussle, France was to offer its hand in monetary matrimony instead.

France has always envisaged a monetary union against, rather than with, Germany. That this was not just one of de Gaulle's fixations has been confirmed repeatedly. Possibly the best example occurred on 18 September 1992, soon after France and a reunited Germany agreed by the Maastricht Treaty to create the euro. The French conservative daily Le Figaro had this to say on its front page: 'In the 1920s it was said that Germany would pay reparations. Now Germany is paying. The Maastricht Treaty is a Versailles Treaty without war!'[66] German officials knew this in 1964 and knew it in 1992. For the French elites, a common currency with Germany was an attempt to neutralize Germany, indeed to conquer the Bundesbank without firing a shot. German decision makers, especially Bundesbank officials, have never allowed themselves to forget that.

But why did Germany eventually agree to a monetary union knowing full well that it was part of a French strategy aimed against it? Conventional wisdom has it that Chancellor Helmut Kohl bowed to French demands for monetary union as the price of German reunification. Though this was not an insignificant consideration, the answer lies elsewhere: in the naked truth that Germany's export-led economy could never afford its own genuinely free-floating currency. The reason is simple: if the Deutsche Mark's international value were to be determined freely by the money markets, Germany's surpluses would create demand for its money, which would push up its value until German goods became so expensive abroad that German surpluses would disappear. The ambition to remain a surplus nation could not be served by a free-floating Deutsche Mark.

While the mark was embedded in America's global plan, its value fixed within the Bretton Woods international monetary system, German leaders and officials could behave like the managers of Europe's gleaming factory. They could concentrate solely on making sturdy cars and impressive gadgets, letting America mind global capitalism – exactly as the United States had planned things in the late 1940s. Alas, once the United States jettisoned Bretton Woods, and Europe along with it, German leaders could no longer treat the global environment as they treated the weather – as a natural system impervious to their actions and beliefs. They had to concede that the international economic environment was no longer divinely ordered and independent of what they decided. They had, in other words, to do something to shape that international environment in ways consistent with Germany's continued economic success.

Reluctant to think globally, or to try to shape the world in their image, German officials took the minimalist position: they surmised that a European Bretton Woods might suffice as a substitute for the American original. And if such a European monetary system could be made to work in the interests of German industry, the common currency that Paris was going on and on about might, eventually, become acceptable to them. But only after they had crushed France's ambitions to remain in the coachman's seat while German industry did all the pulling.[67]

3

Troubled Pilgrims

On a dull autumnal afternoon two men in suits exuding immense authority entered Aachen's cathedral. They were there to pay their respects to the remains of Charlemagne, the ninth-century Frankish king who had briefly reunited the Roman empire and whose spirit encapsulated, at least for traditionalist Central Europeans, the longing for a borderless Christian European realm: *Mitteleuropa* or *Paneuropa*, as they variably called it. Standing above the Christian warrior's grave and next to his ancient throne, the two men sought to quell the considerable trepidation caused by what they had just done: commit their two countries, France and Germany, to bundling their money together. Earlier that day, on the morning of 15 September 1978, they had signed a bilateral agreement to create the European Monetary System (EMS) – the euro's precursor.[1]

'Perhaps while we were discussing monetary affairs,' said one of the two pilgrims to an Italian journalist that same afternoon, 'the spirit of Charlemagne brooded over us.'[2] His name? Valéry Giscard d'Estaing, the finance minister President de Gaulle had dispatched to Bonn in March 1964 to startle the German government with a proposal for immediate currency union and now the proud occupant of the Elysée Palace, France's twentieth president. The second pilgrim appealing to Charlemagne's ghost for its approval of the monetary union was German chancellor Helmut Schmidt, a Social Democrat with a commitment to a United States of Europe as strong as Giscard's.[3]

Acerbic Eurosceptics, especially those of an Anglo-Saxon persuasion,[4] dismiss Giscard and Schmidt's visit to Charlemagne's resting place as another example of Euro-kitsch, as a piece of soap opera intended to win over the support of traditionalist French and German voters. Anyone who has watched the *Eurovision Song Contest* will recognize familiar elements of cheesiness in the notion that the president of France and the chancellor of Germany felt the need to visit the tomb of an ancient king to get his blessing for their attempt at a monetary union. While subsequent statements that Charlemagne's spirit instilled in them the idea of a European central bank stretch credulity beyond breaking point,[5] there is no doubt that the two men had good cause to be very, very worried. Lesser fear has been known to drive significant men to quainter pilgrimages.

Giscard was haunted by the memory of France's late exit from a previous catastrophic experiment with monetary union: the gold standard. Unlike Britain, which had unshackled itself in 1931 from the asphyxiating stranglehold of a fragmenting gold standard, and unlike the United States, which followed Britain in early 1933, France had held on to the bitter end – until 1936. The result was that its economy was crushed by recession,[6] its politics became chaotic, and the nation was so weakened that it could not resist the invasion of Nazi Germany,[7] suffering ignominious defeat in 1940. Of course, monetary union with Germany was Giscard's own idea, which he had unsuccessfully taken to Bonn in 1964. Still, as a thoughtful man, Giscard must have been painfully aware that the most vengeful of gods grant us our sincerest wishes. Would France do better in this fresh monetary union than it had done between the wars? Had he just agreed to an institution that might lose France without winning a united Europe spanning Charlemagne's imperium? I would not be surprised if Giscard did indeed say a little prayer that afternoon appealing to Charlemagne's spirit.

Helmut Schmidt was also a seriously worried man. The memory of what had happened to Chancellor Ludwig Erhard in 1966 weighed heavily upon him. For if the Bundesbank had felt justified in engineering a recession to oust a chancellor during the relative calm of the mid-1960s for the heinous crime of having once disagreed with it on the Deutsche Mark's exchange rate to the dollar,[8] Schmidt had good reason to shiver at the thought of how it would react if it were to get whiff of what he had been up to with Giscard since the previous April. Indeed, Schmidt had kept both the Bundesbank and his own cabinet

in the dark about this European monetary system plan, lest it be scut-
tled. It would not be surprising if, standing above Charlemagne's grave,
Schmidt said a little prayer too, along the lines of, 'Please, Charlemagne,
let the Bundesbank not pounce on me, thinking that I am turning its
authority over German money into a dowry for the French.'

A serpent slithers in a world unhinged

Earthquakes drive snakes out into the open, causing them to slither
about in a daze until the tectonic plates have settled again. The Nixon
Shock had been such an earthquake. It caused fault lines to appear in
Europe out of which, almost immediately, there emerged a noteworthy
serpent. This snake was Europe's initial reaction to the collapse of
the Bretton Woods system.

As the dollar plummeted and the Deutsche Mark soared, Europe's
currencies were in danger of being torn apart. Some managed to keep
up with the mark; others followed the dollar's plunge enthusiastically.
If nothing were done to glue them back together soon, German
exporters would be up in arms. Their cars and washing machines
were becoming prohibitively expensive in Britain, Italy and France,
where there was anger at rising prices and falling living standards.

Prior to 1971 Europe had been lulled into a false sense of American-
managed stability. European nations had become used to their currencies being underpinned by the greenback and varying only very slightly
in value in relation to each other. The institutions of the European
Union were also calibrated to function under the assumption that the
European currencies moved like boats rising or falling as the economic
tide came in and went out, only very occasionally rocked by some
wayward surge.

So, when in 1971 Europe was jettisoned from the dollar zone, and
exchange rates between its currencies started bobbing up and down,
some of them falling as violently as others were rising, the European
Union had real trouble managing the heavy industry cartel and the
common agricultural policy that were its core. Without stable steel,
coal and agricultural prices across France, Germany, Belgium, the
Netherlands and Italy, cartel-like price fixing was impossible. And

without that Central European cartel, the European Union would lose its *raison d'être*, descending into price wars that would undo the established distribution of political power, followed by the dissolution of the Brussels bureaucracies, open antagonism between European capitals and unregulated social upheaval in a continent struggling to put behind it a tumultuous past.

It was in response to this that Europe's 'snake in a tunnel' was born. The idea behind it was to simulate the fixed exchange rates of Bretton Woods within Europe. As Europe could do nothing to convince Washington to reattach its currencies to the dollar, its leaders decided to peg them to the continent's dominant Deutsche Mark. So in 1972 the European Union countries, plus Britain, Ireland, Denmark and Norway,[9] had agreed to restrict the fluctuations in the exchange rates between their currencies within extremely tight constraints.[10] To describe this quasi-fixed exchange rate system the unfortunate metaphor of a snake in a tunnel was employed, to convey the idea that each exchange rate (between, say, the franc and the Deutsche Mark) would be allowed to slither up and down within a narrowly confined space.

Europe's snake wriggled along happily in its tunnel for a few months, its body the surplus economies centred on Germany, its tail comprising deficit nations like France, Italy, Britain and Ireland. Alas, when the dollar price of oil exploded in 1973, the snake's rear end fell off like a lizard's tail in times of trouble.

The reason the snake could not hold on to its tail was the same as the cause of Bretton Woods's demise: in the absence of a leviathan recycling surpluses to parts of the system that nursed debilitating deficits, nations in deficit could not sustain fixed exchange rates with the rest, especially in times of crisis. To remain within Europe's monetary snake, a country with a trade deficit, France for example, urgently needed to attract foreign money to finance its net imports. Foreign money is attracted by high interest rates and deterred by any prospect that the state will not be able to pay its bills or repay its creditors. In other words, to stay in the snake Paris had to make borrowing dearer and simultaneously reduce public spending. But dearer money would reduce investment by French business, which would in turn depress employment and private incomes. And if government spending were also reduced to steady foreign investors' nerves, overall spending (private plus public) would diminish. But what does overall spending equate to? National income of course. In short, for France, just as for Britain, Italy and Ireland, to have stayed in the snake they would have had to crush their economies.[11]

Leaving the snake was not much fun for the deficit countries either. It meant devaluing their currencies in relation to the Deutsche Mark, pushing up not only the price of Volkswagens but also that of the imported machinery that helped Britain's National Health Service function, France's nuclear reactors run, Fiat cars accelerate and the trains arrive on time. Given the rotten choice between pulverizing one's economy and provoking social conflicts caused by inflation, most governments – certainly Washington – would have opted for the lesser evil of inflation caused by leaving the snake. That was certainly Britain's position. However, across the English Channel in France another priority occupied the establishment's collective will: saving what was, for the elites at any rate, a fabulously lucrative Central European cartel and its large multinational bureaucracy in Brussels.

Of course, no economic imperative favouring the interests of a relatively small elite can automatically prevail over the interests of a large majority. To do so, there needs to be a dominant ideology that permits the elites to co-opt the rest, to present their own vested interests on the broader canvas of some general will. The European ideal was, and remains, such an ideology. The image of Charlemagne is, in this context, not as kitsch and insignificant as it may seem to those residing outside Central Europe.

The European ideal, undoubtedly powerful and worthy in its own terms, offered politicians in Paris and Rome a glittering ideological veil with which to disguise their underlying determination to do whatever it took not to cut themselves off from the gravy train of power and funding that the cartel's political-administrative arm offered. Even if it meant a sharp, painful recession for their domestic economies, the national politicians of countries intertwined inextricably with the cartel could usually be counted upon to keep their nations permanently attached to it.

Which raises the question: why was it that, in the event, the French, the Belgian, the Dutch, the Italian elites abandoned Europe's first monetary union experiment, the snake, relatively quickly? Was it the economic cost it was imposing upon their populations, especially on labourers with no unearned income? Judging by the tenacity with which they have held on to more recent reincarnations of the snake,[12] this is a most unlikely explanation. A more convincing answer has to do with the snake's failure to offer worthy job prospects to the ambitious graduates of France's *grandes écoles* and the alumni of other European nurseries bringing up the next generation of Brussels-based bureaucrats. The snake came with no new institutions dedicated to it; there were no buildings with its logo, no army of bureaucrats whose livelihood and perks relied on it, no impressive titles for functionaries whose life's work would be to sing the serpent's praises. In short, the snake was unloved by the elites and thus doomed from the start. Within a year of its birth it had lost its tail, and what was left of it was next to useless for Germany, a living humiliation for France and an embarrassing nuisance for Brussels technocrats.

The European Monetary System that Giscard and Schmidt brought into being in 1978 to replace the deceased snake did more than invoke Charlemagne's spirit in Europe's monetary realm: it came complete with new jobs and opportunities for Brussels's bureaucracy. Unlike the snake, the EMS required central management from Brussels bureaucrats, who would run it in conjunction with bureaucrats in the great capitals of Europe – a mouth-watering prospect for elites seeking a greater battlefield on which to deploy their powers.

A peculiarly decent proposal

Five months before the Aachen pilgrimage Helmut Schmidt had met Roy Jenkins, then president of the European Commission and a former Labour Party government minister.[13] At that meeting Schmidt confided to Jenkins that, if the French Left were to lose the following month's parliamentary elections, as the German Social Democrat hoped they would, he would propose 'a major step towards monetary union; to mobilize and put all our currency reserves in a common pool . . . to form a monetary bloc'.[14]

The difference between such a monetary bloc and the snake could not have been more pronounced. Just as Bretton Woods had been built upon the IMF, and to a lesser extent the World Bank, so the proposed EMS would require a bureaucracy to pool the foreign exchanges of the participating central banks, coordinate their deployment and, hopefully, stabilize the exchange rates. Supranational bureaucrats with the power to make these decisions outside the confines of national governments were clearly necessary. Brussels all of a sudden got a whiff of a new source of power: power over member states' foreign exchange reserves and interest rates.

This was in fact a major shift in the German chancellor's attitude. Only a few months before he had said yes to monetary union but not if it meant German inflation going to 8 per cent. What did Schmidt mean by this condition regarding German inflation? The chancellor was sensibly alluding to Germany's fear of a repeat performance of Bretton Woods's final years, when to stabilize the franc the Bundesbank had to keep printing Deutsche Marks in response to the tendency of the French franc to devalue, courtesy of Germany's trade surplus in relation to France.[15]

The only way the franc's Deutsche Mark value could be kept constant was, indeed, for the Bundesbank to keep doing the one thing it detested: incessantly buy francs using freshly printed Deutsche Marks. Were these marks to remain stashed in the vaults of the French central bank – or anywhere else for that matter – the Bundesbank would not have minded much. Only these banknotes did not stay under lock and key, but were steadily repatriated back to Germany, as the French used them to buy more Volkswagens and speculators converted their francs into marks convinced that at some point the Bundesbank would let the franc slide, netting them a substantial windfall. And why would the Bundesbank let the franc slide? Because the repatriated Deutsche Marks were increasing the quantity of money circulating in Germany, pushing prices up and causing inflation in a nation that despised rising prices with all its heart, a nation that trusted the Bundesbank to prevent this from happening.

Schmidt's fear that a monetary bloc, a fixed exchange rate regime between France and Germany, would lead to increasing German prices and Bundesbank apprehension was conventional wisdom in Bonn and in Frankfurt. Pegging the franc to the mark could easily return the Bundesbank and the federal government to the situation they had so loathed back in the 1960s: having to print German banknotes to prop up the French currency, with Paris constantly pressurizing Germany to print more while at the same time chastising Bonn for not being a good European citizen.

Nonetheless, true to his word, when the French Right, Giscard's ruling coalition, unexpectedly won that election on 2 April 1978, Schmidt met Giscard in Rambouillet and told him of his change of heart. Giscard's face lit up, and together they plotted the next steps that led them, a few months later, to paying Charlemagne's tomb a visit after first signing the Franco-German EMS accord. Which raises several questions.

What caused Helmut Schmidt to make Giscard the peculiarly generous proposal he had mentioned in passing to Roy Jenkins? Were there new grounds for adopting Giscard's 1964 idea, the very one Chancellor Erhard had unceremoniously rejected? Was there a reason for the proposal being conditional on a defeat of the French Left? And where did Schmidt find the courage to go behind the Bundesbank's back and risk provoking its fury?

Chancellor Schmidt was a committed Europeanist, without a doubt. This explains why he wanted monetary, economic and political union, though not necessarily in that order. But it does not explain his sudden change of heart, his setting aside of inflation jitters and his apparently careless disregard of a potentially vengeful Bundesbank. To understand his generous offer to the French president one needs to recall that Schmidt was, in addition to being Europeanist, also a committed Atlanticist.

While talking to the French and arguing with the British, Schmidt's eyes were trained on the other side of the Atlantic, tuned in to how the hegemon which had shaped postwar Europe was deploying its extensive means to achieve its undiminished hegemonic ends. Schmidt had set aside his reluctance to risk German inflation and the wrath of the Bundesbank because of a historic development that he thought made the creation of the European Monetary System timely: the birth of a new type and a new era of American financial predominance that would establish itself in the 1980s and beyond.

That 'goddamn Volcker', again

The year was 1960. Postwar American monetary supremacy, in the form of the Bretton Woods system, was rock solid. One morning a young Chase Manhattan banker was startled when an aide stormed into his office with terrible news: 'Gold rose to forty dollars!' In a world made in America's image, where gold was supposedly fixed ad infinitum at $35 an ounce, the news struck Paul Volcker, the young banker of our story, as apocalyptic. On that day Volcker got it: the Bretton Woods system was on its way out. Would American hegemony perish with it? Not necessarily, he surmised.

As the 1960s ran out of puff, youngsters all over the world were rebelling against the uneasy affluence Bretton Woods had brought and revelling in every sign of its faltering. The Paris 1968 rebellion, Woodstock even, were political and cultural signs of a global system in trouble. By then Volcker had risen through the ranks of successive Democratic and Republican administrations to become instrumental in the dismantling of the Bretton Woods system. The 1971 announcement of the Nixon Shock may be remembered in John Connally's Texan accent but it was 'probably that goddamn Volcker', as President Nixon once referred to him, whose intellectual and technical work underpinned it. Volcker's concern and purpose? To ensure that the demise of the Bretton Woods system, made inescapable by America's slide from surplus to deficit nation status, should bestow more power upon the United States of America, not less.

A few short weeks after Giscard and Schmidt made their pilgrimage to Charlemagne's tomb, having signed the Franco-German European Monetary System agreement, Volcker gave a momentous speech to students and staff at the University of Warwick.[16] It was 9 November 1978, seven years after the Nixon Shock, and Volcker addressed his audience in his capacity as president of the New York Federal Reserve. Ten months later President Carter was to appoint him chairman of the Federal Reserve system, giving him the opportunity to put into practice what he had preached at Warwick.

Volcker's Warwick speech[17] is relatively unknown but it must surely go down as one of the most significant ever in central banking history.[18] 'It is tempting to look at the market as an impartial arbiter,' Volcker said, using a phrase so banal that even first-year economics students might have yawned at it. Of course the sting was in 'tempting', as Volcker is not a man often tempted by blandness. His next sentence was crafted to prove this, utilizing a degree of brute honesty that central bankers are not known for: 'But balancing the requirements of a stable international system against the desirability of retaining freedom of action for national policy, a number of countries, including the US, opted for the latter.'

And as if such unbridled veracity was insufficient, Volcker added a phrase equivalent to undermining all the assumptions on which Western Europe and Japan had erected their postwar economic miracles: 'controlled disintegration in the world economy is a legitimate objective for the 1980s'. It was a fitting epitaph for the Bretton Woods system and the clearest exposition of the dawning second postwar phase, which Volcker had been busily working towards. But why would a 'disintegration in the world economy' even if 'controlled' help the United States in the 1980s?

Volcker had been trying to answer the questions he had asked himself in 1960, when out of the blue the price of gold had shot up to $40. How could America retain its hegemony once it went into deficit in relation to Japan, Germany and later China? If the United States had no surpluses to recycle, how could it dominate global capitalism? It took Volcker some time to develop a fully fledged answer, but by 1978 he was ready to present it to his Warwick audience, just before moving from the powerful New York Federal Reserve to the almighty Fed.

The essence of his Warwick lecture was, if America cannot recycle its surplus, having slipped into a deficit position back in the mid-1960s, it must now recycle other people's! But how, one may reasonably ask, can a deficit nation recycle other nations' surpluses? Surely those with the money – the surplus owners – have the power to do as they please with it, paying next to no attention to the musings of those in deficit? Usually, but not always, thought Volcker. The trick, he believed, was to persuade foreign capitalists to send their capital to Wall Street. Tricky but not impossible. The way to do this was to hit two usually contradictory targets at once: on the one hand push American interest rates through the roof, while on the other ensure that Wall Street offered a more lucrative market for investors than its equivalents in London, Frankfurt, Tokyo, Paris or anywhere else.

High interest rates are wonderful for those living on unearned income, so-called rentiers,[19] but not so good for manufacturers, who see their investment costs skyrocket and the purchasing power of their customers plummet. For this reason, combining high returns to financial capital (requiring high interest rates) with high profit rates for American businesses (requiring low interest rates) was never going to be easy, and Volcker knew this. It was a combination that could only come about if another way of providing that profit could be found. And one way to do that would be to reduce wages. The Fed would push interest rates through the roof; meanwhile the federal government would turn a blind eye, indeed promote, policies that crushed the real wage prospects of American workers.

For the first time in American history, including the Great Depression, American blue-collar workers were to face an age of declining real wages.[20] That decline, in a global economy buffeted by the 'controlled disintegration' Volcker unashamedly spoke of, was the price poorer Americans were to pay so that the United States could maintain world dominance despite being a deficit nation. Soon the fate of America's working class was to infect the circumstances of weaker citizens in Britain, France and, by the 1990s, even Germany. As for Africa and Latin America, the weak there suffered losses that only the great novelists can begin to recount.

Once ensconced as chairman of the Federal Reserve, Volcker lost little time in putting his plan into action. Dollar interest rates topped 20 per cent; American inflation was defeated; the Third World went bankrupt; Africa's sputtering industrialization ended; Soviet satellites that had borrowed heavily from the West in greenbacks such as Yugoslavia, Poland and Romania failed, and workers everywhere were forced into a race to the bottom, having to choose between undercutting the wages of workers living elsewhere and unemployment.

Disintegration was in the air, and the majority of people in the majority of countries eventually acquiesced in the notion that labour was overvalued and overprotected, manufacturing was overrated, while finance was undervalued and in need of unshackling. Everything became increasingly reducible to its financial value. Manufacturers of note, like General Motors in America and Cadbury's in Britain, were reduced to their stock exchange value, losing their place in the public conscience as venerable institutions. Engineers lost out to young brash MBA graduates, who despite their inexperience rose to lead giants like Ford and General Electric. Workers were financialized too, forced to take increasing risks in the housing market and with their pensions. A new mantra – 'There is no alternative' or TINA – was born, soon to be given an ideological wrap by Margaret Thatcher in Britain and Ronald Reagan in the United States. Financially stressed citizens, made so by their lack of access to capital goods and unearned income, were facing an onslaught they had not experienced since the 1930s, an onslaught that New Deal and Great Society programmes in the United States, and the social contract implicit in the European Union's cartelized economy had supposedly made impossible in the postwar era.

In continental Europe a borderless cartelized economy comprising different currency jurisdictions faced special challenges. Volcker's disintegration inserted the thin edge of a large wedge into its flesh. With every interest rate rise, every jolt of divergence in the value of the currencies of surplus and deficit European nations, the Europe that America had built up in the late 1940s was torn apart. Central European politicians, like Schmidt and Giscard, held on to the hope that their European Monetary System would act as the cement keeping their postwar realities together. History was to prove them badly mistaken.

Not by choice

History has no time for the democratic process, but surges ahead like a steamroller bent on flattening our collective preferences. Occasionally this is a good thing. If Europeans living under feudalism had been asked to choose the Industrial Revolution over serfdom, they would have almost certainly declined. The collapse of Bretton Woods was not such a development. Even Paul Volcker, who had played a major role in its demise, would have preferred it to survive. And he would have been right.

Bretton Woods was meant as a balanced system of international trade and financial flows. The New Deal that stabilized 1930s America, albeit imperfectly, was internationalized after the war, extending its righteous reach to the four corners of the so-called Western hemisphere. The fact that inequality between and within nations shrank during Bretton Woods was a design feature.[21] As a result, in the 1950s and 1960s the poor had, as the phrase goes, never had it so good, courtesy of a leviathan keenly aware that its self-interest was best served by an enlightened equilibration of world capitalism, involving controls on finance, limits to all sorts of profiteering and the active redistribution of incomes to the have-nots.

Central to that global plan, of which Bretton Woods was the monetary component, was America's surplus position – the fact that the United States exited the war exporting a great deal more manufactures and agricultural products than it imported. To stabilize its global dominion it used its trade surplus judiciously, politically and hegemonically, fully aware of the profound difference between hegemony and authoritarianism. In that world bankers like Paul Volcker were kept in a box. During the 1950s and 1960s American bankers were forced to labour within strict confines set by the New Deal institutions. Their salaries were substantial but no more than six or at most seven times that of their building's janitor, compared to today's obscene factors of three hundred and beyond. They paid taxes at rates today's bankers would laugh at and with no recourse to an archipelago of tax havens. Interest rates were fixed, at close to 5 per cent, and opportunities for gambling with depositors' money were severely circumscribed by draconian restrictions harking back to Franklin Delano Roosevelt's administration.

Bretton Woods had kept Paul Volcker and his fellow bankers within shackles forged in the workshops of the Great Depression and designed to prevent another bout of 1920s-style financialization (in which the trade in financial products outweighs all others, such that more profit is made from loans and debt than from capital) from wrecking capitalism again.[22] It would be a grave error, however, to imagine that Volcker worked towards demolishing Bretton Woods because of these restrictions on his liberty to profit. Unfettered banking was not his thing. Indeed, Volcker was himself a New Dealer who cut his teeth defending, upholding and attempting to stabilize the Bretton Woods system. It was only when he was convinced that Bretton Woods's global balancing act was doomed by forces beyond America's control that his pragmatism kicked in.

Instead of retiring into a bunker to defend a system crumbling around him, as Europeans habitually do, Volcker and many others of his ilk did what they knew best: they tried to overtake events, to lead them, to forge the next global financial system out of the debris of the one they had destroyed once they had realized that it was pointless trying to save it. Volcker symbolizes the self-confident American policymaker whose greatest fault is an unquestioning conviction that what is good for the United States is good for the world; a foible compensated for with an astonishing capacity to look into the future and distinguish between that which is desirable and that which is feasible.

If Volcker had had a choice, he would have opted to repair and retain Bretton Woods despite the restrictions it placed upon his banking activities. Why? Because he understood that true and sustainable hegemony requires a rejection of the Athenian generals' logic in Thucydides's *Peloponnesian War*.[23] The New Dealers may have seemed unbearably arrogant in the eyes of Europeans like President de Gaulle, but they nonetheless recognized a simple truth: that if 'the weak suffer what they must', their very capacity, let alone willingness, to reproduce the power of the strong declines precipitously.

Condorcet's little secret

Do the weak really reproduce the power of the mighty? Don't the strong do what they can with no help from the weak, for whom solace comes from a moralistic glorification of their misery? In 1794, as the French Revolution was preparing to give way to a new despotism, the Marquis de Condorcet alluded brilliantly to 'the secret that real power lies not with the oppressors but with the oppressed'.[24] It was a point the New Dealers were painfully aware of but which European elites have still to grasp.

The power to accumulate trade surpluses, to amass a large part of the jointly produced wealth, to set the agenda – these are not forms of might that can be maintained for long on the basis of brute force or authoritarianism. Crushing those in deficit when they cannot meet their obligations is bound to destroy the surplus position of their stronger trading partners. Putting defaulters into debtors' prison guarantees that their debts will never get paid. Moreover, only when the weak have reasons to defend the system that promotes their subservience will the empire of the powerful survive.

Volcker, like all New Dealers, harboured a deep appreciation of power's capacity to undermine itself, both at the level of a national economy and, even more so, internationally. He had seen in his youth how unbridled financialization had led to the wholesale liquidation of capital and how unfettered international relations had brought on the annihilation of millions of people on battlefields, in concentration camps, in the dustbowls of the Great Depression. It is unlikely that Volcker ever read Thucydides' account of the Melian representatives' speech or indeed Marquis de Condorcet's insight. However, he was of a generation for whom the weak could be trampled upon only at the peril of the mighty. And yet by 1978 he had surmised that America's postwar attempt to create a system that protected economically weaker citizens and nations was dead in the water.

To salvage the American way of life, and its global dominion, the world economy had to be disintegrated in a controlled fashion. And monetary policy, over which Paul Volcker was about to acquire decisive authority, was to be his weapon of mass disintegration.

Volcker's gauntlet picked up

Volcker felt it his duty to raise interest rates to levels hitherto unknown in leading capitalist economies. The standard interpretation is that he was firing a silver bullet at the inflation bogeyman: by raising interest rates substantially he would encourage Americans to save. Since higher savings can only be achieved by cutting down on spending, consumers would reduce their demand for goods and services, thus causing a slowdown in price inflation. But this is a very small part of the story. Volcker's reasons were much deeper.

The postwar system that had constrained the exercise of financial power by the strong over the weak, people and nations alike, was kaput. And it was so because America had lost its surplus, that great stabilizing instrument that had kept the postwar world order together. When John Connally explained to President Nixon, relying on Volcker's underlying analysis, that 'all foreigners are out to screw us and it's our job to screw them first', what he meant was that the Bretton Woods balancing act was being unbalanced by the surpluses of countries like Germany and Japan.

Impervious to the global responsibility that comes with large trade surpluses, these foreigners were trying to take advantage of the United States' commitment to global balance, the result being a collapse of the postwar equilibrium. Like immature children who don't know what is good for them, they were taking advantage of America's difficulties, with detrimental results for everyone. They had to be put in their place.

And put in their place they were, not once, not twice but three times. Once in 1971, when the European currencies were jettisoned from the dollar zone. A second time with the oil crises of 1973 and 1979, which limited the cost advantage of European and Japanese industry vis-à-vis America's. And last but not least Volcker's interest rate hikes between 1979 and 1982, which hit Europe and Japan far harder than they hit America's more tenacious economy, their effect being a stupendous collapse in economic activity as the cost of *not* sending capital to Wall Street skyrocketed.

Volcker's 1978 Warwick speech had given the Europeans ample warning. He effectively threw down the gauntlet before Bonn, Paris, London and Tokyo. Between the lines he was foreshadowing the second phase of America's postwar global dominance. In 1971, Volcker implicitly told his audience, America had dismantled the monetary system whose integrity the Europeans had foolishly undermined. Its next move would be to bring about a highly unbalanced global system that the United States controlled because, rather than in spite, of its twin deficits – in trade and the federal government budget.

The price for that new system, which would extend America's dominance, was high: weak people and fragile countries were once more left to their own devices, suffering not what was globally optimal but that which they 'must' in a world economy unrestrained by New Deal-like rules and institutions. Politics would become toxic; social solidarity would weaken; international relations would turn nastier; poverty would multiply in Latin America and Africa. Nonetheless, the United States was bound to emerge as a net beneficiary of this painful change, a thought that consoled Volcker despite his hand in deconstructing the universalized version of the New Deal that had shaped him as a young man keen to devote his life to public service.[25]

The dawn of this new, less confident era was what made 1978 such a significant year, motivating Chancellor Schmidt to rethink the idea of the Franco-German monetary union initially proposed by Valéry Giscard d'Estaing in 1964. The new American global design, founded on a Washington-led controlled disintegration of international trade and banking, suddenly added appeal to the idea of an institutionalized monetarily united *Mitteleuropa*.

Charlemagne's spirit was to get a postmodern spin as Chancellor Schmidt, with President Giscard in tow, picked up Volcker's gauntlet.

A triumph of optimism?

As Volcker readied his controlled disintegration the German chancellor diagnosed that, in this brave new financial world, the European Monetary System might deliver more than just lucrative jobs for Central Europe's elite boys in fancy new Brussels directorates. Within the circumstances of America's new role, it was just possible that the EMS might work, proving more than another triumph of hope over experience.

Chancellor Schmidt knew that the Americans were about to put the global economy through the rapids of financialization, using US interest rates as the lever. Since Erhard's time Bonn had always been more attuned to Washington's ways, at least compared to the self-satisfied Elysée officials, by whom America was more scorned than second-guessed. While Giscard's team were preoccupied with the goings-on in Brussels and absorbed with Germany's attitude to their plans, German officials were busily working out the likely impact of a monetary bloc that had to thrive within Volcker's new design.

The snake, they knew, had failed for two reasons, each of which on its own was perfectly capable of causing its early demise. The first was its lack of joint institutions to pursue a common monetary policy. The EMS would have those in the form of brand new Brussels committees. The second, potentially more important, reason was the same feature that had doomed Bretton Woods in the late 1960s: the absence of a mechanism for supporting the fixed exchange rates via recycling surpluses; that is, taking profits from the countries that produced (or least received) them and redirecting them to the deficit regions or nations.

The Bretton Woods system had had the institutions necessary to coordinate interest rates and the central banks' interventions in money markets. But this did not help alleviate the tensions between the Bundesbank and the German federal government after America lost its capacity to regulate trade and financial flows through exporting its own surplus. Why would the EMS, even if it possessed the right institutions, succeed in the late 1970s and early 1980s where Bretton Woods had failed in the late 1960s?

Here is a thought that gave Chancellor Schmidt hope: if Volcker's global design occasioned a constant torrent of German capital gushing into Wall Street, maybe a monetary union with France could be made to work. *This time things might be different* was the hope that explains, at least partly, Schmidt's change of heart. Was this optimism sensible prescience or pie-in-the-sky wishful thinking?

The 1980s, 1990s, even the 2000s, confirmed that there was some sense in the optimism behind the EMS. Volcker's disintegration, effected initially through sizeable interest rate increases, enabled the United States to accomplish a feat unique in history: to enhance the power of its empire by increasing its trade and budget deficits. 'But who would pay for them?' the Calvinist might ask. 'The rest of the world!' Paul Volcker would retort. 'How?' 'By means of a permanent transfer of capital' was the answer America's policymakers gave in practice, even if never in so many words.

While German officials would rather die than emulate America's designer profligacy, Helmut Schmidt's team could see an opening for a European Bretton Woods within this new phase of American dominance. The ever-expanding US deficits would operate like a giant vacuum cleaner, absorbing Germany's surplus goods and capital. Under these conditions, there was a possibility that the French franc could be harmlessly pegged to the Deutsche Mark.[26] As in the late 1960s, the

Bundesbank would have to print Deutsche Marks to buy francs to stop the French currency's decline. But unlike in the late 1960s, German inflation was less of a threat with Volcker on the loose. The American vacuum cleaner, powered by Volcker's high interest rates, could now be counted upon to suck the fresh Deutsche Marks in, preventing them from making their way immediately from France back into Germany. The Federal Republic could thus, for a second time since Byrnes's 1946 Speech of Hope, look to America for assistance in cementing its position, and reputation, as Europe's powerhouse.

Chancellor Schmidt, in acceding to President Giscard d'Estaing's monetary union plans, could look forward to the benefits of stabilizing the European Union along the Franco-German axis, bolstering the Central European industrial cartel and maintaining a constant demand for German industrial goods from France and the other Latin countries attached to it. And all that without the earlier worries of German inflation that enraged the Bundesbank.

That the Bundesbank's anger was not, in the event, averted confirmed that Schmidt had good cause to be worried as he put his signature on the EMS agreement. Still, it was not totally rash to anticipate that this time things might be different. Powered by America's deficits, the world's leading surplus economies, Germany, Japan and, later, China, kept churning out the goods that America absorbed, and yet almost 70 per cent of European profits were being transferred back to the United States in the form of capital flows to Wall Street. And what did Wall Street do with them? It funded the rise of financialization.

The bankers' emancipation from their New Deal fetters was both a symptom and a prerequisite for this new phase of American dominance. Who else but the bankers could facilitate the vast capital transfers, the perpetual tsunami of capital, necessary to satiate American deficits, which had to keep growing in order to maintain the illusion of what Ben Bernanke, one of Volcker's successors, named the Great Moderation? Fair-weather recycling, writ large, had taken over globally from the planned political recycling that was the essence of the Bretton Woods system. Though this was never going to end well, it had the capacity to put the global economy on a spending spree that lasted three decades before crashing in 2008.[27]

French and German banks participated joyfully in all this and, through their frenzied lending, underpinned Europe's attempt at monetary union – first via the EMS, later the single currency. It was only in 2008 that Europe was to come face to face with the tremendous damage its bankers had done to the project of monetary union. Two years later, in 2010, the euro crisis was in full swing and Europe in disarray.

A timeless beast

Once upon a time, as a famous Greek myth has it, the reign of King Minos of Crete secured peace, enabling trade to criss-cross the high seas in heavily laden ships and spread prosperity's benevolent reach to all corners of the known world. Alas, a terrible secret was buried deep inside the foundations of the good king's palace. For inside its maze-like basement, known as the Labyrinth, there lived a creature as fierce as it was wretched. The product of the queen's miscegenation with a sacred bull, the creature's intense loneliness was comparable only to the fear it inspired far and wide. The Minotaur, for this was the tragic beast's name, had a voracious appetite that only human flesh could satiate. And satiated the fiend had to be or the king's reign would be cut short by the gods' wrath. Every now and then a ship loaded with youngsters left faraway Athens, a city that Minos had subdued in battle. Docking in Crete, the ship delivered its human tribute to be devoured by the Minotaur. It was a gruesome but essential ritual for preserving the era's peace and ensuring its prosperity.

The spectre of the Minotaur, confined for millennia to mythology, emerged again to haunt Europe as Paul Volcker delivered his University of Warwick speech. Unwittingly, Volcker was presenting a narrative that bore a striking resemblance to the Cretan myth: both were accounts of how a terrible secret underpinned a seemingly stable world order.[28] In both narratives equilibrium and trade-based prosperity were built on tributes flowing from the periphery (Athens in mythological times, Europe and Asia in Volcker's version) to the seat of power (Crete and Wall Street respectively). These tributes fed the story's menacing aberration, the Minotaur in one case, America's trade deficit in the other, devouring the rest of the world's net exports and keeping its industries humming nicely. Volcker was presiding over the birth of a new, global, Minotaur, its Labyrinth located deep in the guts of America's economy.

What to Ben Bernanke was the Great Moderation was in fact the most immoderate, least stable equilibrium the world economy had experienced. The open secret no one dared discuss was that the new global order depended on the constant inflation of America's twin deficits. In other words, the Great Moderation rested on the thin walls of a constantly expanding gargantuan bubble. The more US deficits grew, the greater the global Minotaur's appetite for Europe and Asia's capital. Its truly global significance was due to its role in recycling financial capital (profits, savings, surplus money) through the international circuits that Wall Street had established. It kept the gleaming German factories busy. It gobbled up everything produced in Japan and later in China. And, to complete the circle, the foreign (or American) owners of these distant factories sent their profits, their cash, to Wall Street – a modern tribute to the global Minotaur.

What do bankers do when a tsunami of capital comes their way daily? When billions of dollars, net, run through their fingers every morning of each week? They find ways to make it breed. Throughout the 1980s, the 1990s and all the way to 2008 Wall Street took in the daily influx of foreign capital and on its back built mountains of derivative trades, which in time acquired the properties of private money. Financialization, as we now call this process, was the critical by-product of maintaining and enhancing US dominance on the back of increasing trade imbalances and in the interest of financing America's ever-expanding twin deficits. It began as froth on top of the stream of profits flowing from Germany and Japan to Wall Street, once Volcker's controlled disintegration of the world economy took effect. But soon the froth took over, usurping the underlying stream of actual values, turning finance into the driver and industry into its servant.

Just like its mythological predecessor, the global Minotaur kept the world economy going. Until, that is, in 2008 the pyramids of private money built upon the Minotaur's feeding frenzy caved in under their own impossible weight. Europe's monetary system, born in 1978, was to suffer a terminal blow. America was to feel its impact too, but it was Europe's weakest link, Greece, that was flattened.

Athens pilgrimage

The Greek dictatorship collapsed in the summer of 1974, at the end of my first year in high school. As the military regime melted away, the presidential plane of Valéry Giscard d'Estaing carried a Greek politician, a personal friend of the French president, to Athens to take over the reins of government. Five years later, a year after the signing of the Franco-German European Monetary System agreement, the same plane carried Giscard to Athens.

During the preceding night and day the Greek authorities had proved their capacity for brutal efficiency by completing at breakneck pace a multi-lane thoroughfare connecting the old airport to the centre of Athens. It was a gesture – for the benefit of the French president – towards Greece's modernizing intentions, for Giscard was visiting the Greek capital in order to sign the treaty by which a year later, in 1980, Greece would become a full member of the European Union.

Here is how Giscard was to relate to France's leading daily newspaper the reasons behind his pilgrimage to Athens in 1979.

> Our partners were extremely reluctant. The country [Greece] was disorganized, its democracy had not yet solidified and it lacked a common border with any member state. I took the decision emphasizing that we had to do this [induct Greece into the European Union] in order to reinforce democracy. And since at the time I held the rotating presidency of the European Common Market, I signed the act by which Greece was admitted into the community on 28 May 1979 in Athens. The logic of my decision was purely political. It was imperative that Greece was supported after shedding dictatorship. But it also had symbolic importance. My education, the education of my generation, was based on the idea of democracy, of politics, all ideas that came from that country. To us, Greece is

synonymous with civilization. In this sense, the idea that it would remain outside the gates of Europe was unbearable.[29]

Thirty-six years later, less than a month after I had become Greece's finance minister, Giscard was to give an interview to another French newspaper to argue that, while 'Greece belongs to the European Union', it should leave its monetary union – the single currency that was the 'natural' conclusion of his and Schmidt's 1978 EMS treaty.[30] Just as Volcker, Connally and Nixon began to think of Eurexit as the solution to the dollar zone's troubles, so today some of the pioneers of the eurozone are toying with Grexit as the way to fix the common currency.[31] Clearly something had gone terribly wrong.

Irrespective of whether Giscard was right to bring Greece into the European Union in May 1979 or to advocate Grexit in February 2015, a splendid irony was unfolding: the monetary union he and Schmidt inaugurated in September 1978 first asphyxiated the Greek government during the spring of 2015 and, then, on 12 July 2015, with the Euro-summit 'agreement' on Greece, unthinkingly crushed the very same democracy that Giscard had worked so hard to protect by bringing Greece into the European Union.

The 1980s and early 1990s were not kind to Europe's monetary system. The decade kicked off with a major global recession (1979–82), complicating the task of keeping Europe's currencies pegged to each other, and by the time some stability had returned, causing Europe to attempt to tighten its monetary union, a fresh recession in the early 1990s devastated it. After almost two decades of trying and failing to fix their exchange rates, to create a European Bretton Woods following the Nixon Shock, a stark choice was imposed on Europe's leaders: abandon monetary union altogether, or go all out, turning a system of many currencies with quasi-fixed exchange rates into a single currency: the euro.

At that juncture, between 1991 and 1993, it was Giscard and Schmidt's direct successors, President François Mitterrand of France and Chancellor Helmut Kohl of Germany, who were the driving force behind the euro project. Mitterrand's former finance minister, Jacques Delors, by then the all-powerful president of the European Commission, warned Mitterrand that a proper monetary union required more than rules and Brussels-based committees. At the very least, it required some common public debt (as Alexander Hamilton, the first secretary of the treasury, argued at the founding of the USA) and a common investment policy (as the New Dealers knew well).

Mitterrand's reaction circa 1993 was typically nuanced. Yes, he acknowledged, we need both some common debt and a union-wide investment programme. But this required a degree of political union that he and Helmut Kohl did not have the power to impose on France and Germany's powerful elites. Mitterrand's solution, such as it was, was deliberately to put the cart before the horse and wait for a large bump in the road to convince Europe's backseat drivers that the configuration needed changing. European currencies would be glued together first. And when the next global financial crisis came along, it would persuade France and Germany's power brokers to merge their political systems into some sort of federation.

Mitterrand appreciated that a single currency without common debt, or an aggregate investment policy that took capital from the surplus countries to invest into the deficit ones, was asking for trouble. At least that is what he conceded to Jacques Delors in private.[32] He realized that a sharp financial crisis would find the euro wanting. But he also believed deep in his bones that, when that next global crisis came, his and Kohl's successors would have no alternative but to acquiesce in the political union necessary to salvage it. If they did not, the euro would shrivel and die.

Heartbreakingly, Mitterrand and Kohl's successors came up particularly short when the mother of all financial crises hit in 2008, putting the euro into a tailspin eighteen months later. During the spring of 2015 I was privileged (if that is the word) to endure long meetings with them and to listen in during teleconferences that went on until the wee hours of the morning. Mitterrand and Kohl must have been spinning in their graves at how their heirs failed to rise to the occasion once the euro crisis hit. They had plenty of opportunities to help build the political union Mitterrand had hoped for, but they missed every single one of them (see Chapter 5). The question is why. Why did

Europe fail to consolidate in response to its long post-2008 crisis? The United States came out of every financial crisis from the early nineteenth century onwards stronger and more united. Why not Europe?

It is nowadays common for Europeans to bemoan a lack of quality leadership and to long for the leaders of decades past. 'If only we had a Mitterrand, a Giscard, a Kohl or a Schmidt in government' is a standard lament in Europe's bars, taxis and even parliaments, the implication being that, if we did, Europe would be uniting now as America did after 1929 under the stewardship of Franklin D. Roosevelt. But things are not that simple. First, for reasons outlined in the previous chapter, Europe's union is nothing like America's: it was founded as an administration for an industrial cartel, rather than as a political mechanism by which to balance competing interests in a democracy.[33] Second, there are reasons why political leadership is not what it used to be across the world.

This is not due to some deterioration in the current generation's leadership gene. Rather, the depoliticization of political life, itself aided and abetted by Europe's technocratic monetary union, has turned naturally gifted political animals away from politics. The more the crucial political decisions are turned over to unelected second-rate technocrats, the fewer gifted men and women enter politics. Would the young Mitterrand, I wonder, have entered politics in a Europe where questions of interest rates, taxation and social welfare policy were deferred to faceless bureaucrats?

Inadvertently, Mitterrand and Kohl contributed to a technocracy revolving around a monetary union that eradicated the type of political leadership necessary to step in during a crisis and complete their creation. Adding a political amalgam to the monetary union that Schmidt and Giscard began and took so much further requires leaders that their monetary union weeded out. It is not therefore a simple case of heirs and successors proving unequal to the task bestowed upon them by the pioneers. It is, rather, a case of pioneers who put into place monetary institutions which at once needed future politicians to complete them, while at the same time ensuring that this calibre of politician would be driven out of politics. The stuff of tragedy had been woven into Europe's monetary union from the outset.

There is a sense in which the euro's pioneers, from Giscard and Schmidt to Mitterrand and Kohl, could be excused. The European Union began as a cartel of heavy industries whose excellent by-product was the impossibility of orchestrating another European war once the instruments necessary for its waging had been Europeanized. Why should they not imagine that political union would follow from the Europeanization of money? Could Mitterrand have known that monetary union would have the opposite effect to that which he anticipated? That it would make political union harder, rather than a natural development of a single currency? That it might even crush democracy sequentially, beginning with weak links like Greece before doing immense damage to France and Germany?

The answer is, I submit, that not only could Mitterrand and Kohl have known but that they should have known.

'[I]t is a dangerous error to believe that monetary and economic union can precede a political union or that it will act (in the words of the Werner Report[34]) "as a leaven for the evolvement of a political union which in the long run it will in any case be unable to do without".' These words were penned by Cambridge economist Nicholas Kaldor not in 2015 or 1993 but in 1970, at a time when the good professor could see the Nixon Shock coming and Europe itching to respond by putting the cart before the horse.[35] Kaldor had seen enough evidence that the Europeans were about to commit a 'dangerous error'. A clash between France and Germany was developing even at that early stage and Kaldor's sensitive antennae had picked it up.

The Werner Report, which Kaldor read and referred to, explicitly talked of the need to 'coordinate national spending and taxation' as a prerequisite to a workable monetary union. This reference was put in the report by the German representatives, with support from their Italian and Dutch colleagues but against the express wishes of the French. France, reflecting de Gaulle's vision of using Europe as a means of enhancing (rather than diminishing) the French nation state, opposed this federalist dimension. Paris wanted to have its cake (a Europeanized Deutsche Mark) and eat it too (retain national sovereignty over budgetary matters). When the European Commission backed Paris, as it usually did in pre-euro days, Germany's enthusiasm for the whole idea crumbled, although only eight years later, in 1978, Chancellor Schmidt, influenced by America's new game, revived the idea.

Kaldor took a quick look at this emerging opposition along the Franco-German axis and, well before Giscard and Schmidt had risen to the top, issued a clarion warning: '[If] the creation of a monetary union and Community control over national budgets generates pressures which lead to a breakdown of the whole system, it will prevent the development of a political union, not promote it.'[36]

Rather than take heed of such wise counsel, official Europe chose to bob merrily across a sea of self-satisfying myths. Denial of basic economic laws had become its foundation stone and hubris its response to reality's protestations. Nemesis, as Greek tragedians might have warned, was biding her time, waiting for her moment in history.

4

Trojan Horse

London, November 1990. After weeks of bitter struggle fending off a pack of toffee-nosed cabinet ministers hell-bent on toppling her, Margaret Thatcher made her last stand in a now famous cabinet meeting at 10 Downing Street. The issue that had allowed Conservative Party grandees to unite against their prime minister was Europe's monetary union. She wanted none of it; they were keen to hook sterling to the European Monetary System.

Soon after the cabinet meeting began it was clear that her eleven-year reign was over. One after the other even her hitherto loyal ministers abandoned ship with all the cowardice that one expects of politicians sensing that their bread will be better buttered and their seats made safer by a new leader. It has been said that the Iron Lady shed a single tear, a sign of her humanity over whose existence many had expressed doubt.

That same evening she made her penultimate appearance in the House of Commons as prime minister. It was a memorable performance. Pressing into service her impressive command of Parliament, Thatcher was never going to miss the opportunity to avenge herself on her colleagues by demonstrating that none of them would ever dominate the opposition the way she could. Her earlier tear became a cataract of rhetoric peppered with humour, flattening her opponents.

The leader of the opposition, Neil Kinnock, must still regret that he chose Europe's monetary union as the topic on which to score points against the outgoing premier. 'Will the prime minister tell us,' asked Liberal Democrat Alan Beith, in the misguided expectation that Thatcher would be discomfited by the subject, 'if she will continue her personal fight against a single currency and an independent [meaning European] central bank?' Before she could answer, another opposition MP mischievously interjected, 'No, she's going to be the governor!'

'What a good idea!' Thatcher replied after a great deal of merriment had filled the House. And then went on to say playfully, 'I had not thought of it. But if I were, there would be no European central bank accountable to no one, least of all to national parliaments. Because *under that kind of central bank there will be no democracy*, [and the central bank will be] taking powers away from every single parliament and be able to have a single currency and a monetary policy and an interest rate policy that takes away from us all political power.'[1]

It was perhaps the first and last time the prime minister of a major European nation hit the nail on the head regarding the nature of Europe's monetary union. The notion that money can be administered apolitically, by technical means alone, is dangerous folly of the grandest magnitude. The fantasy of apolitical money was what rendered the gold standard in the interwar period such a primitive system whose inevitable demise spawned fascist and Nazi thugs with effects that we all know and lament.

The gold standard was underpinned by the idea of depoliticizing money by linking its quantity to the amount of gold – a metal that politicians could not conjure up from thin air since it was provided exogenously by nature. Today the same fantasy of apolitical money can be found not just in the construction of a European central bank that is answerable to no parliament (as Thatcher pointed out so astutely) but also in newfangled digital currencies like Bitcoin, whose selling point is the absence of political authority over them. Margaret Thatcher's precious point was that controlling interest rates and the supply of money is a quintessentially political activity which, if removed from the purview of a democratically elected parliament, would occasion a steady descent into authoritarianism.

Her final phrase on the matter resonated in my mind during the five months I served as Greece's finance minister. Every time I looked across the aisle in Greece's parliament to see the thugs of the Golden Dawn sneering at me, and at every Eurogroup meeting, in which Mario Draghi, the European Central Bank's president, would set the parameters within which we politicians had to labour with no recourse to any parliament or any process that might be thought of as demo-cratic,[2] Thatcher's words rang true: 'A single currency is about the politics of Europe.'[3]

Occasionally I return to the faded clip of Thatcher's final parlia-mentary performance as prime minister to extract some bitter joy. 'I am enjoying this! I am enjoying this!' Thatcher concluded happily before sitting down, satisfied that her executioners were reminded of their mediocrity.

Having spent my formative years joining every demonstration I could find against Mrs Thatcher and her government's policies, my appreciation of her prescient critique of the euro's built-in democratic deficit is particularly delightful. Politics, I now understand, is at its best when it enlightens us via an opponent's insight. In meetings I addressed in London in September 2015 to celebrate Jeremy Corbyn's elevation to the leadership of the Labour Party I dared mention my appreciation of Margaret Thatcher's critique of apolitical money. To my great relief, audiences seemed to welcome my tribute to a polit-ician who, for us left-wingers, symbolizes everything that we had stood against.

Thatcher's error

That European monetary union was a political project was never in dispute. Its pioneers openly and proudly wore their political agenda on their sleeves. President Giscard and Chancellor Schmidt alluded in 1978 to the creation of a Central European realm that Charlemagne's spirit would approve of. In the late 1980s and early 1990s François Mitterrand imagined the single currency as a prelude to federation. The euro was always, in Thatcher's words, 'about the politics of Europe'. The question was, what kind of politics? The kind that promotes the idea of common prosperity within a democratic Europe? Or the kind that divides Europeans and turns their democracies into empty shirts hanging out to dry on an unaccountable central bank's clothes line?

Alas, that was a question never seriously put. The political dimen-sion of monetary union was confined to sermons on how it was part of Europe's historical duty towards ever closer union. Any concerns that a shared currency might, perhaps inadvertently, cause ruptures in Europe's social economy were dismissed instantly as the mutterings of dangerous, deluded populists unfit for admittance to polite society. Indeed, during the run-up to the euro's establishment, the slightest doubt about the solidity of the new currency's architecture was routinely used as evidence that the doubter was un-European, nationalist, a charlatan perhaps. It was not too different to the treatment reserved in the United States for critics of the Pentagon's plans prior to the invasion of Iraq or Afghanistan.

While establishment politicians dared not offer nuanced views on monetary union, bureaucrats did occasionally call a spade a spade. In 1991, a year after Thatcher's performance in the House, German economist and politician Wilhelm Nölling, a member of the Bundesbank's governing council, confirmed her assessment: 'We should be under no illusion that the present controversy over the new European Monetary Order is about power, influence and the pursuit of national interests.'[4]

It is bewildering that Europe had fallen into the illusion that criticism of its monetary union was necessarily driven by nationalism and, conversely, that championing the common currency was restricted to those who had shunned their own national interest in favour of Europe's. Nölling's point was, correctly, that its French and German champions saw monetary union as a means of gaining power and pursuing what they perceived to be in their national interests, often against the interests of their European partners. War by other means – as President de Gaulle considered his own plan for monetary union with Germany back in 1964.[5]

Ideally, Europe's institutions should have harmonized the national interests of its members into a common European will. But to assume that monetary union would automatically achieve this harmony was a dangerous flight of fancy. That monetary union is good for Europe's economy and consistent with European democracy ought to be a theorem. Europe, however, decided to treat it as an axiom.

Margaret Thatcher's objections, which incidentally coincided with those of Europe's radical Left, were twofold: monetary union would produce an economic disaster. And it would undermine parliaments together with their hard-won democratic rights. In an interview she gave a few months after her removal she prognosticated that 'this single currency, like all fixed exchange rate regimes, will crack in the end. It will not result in harmonious developments.' In other words, large-scale crisis is inevitable when control over different nations' money is deferred to technocrats unchecked by a parliamentary process to keep them in awe or to back them up when necessary. Once the inevitable crisis hits, national interests resurface with a vengeance. Considerable naivety is required to agree with Mitterrand that political union would somehow subdue nationalist bigotry.

Thatcher was, in short, echoing Nick Kaldor's prophecy (recounted at the end of the previous chapter) that monetary union would impede, rather than enable, the formation of a democratic political union across Europe. The moment control over the money of separate political jurisdictions is depoliticized, decision-making over things that matter is removed from parliaments; parliaments then lose their *raison d'être*, democratic legitimacy wanes and, when the inescapable economic crisis hits, authoritarian, highly political solutions appear as the only alternative. Thatcher's beloved TINA – 'There is no alternative' – emerges then in its most horrendous form – one that even Thatcher feared.

There is, however, one crucial matter on which Thatcher was in error. Referring to the single currency in that House of Commons debate, she claimed that it constituted 'European federation by the back door'. It is true that some of her foes on the other side of the English Channel had that intent. President Mitterrand, Thatcher's charming antagonist, did indeed intend the euro as a Trojan horse with which to smuggle through Europe's defences a federation that Europeans would have otherwise rejected, unready and unwilling to transfer political authority from their national parliaments to some federal institution in Brussels.

Thatcher's mistake was to assume that Mitterrand's scheme would succeed. She failed to recognize – as Mitterrand also failed – that the ability to create a federation out of its monetary union's troubles was not in the European Union's DNA. The monetary Trojan horse would deliver no federation. As I explain below, the euro and its bureaucratic minders were not capable of producing such an offspring. Only inefficient, sweeping authoritarianism could emerge from its wooden underbelly.

Not in its nature

If the custodians of Europe's monetary union were crypto-federalists, as Thatcher feared and Mitterrand hoped, why is a European federation further away today than it has ever been? François Mitterrand, and probably German chancellor Helmut Kohl too, knew that the common currency would spearhead unsustainable flows of money from the surplus to the deficit countries. They could see that a large-scale crisis was inevitable. But they hoped that the crisis would create the political momentum towards a federal Europe. It did no such thing.

The euro crisis that hit hard in 2010, beginning with Greece, was the perfect opportunity for politicians and bureaucrats desirous of federation to make their move. As banks went under, taking with them the governments that had to bail them out (such as in Ireland and Spain), and other banks were being bankrupted by the insolvent states in which they were domiciled (such as in Greece and Portugal), the creation of federal institutions would have been the perfect medicine.[6] Instead, European officials are, even today, doing everything in their collective power to avoid moves towards federation. At the cost of unnecessarily inflaming the crisis, a series of ramshackle simulacra of federal institutions were created, always taking care to ensure that they looked federal when in essence they were anything but.[7] A confederacy of incompetence thus rose from the clamour of stressed social economies in disconfirmation of Thatcher's anxiety.

Were the crypto-federalists that Mrs Thatcher saw everywhere in 1990 gone or silenced by 2010? Or were they never dominant in the first place? I have already taken sides on this question, arguing in previous chapters that the European Union's genes were geared from the outset – from 1950 – towards the depoliticization of political decisions. Europe's elites wanted a mega-bureaucracy in cahoots with large, oligopolistic business without the vagaries of federal democratic politics. In this vein, a 'Europe of states' was set up in intentional opposition to a 'Europe of citizens'. Brussels was built along the lines of 'We the governments . . .' to preclude the ideal of 'We the people . . .' This mega-bureaucracy was invented to serve a cartel of large businesses seeking common rules and industry standards in perfect freedom from any parliament with real power over its actions. It is no accident that the European Parliament, once instituted to give the European Union a semblance of democratic accountability, lacked the capacity to legislate.[8] The great hope among European democrats was that democracy would slip inconspicuously into the European Union exactly as it had into the institutions of nation states such as Britain and France. Nation states of this sort began as the instruments of the powerful but in time became democratized. If Britain, the United States and Germany could turn into liberal democracies, why could not the same fate transform Brussels?

English Euroscepticism retorts that authentic parliamentary democracy is built on a bedrock of common bonds and evolving conventions that only a nation can generate. If so, a multinational Europe will never evolve into a democratic realm. In this sceptical view 'European' is a geographic and possibly cultural signifier that cannot act as the cement of European democracy because it will always be trumped by its underlying French, Italian, German or Greek identities.

But this view is either logically incoherent or grossly offensive to, say, the Scots. For if true, it must mean that the United Kingdom either lacks democratic legitimacy or that the Scots and the English are no longer bona fide nations. Think about it for a moment. If the Scots are indeed a nation, the view that a single parliament must correspond to a single nation leads to the sole conclusion that the London-based House of Commons is unrepresentative of the Scottish nation and merely helps project England's illegitimate authority north of the border.[9] The only alternative consistent with the one-nation-one-sovereignty perspective is that the Scots are no longer a nation in their own right, but have been subsumed into a British nation. But if so, the English do not constitute a nation either, the two separate identities (English and Scottish) having merged some time ago into an overarching British identity capable of buttressing British parliamentary democracy.

So, one-nation conservatives, whether they are British Tories or Madrid-based opponents of Catalonia's independence from Spain, had better make their minds up. If a joint European identity and a sense of supranational belonging is impossible, the European Union ought to be disbanded and Scots and Catalans should also be granted independence from London and Madrid. On the other hand, if a supranational European identity is possible and capable of generating a European sovereign people, then a democratic European Union is possible.

Most Europeans (including this writer) side with the second view, convinced that the European Union's troubles cannot be due to the impossibility of forging an overarching European identity that incorporates but does not usurp their separate national identities. They are simply bamboozled as to how the European Union can evolve from bureaucratic institutions in the service of an economic cartel to a democracy serving a sovereign European people.

The nineteenth century is brimming with examples of how commodification, the triumph of capital accumulation over feudal authority and the concomitant removal of internal borders put into the blender of identity creation a variety of regional characters to construct new national identities. German unification, effected by Prussia's iron hand, is an excellent example. The notion that economic union could one day spawn a European identity, a 'We, the people of Europe . . .' is neither far-fetched nor unwholesome. Indeed, the path of institutional consolidation that began in the 1950s might well have gone that way. Student exchange programmes are the best example of a Brussels-guided process cultivating the promise of instilling a European identity among Europe's young.

The European Union's prospects of evolving into a democratic federation built on the shoulders of an advancing European identity were damaged badly by monetary union and its discontents, rather than by the impossibility of such an evolved identity. The unification of Europe's money amplified both the power of the bureaucrats over elected officials and the force of any future economic crisis. One fed incessantly into the other, with the prospect of democratizing the European Union the ultimate victim.

Monetary union, as both Margaret Thatcher and François Mitterrand had predicted, generated a large-scale crisis. What neither of those astute politicians had seen coming was that the crisis in turn empowered the bureaucrats to increase the authority with which they fended off all democratic pressure to reduce their power.[10] In a never-ending cycle of mutual reinforcement, monetary union, economic crisis and the democratic deficit were to coalesce. No federation can spring out of such a toxic brew. And none, therefore, did.

Frankfurt's long shadow

The German central bank, the Bundesbank, could see the purpose of lessening exchange rate fluctuations, even actually fixing exchange rates. What it detested was the idea that politicians would be doing the fixing, even if they were German. When Helmut Schmidt announced his and Giscard's intention to create the European Monetary System, the Bundesbank went into overdrive to place limits on the EMS, on politicians and of course on the Brussels bureaucrats. It also began a campaign to overturn Schmidt's promise to Giscard of a bailout fund, to be called the European Monetary Fund, whose purpose would be to lend to member states temporarily unable to stay glued to the Deutsche Mark.

The value of German money would be determined by the Frankfurt-based Bundesbank, its governing council insisted. Full stop. The burden of any adjustment to the value of other currencies, to keep the EMS going, should fall on the weaker currencies, not on the Deutsche Mark. Put simply, the Bundesbank demanded control of the mark's exchange rate with the dollar and the yen; Europe's stragglers, especially France, would have to do what they could to keep up. Frankfurt's demand was tantamount to a declaration that it would never push the Deutsche Mark's value up to help Paris.

If the French franc was falling behind its EMS minimum value, the French had to suffer more recession, courtesy of significantly higher interest rates, to push the franc up to where the EMS treaty said it should be. Frankfurt refused point-blank to lower its interest rates to give the franc a helping hand. It is for this reason that the unlikeable Norman Tebbit, Margaret Thatcher's favourite cabinet minister, would refer to the Exchange Rate Mechanism (ERM – the part of the EMS meant to keep exchange rates stable) as the Eternal Recession Mechanism.

Chancellor Schmidt tried his best to placate the Bundesbank in 1978. At some point, driven to exasperation, he resorted to blackmail, telling its president that further recalcitrance from Frankfurt would force him to legislate to curtail the Bundesbank's coveted autonomy. His successor, Helmut Kohl, would have to repeat this threat fifteen years later, in 1993, to get Germany's central bank to play ball in the formation of the euro. It would be a gross understatement to say that the relationship between Germany's political leaders and their central bank counterparts was an uneasy one.

Unexpectedly, at least from Frankfurt's perspective, the EMS, and the ERM embedded within it, worked well at first. The reason? Volcker's design was functioning in a manner that Chancellor Schmidt had shrewdly anticipated. Shopping malls across the United States filled with imported German, Japanese and later Chinese goods while Wall Street was awash with money gushing in from the rest of the world. American blue-collar workers fell off the escalator of increasing real income that they had climbed for more than a century but could now rely on readily available credit instead and on the hope that their mortgaged home would appreciate magnificently in price. From Helmut Schmidt's perspective, the American economy had begun to operate like a vacuum cleaner, sucking into the United States Germany's surplus money, thus preventing inflationary pressures from building up in the Federal Republic.

The dollar's appreciation, following the imposition of Volcker's exorbitant interest rates, was a godsend for the Bundesbank and improved its attitude towards the EMS. As the Deutsche Mark declined in value relative to the greenback, it slipped even in relation to the Italian lira and the Spanish peseta, currencies traditionally more responsive to the dollar. Basking in the warmth of the mid-range of its target value vis-à-vis its Latin counterparts, the Deutsche Mark experienced between 1978 and 1980 two or three years of comfort in the bosom of Europe's fledgling monetary union.

The downside of Volcker's disintegration was not far beyond the horizon, though.[11] By 1980 it was causing a global slowdown. France's prime minister, Raymond Barre, took the task of sticking to the EMS-ERM project seriously, determined to trade jobs and economic activity in France for a stable franc value.[12] So, while French unemployment was rising, he adopted what we now know as austerity – cuts in benefits, increases in sales tax, reductions in public investment – thus sacrificing many more jobs on the altar of keeping the franc's Deutsche Mark value within the agreed limits. A year later, in 1981, Barre's fiscal parsimony cost Giscard the presidency and brought socialist François Mitterrand into the Elysée.

On the other side of the Rhine, Chancellor Schmidt was fretting. Worried that he would suffer the same fate, he went in the opposite direction. Keen to boost employment, he allowed Germany's federal budget to go into deficit. Even though employment held up, as planned, the Bundesbank's deficit phobia meant that Schmidt's chancellery days were numbered. With inflation picking up and the German trade balance going unprecedentedly into the red, the Bundesbank responded violently. When prices rise fast and net imports balloon, there is only one short-term remedy that deficit-phobes appreciate: an increase in the cost of domestic money (i.e. of the interest rate), which douses local demand, puts a lid on both prices and imports but pushes the domestic economy into recession.

Helmut Schlesinger, the Bundesbank's vice president, convinced the board to out-Volcker Volcker and push short-term interest rates up to an astounding 30 per cent. Meanwhile, Schmidt's coalition partner, the Free Democratic Party (FDP), demanded austerity. The combination of extraordinary central bank interest rates and federal government spending cuts ensured that by 1982 German unemployment had doubled. At which point the German federal government's tail shed its main body: the small FDP abandoned Schmidt and his Social Democrats, going into coalition with Helmut Kohl's Christian Democrats instead. Alongside Schmidt's government, Schmidt's pledge to the French to add a European Monetary Fund to the EMS bit the dust. Any chance that Europe's Bretton Woods might resemble America's original design had perished.

By 1982 Volcker had unwittingly caused the replacement of the Giscard–Schmidt axis in Europe with another pivotal Franco-German pairing: François Mitterrand and Helmut Kohl. As America began to play in earnest its role of Minotaur on the world stage, the twosome who had instituted monetary union in 1978 passed the baton on to another pair, who in 1994 would found the European Central Bank and christen its offspring the euro. And never too far distant from this long string of concessions, deals and shenanigans, and against the backdrop of momentous world events – like the end of the cold war – the Bundesbank was always there, guiding, enabling and actively undermining the Franco-German axis around which the European Union rotated.

Aspirational riff-raff

The Franco-German axis is the European Union. While no one will ever admit this, in truth the other member states merely add liturgical sanctification to whatever the German and French leaders decide. This is because the influence of its Franco-German origin and centre has never waned, even as the union's borders have expanded, giving rise to an ever-growing European periphery. Following Giscard's pilgrimage to Athens in 1979, which brought Greece into the fold in 1980, the European Union expanded from ten to twenty-eight member states and counting. After incorporating former right-wing dictatorships (Greece, Spain and Portugal), the parting of the Iron Curtain opened up an expansive hinterland that was steadily assimilated, including three former Soviet republics.

With Germany and France busily struggling to keep the flame of monetary union alive, the new member states eagerly jettisoned their monetary independence to throw their lot in with whatever emerged from the Franco-German monetary laboratory. Paradoxically, monetary union was reinforced by the aspirations of those least capable of surviving, let alone thriving, within it.

The predilection of European powerhouses for a common currency is easy to understand.[13] But what of the penchant of weak societies, like Greece, for a hard currency that threatens to squeeze the living daylights out of them? Following the Nixon Shock and the great bouts of inflation that ensued in the 1970s, the elites in places like Milan and Athens grew tired of currency devaluations. Their yachts, townhouses, country mansions, shares in local businesses, as well as the contents of their domestic bank accounts, constantly lost value when accounted for in dollars or Deutsche Marks. Every time they visited London for the theatre season or went skiing in Switzerland, they realized the net worth of their domestic fortunes had diminished. Their recourse was to liquidate assets at home and find ways of violating their country's capital controls to export capital to Geneva, London, Wall Street or Frankfurt. If only there was a single currency and free capital movement; if only the hard Deutsche Mark were everyone's currency, all these cares would disappear.

The working class in Greece, Italy, Spain and elsewhere also grew impatient with their national currencies. Immense effort – costly industrial action, tiresome organizing, the fatigue and bitterness involved in mobilizing fellow workers and so on – was invested in collective bargaining with employers to achieve higher wages. Then, the moment the nation's central bank announced yet another devaluation, any gains that had been secured went up in a puff of smoke as inflation burgeoned in response to increases in the imported oil that in turn caused most prices to rise. While devaluations allowed workers to keep jobs that would otherwise have disappeared, protecting the products of their labour from being swamped by competing imports from places like Germany, devaluation-weariness set in and was ably exploited by elites eager to enlist their working classes in the cause of monetary union.

Politics came into the equation too, differently but forcefully in each member state. Ireland's government was keen to do something that made little economic sense but which packed political and symbolic power: to decouple the Irish punt from the British pound and have it shadow the Deutsche Mark instead. The German government, grateful for Dublin's endorsement of the EMS, offered financial help. That aid did not compensate for the fact that most of Ireland's trade continued to be with Britain, but added political utility to a government seeking independence from London and a backdoor through which to bring the European Union's influence to bear on the Northern Ireland question. Italian, Spanish and Portuguese politics were also crucial to the monetary union project. Chancellor Schmidt had invested enormous political capital, in collaboration with Washington, to ensure that the Left failed in its bid for power in the Iberian peninsula[14] and of course in Italy, where a resurgent communist party under the enlightened leadership of Enrico Berlinguer was working on a 'historic compromise' with progressive elements of Italy's Christian Democrats.

Monetary union and the prospect of a common currency were political gifts of great value to conservative forces on the periphery of Europe, but the lure of the EMS was also used with dexterity by French and German leaders to circumvent peripheral European governments, offering lucrative contractual arrangements to local businessmen on behalf of French and German multinational corporations. The combination of Brussels-sourced money and business links was pressed into the service of monetary union with zeal, preventing serious challenges to the logic of monetary union. Together with their political agents, employers reaped great benefit from these deals, placating hitherto unruly labour unions along with national intelligentsias seeking reasons to rebel against what they saw as European homogenization.

In countries such as Italy and Greece domestic kleptocrats used the monetary union card cleverly to extend their rule. Cheekily confessing to their culpability for the inflation, administrative incompetence and corruption besetting their nations, they asked for more time until Rome, Athens, Madrid and Lisbon could be governed directly by Brussels and Frankfurt as part of a monetarily united Europe. Greek and Italian politicians representing shady local interests, such as Giulio Andreotti and Bettino Craxi, two of Italy's most infamous prime ministers, and leading members of the New Democracy and PASOK Greek governments, extended an intriguing offer to voters fed up with them: Keep voting for us and we shall soon rid you of . . . our rule! Once monetary union is complete, our country will be administered de facto by Northern Europeans. So bear with us for a little while longer and we shall deliver you from . . . us! Modernization is coming. Calvinist administrators will take over our nation's reins, turning it into a Germany, or perhaps a Denmark, on the Mediterranean!

Most Greeks I know secretly welcomed that offer, even if they protested for show and for the benefit of their wounded pride and guilty conscience. I suspect the same applied in Italy, Spain, Portugal, even Ireland.

Northern Europe was different, but not much. Here too political factors determined attitudes towards monetary union. Belgium is a good example. Before the Great War, Belgium was in France's sphere of influence, tied for decades to the Latin Monetary Union, a nineteenth-century attempt to create a European common currency around the French gold franc which caused it to fall behind the Netherlands and Germany at a time when those two countries were industrializing rapidly. Later on, in the 1930s, Belgium's fate was again bound to France's, as both nations foolishly remained tied to the dying gold standard until the high value of their currencies decimated their economies. For decades Flemish areas protested against the damage done by Belgium's over-reliance on France, so, when the United States reconfigured Europe after the Second World War, the Benelux Treaty tied Belgium to the Netherlands and pegged its franc to the Deutsche Mark. Still, given the ethnic divisions between the Dutch- and French-speaking communities, a Franco-German monetary union was exactly what the proverbial doctor ordered for Belgium, independently of economic arguments and realities.

After the Berlin Wall came tumbling down, a different species of member state appeared. Former Soviet satellites, having undergone massive retrenchment, deep recession, unprecedented poverty levels and often outright desolation, queued up to join the European Union, applying at a time when monetary union was the main game in town. Keen to be let in, and to leave behind the memory and fear of the Soviet bear, they embraced the new mantra enthusiastically. A tradition of following faithfully the geopolitical hegemon's party line, coupled with extensive use of recession as a way to regulate social conflicts, meant that countries such as Slovakia and Latvia were prepared for the logic, such as it was, of a monetary union lacking the politically administered surplus recycling necessary to stabilize it properly. German politicians eager to spread the Deutsche Mark's reach as far as possible seized the opportunity.

At the same time the inclusion of even weaker and more impoverished member states allowed Germany to justify a reduction in state support for the aspirational riff-raff of countries such as Greece and Italy. 'How can you argue for Greek monthly pensions of seven hundred euros when Lithuanians and Slovenians have to do with three hundred euros?' was a question I was repeatedly berated with in Eurogroup meetings in 2015. My response was that this question precluded allowing Albania into the EU, lest Lithuanians and Slovenians suffer a 60-per-cent pension cut to fall into line with their Albanian counterparts. The logic of their argument would be a race to the bottom. This cut no ice. While arguing my case, though, I couldn't help but notice the French finance minister's worried expression. For he knew that the pressure exerted upon me by a German-led alliance of predominantly Eastern European finance ministers to accept inhuman cuts in already low pensions and ridiculous hikes in sales tax on basic goods would soon be applied to him.[15]

What was it that had diminished France's power so significantly since the days when Helmut Kohl and François Mitterrand were plotting together to push forward the Maastricht Treaty and create the euro? In the 1980s and 1990s, despite many stand-offs between France and Germany over control of their bold project, there had been close collaboration between German and French officials. Immediately after the creation of the EMS in 1978, France's position was bolstered by the first phase of European Union expansion, when nations with strong left-wing opposition parties (Greece, Spain and Portugal) were inducted. However, the second phase of expansion, which saw the European Union move east into a vast ex-communist dominion ravaged by recession and used to deferring to a hegemon, altered the balance of power at France's expense. These entrants – for example, the Baltic states and Slovakia – were also deficit countries (like France) but had no social security systems to protect (unlike France), had already practised severe austerity and were keen to demonstrate their credentials as worthy followers of Berlin's lead in the Eurogroup. Fast-forward to 2010, and France was suddenly outnumbered at precisely the point in time when the euro crisis was pushing its national budget into the red.[16]

France's slow-motion defeat

Being the deficit partner of a deficit-phobic Germany whose budget was moving into the black precisely because of the same crisis undermined France's position immensely.[17] Meanwhile, its finance minister's failure to make a difference in the Eurogroup was an almost natural consequence of the expansion of the eurozone. But the libretto of France's defeat had been written back in 1983, even though it took another ten years to be performed on the stage of Europe's monetary union.

As we have seen in Chapter 2, in the 1960s President de Gaulle had the idea of a common currency to smother a resurgent Germany and remove it from Washington's direct control. And as we have seen in Chapter 3, in the 1970s President Giscard d'Estaing signed the EMS treaty to energize a wider European federation and use a franc–mark peg to bring the powerful French trade unions under the moderating power of the Bundesbank's discipline. A decade later President Mitterrand combined de Gaulle's and Giscard's projects into a new daring plan: to use the Bundesbank as an instrument for realizing at the European level an economic programme that was impossible at the level of the French nation state. To understand the logic of this outrageous plan, which ultimately failed epically and led to a great diminishing of French power, we must return to the beginning of his administration.

François Mitterrand was elected in May 1981 on a ticket to form a socialist–communist coalition government with the express purpose of ending austerity, restoring equality and promoting growth. Trusting that the new government would place growth and jobs above the maintenance of the relatively high value of the franc within the EMS arrangements – which Giscard, Mitterrand's predecessor, and Schmidt had agreed to in 1978 – City of London and Wall Street speculators started taking out bets that Mitterrand's administration would allow the franc to slide. The power of the speculators' prophecy was taken seriously even by small investors who, anticipating a fall in the franc–Deutsche Mark exchange rate, sent their cash to Germany. Thus, shortly after Mitterrand moved into the Elysée Palace, an exodus of capital from France to Frankfurt, Germany's financial centre, took place.

Mitterrand was not keen to tear up the EMS treaty with Germany in the first week of his presidency. Hoping to buy time, he authorized France's central bank, the Banque de France, to push interest rates up to 25 per cent as an incentive to French savers to keep their cash in the country but also in order to attract foreign money into France. Meanwhile, his finance minister, Jacques Delors, introduced a price freeze to contain inflation. Neither worked, and Mitterrand instructed Delors to negotiate with Germany a devaluation of the franc within the EMS. The German authorities agreed on condition of an immediate wage freeze throughout the French Republic. This prompted France's Left to demand an immediate exit from the EMS, lest Mitterrand's government be reduced to the agent of Germany's policy choices for . . . France.

Mitterrand had to choose between dropping out of the EMS with a unilateral devaluation of the franc, and dropping his anti-austerity programme in order to stay within the system. To the outrage of the Left, the president opted for the EMS, but sticking to that proto-euro necessitated attracting foreign money into France, which in turn meant higher interest rates, lower public expenditure and in essence shrinking the French economy in order to maintain a stable franc–mark exchange rate. It was the first time a left-leaning government was to discard an anti-austerity agenda in favour of remaining true to the iron logic of Europe's monetary union.[18]

However, Jacques Delors, a master tactician, convinced his president that their socialist agenda was compatible with a U-turn on austerity. His point was that to fight austerity they first had to embrace it, in the context (and this is my term, not Delors's) of an enhanced anti-austerity strategy. Delors's argument was as follows: for as long as France insisted on pro-labour policies, such as targeting unemployment through public works and protecting wages, the Anglosphere's financial markets would bet against the franc, drive the state's borrowing costs up, cause a flight of capital to Germany and elsewhere, and force the devaluation of both the French currency and the French state. Inflation would follow and, before they knew it, the government would fall. Did that mean that they should give up, though? No, answered Delors. It meant that their anti-austerity policies, which could not be implemented at the level of France's nation state, should instead be implemented at the level of the EMS area, today's eurozone. As the currency of a deficit country, the City of London and Wall Street could treat the French franc as their plaything, but not if the franc was indivisibly connected to the formidable Deutsche Mark. The way to implement their 1981 agenda, concluded Delors, was to 'capture' the Bundesbank and somehow convince the German government to adopt the socialists' agenda at a European level.

Merely stating this proposition today is enough for its implausibility to shine through; Germany's elites would never roll over and adopt the

French socialists' agenda. Nevertheless, in 1983 this outrageous ambition carried significant weight in Parisian circles. French elite administrators of all political persuasions believed deeply that France's civil and military nuclear capabilities, their superior administrative systems, their relatively (compared to Frankfurt) more sophisticated banks, plus a divided Germany's reluctance to lead Europe, sufficed to keep them in the continent's driving seat. Jacques Delors's crusading mindset just added an anti-austerity veneer to this sense of entitlement, leading him to persuade himself that German officials could be convinced of the wisdom of French Keynesianism as long as Paris demonstrated to the Germans the capacity to discipline itself sufficiently to keep the franc as strong as the Deutsche Mark, whatever the cost of doing so.

And so President Mitterrand's government abandoned anti-austerity policies on the dubious grounds that austerity could only be defeated Europe-wide once the French economy was subjected to doses of austerity sufficiently large to placate the money markets and to convince Germany's elites to bow to the superior wisdom of French economic policymaking. French 'socialist' austerity would, according to this ill-fated plan, lull the Bundesbank into a sense of security that would deliver it into Delors's arms, allowing French bureaucrats to erect a European central bank in France's image. From there the single European currency would spread Mitterrand and Delors's expansionary growth-oriented anti-austerity policies – the same ones they had just abandoned at home – throughout the union. Or so the fairy tale went.

By 1983 Helmut Kohl was German chancellor and liked what he saw over the border – Jacques Delors's readiness to prop up the franc in particular. The two governments then embarked on a project that is with us to this very day: to convince German voters that monetary union was Germanizing France and exporting Teutonic discipline to Latin Europe, turning grasshoppers into ants rather than importing French sloth into Germany. Moreover, two years after Kohl's election and Delors's abandonment of his anti-austerity stance, Delors moved from Paris to Brussels as perhaps the European Union's most powerful commission president ever.

One of history's curious habits is humanity's tendency to be influenced more by its failures than its desires. François Mitterrand entered the Elysée with the best anti-austerity intentions, but it was his failure, and subsequent volte-face, that left an indelible mark on Europe and of course France. Today's Eurogroup meetings, in which the French finance minister carries next to no weight, are the direct consequence of that failure.

The importance of the Delors-inspired recourse to French austerity as a ram with which to batter down the Bundesbank's gates was amplified by Mitterrand's unique achievement of co-opting much of the traditionally recalcitrant French Left to Delors's cause – effectively into support for the conservative North-Central European cartel. Instead of the socialism-in-one-country that he had promised French voters in 1981, he ended up espousing cartelized-corporatism-on-one-continent, or along the Paris–Berlin axis to be a little more precise. And yet a large number of French Marxists were impressed by Mitterrand's crushing determinism, which surely reminded them subliminally of the Stalinist enthusiasm for being on the right side of an inevitable historical process. Some would become his loyal companions on the path to monetary union.

Between 1983 and 1986 the EMS worked to the Bundesbank's satisfaction, allowing the Mitterrand–Kohl relationship to flourish. Volcker's vacuum cleaner continued to function as planned, siphoning off excess German capital to the United States, keeping the dollar strong and permitting, as Chancellor Schmidt had anticipated in the late 1970s, the franc–mark peg to survive, aided occasionally by a new dose of austerity in France.

But things began to go awry after 1986, when the American authorities decided to turn down the vacuum cleaner, limiting the rate at which US deficits grew. The recession of the early 1980s caused by Volcker's sky-high interest rates and Ronald Reagan's early budget cuts frightened the Reagan administration. Using the US military budget as its main instrument, Washington effected the most Keynesian macroeconomic expansion in America's history. It was quite extraordinary. The president who had won the 1980 election by preaching against public spending and in favour of shrinking the state won re-election in 1984 declaring, 'It is morning in America again,' on the basis of a massive spending spree.

The Minotaur subsequently went crazy – in fact a little too crazy, with imports ballooning and US exports severely hampered by the dollar's high value. Keen to keep foreign money flooding into America, Washington did not wish to reduce interest rates significantly. But how could the US authorities force the dollar's international value down (to boost US exports and curtail the import spree) without reducing the dollar price of borrowing and lending, which the Minotaur needed to be kept at high levels? Washington's answer was typically American: it employed brute political power on the world stage.

By the Plaza Accord, struck in 1985, Tokyo was forced to appreciate the yen substantially in relation to the dollar, with the Deutsche Mark compelled to follow suit. Japan's exports took a major hit, Germany's less so. Washington's objective was achieved except that the 'correction' proved larger than desirable. By 1987 the dollar had devalued to levels that were jeopardizing Wall Street. In the same year a G7 meeting was held in Paris at which American officials pushed the opposite way, towards a strengthening of the dollar. At that meeting, which is now known as the Louvre Accord, Washington bullied the Europeans into accepting coordinated efforts to strengthen the dollar.

The Bundesbank was unhappy that politicians out of its direct control were messing about with the Deutsche Mark's international value. It was not long before it made its unhappiness shown in the form of destabilizing the EMS-ERM system at the expense of France. To do so, the German central bank simply had to signal to markets through rumours or small adjustments in a number of the interest rates it controlled that it was not going to act when necessary to stabilize the value of the franc, the attitude that had caused so much tumult in the days of Bretton Woods (recall Chapter 2).

The French government did its best to continue to demonstrate to the Bundesbank its austerity credentials by using every available lever with which to push French inflation below German levels, bringing France's interest rates in alignment with those prevailing in Frankfurt and showing that the franc was on a par with the Deutsche Mark. French officials were adopting a new refrain: they spoke as if monetary union between France and Germany had already been attained, save perhaps for the fact that the French and German banknotes had different pictures on them. The more the

Bundesbank's unhappiness grew, the greater the show of harmony French officials put on. France's treasury director at the time, a certain Jean-Claude Trichet,[19] expressed the French authorities' hubris admirably. In a bid to refute the plain truth that the Deutsche Mark was the anchor keeping the EMS-ERM system grounded, he denied the dominance of the German currency with the extraordinary statement that 'the anchor of the [EMS] system is the system itself'.[20]

Incapable of grasping the finer aspects of French postmodern sophistry, Bundesbank officials were aghast. *No fixed regional exchange rate system can anchor itself!* they must have thought, correctly. Even Bretton Woods had required the gold–greenback link to do the anchoring. Trichet's denial that the German mark anchored Europe's monetary union would not go unpunished. Punishment had, however, to be delayed because of German reunification. Chancellor Kohl instructed the Bundesbank to sit tight while the Soviet Union, under President Mikhail Gorbachev, and President Mitterrand were indicating their willingness to let West Germany absorb the German Democratic Republic. France had to be allowed its illusions for the present, even if this required that the Bundesbank be caged like a wild animal in case it pounced on Delors and Trichet.

Frankfurt got its chance after reunification was safely in the bag. The Bundesbank's pretext was the cost of reuniting Germany, which gave it the opportunity to push German interest rates up to such an extent that Paris was forced into a fresh dilemma not so different from the one Delors and Mitterrand had faced in 1983: devalue and therefore confess that the franc's permanent parity with the Deutsche Mark was a soothing lie, or push French interest rates to a level that would double unemployment in a few months? Confess to the Deutsche Mark's EMS leadership or go into recession?

That was the choice Frankfurt gleefully gave Paris after long months of biding its time and suffering silently the self-congratulatory statements of French officials. But humbling France, however satisfying in itself, was not the Bundesbank's sole concern. It was also keen to exact revenge upon those German politicians, Kohl in particular, who had disregarded its objections to a monetary union between the two Germanies that had given East Germans one (West German)

Deutsche Mark for each worthless East German mark they handed over.

Under Helmut Schlesinger, its new boss, the Bundesbank soon killed both birds with one stone. The European Exchange Rate Mechanism, the EMS's main engine, was Paris and Berlin's pet political project, its 'glidepath' towards a single currency. By early 1993 the Bundesbank had wrecked that particular glidepath. Why? Because it had never forgiven Berlin's federal politicians for reaching an agreement with Paris to effect a monetary union behind its back and without its full approval. And how did the Bundesbank do this? Through an interest rate policy and subterranean machinations that intentionally disembowelled the EMS-ERM system.[21]

Once Berlin politicians had got their comeuppance, and had learned (again) the hard way that sidelining the Bundesbank in their dealings with Paris was a terrible idea, the Bundesbank was happy to consider a common currency. But under its terms and direct control. Only after Berlin and Paris had acknowledged Frankfurt's authority and priorities, and even then with considerable reluctance, did the Bundesbank feel ready to grant politicians their wish to replace the EMS-ERM with something even more ambitious: the single currency known as the euro.

As for France, it had been subjected to yet another politically engineered recession during which a large section of its population saw their prosperity and prospects sacrificed on the altar of a flimsy monetary union between France and Germany. That recession was particularly hard to take since it did not even succeed in keeping alive Delors and Trichet's dream of a monetary union between equals.

When the euro's time came, after Europe's pitiful attempts at fixed exchange rate regimes were abandoned, it was evident that the franc and the Deutsche Mark were not entering into a romantic marriage. 'Takeover' comes closer to describing the proceedings than 'union'. Indeed, the eurozone's formation recalled both versions of German reunification: that of 1871, dominated by Prussia, and the second one in 1990, when East Germany was absorbed into West Germany. Perhaps the only silver lining for France's politicians was that at the dawn of the euro project their German colleagues were also nursing Bundesbank-inflicted wounds.

Cruel glidepath

On 8 December 1991 the Soviet Union expired. On that same day European leaders began their journeys to the Dutch city of Maastricht, where over the next couple of days they were to draft the euro's birth certificate: the Maastricht Treaty. As the red flag was lowered for the last time at the Kremlin, Europe's currencies were committed to a new glidepath meant to guide them smoothly onto a common landing strip, a common currency that would end twenty years of turmoil caused by the 1971 Nixon Shock. Unfortunately, the path to the single currency proved more of a botched bungee jump than a glide.

The original idea was that fluctuations between the value of Europe's other currencies and the Deutsche Mark would be eliminated within a few years with a view to locking them securely together. Once they began to move in perfect synchronicity, all rising and falling at exactly the same rate vis-à-vis the dollar, they would be replaced by the euro. At least, this was the plan, to be realized by 1997.[22]

It is a remarkable trait of the Brussels commentariat that its professional success seems to be inversely related to its predictive capacity. Daniel Gros, an economist and commentator whose opinion is regarded to this day as the ultimate conventional wisdom regarding the European Union, had this to say on the agreed process: 'Overall, there is therefore little reason to believe that the EMS would be destabilized by random self-fulfilling attacks in the 1990s . . . the basic ingredient for exchange-rate stability [is] a firm and credible commitment to subordinate domestic policy goals to the defence of the exchange rate.'[23] Could anyone really expect France or Germany to subordinate its goals to the defence of indefensible exchange rates? The events of 1992 would soon demonstrate that such faith was misplaced.

To qualify for the euro, a nation would have to eliminate all controls over the movement of money in or out of the country for at least two years and, during that time, prove that its currency's Deutsche Mark value could stay within a narrowing band of upper and lower limits until it stabilized fully. Additional criteria, also known as the Maastricht Criteria, specified common rules governing the total amount of public debt and the maximum budget deficit the member state was allowed.[24] So Germany would give up the Deutsche Mark, or allow the other countries to use a version of it, if the rest of Europe committed to fund their own deficits without counting on Germany or the new central bank.

The Maastricht Treaty was signed a couple of months later, in February 1992, foreshadowing the creation of a European central bank whose charter would mirror that of the Bundesbank and whose job would be to ensure that grubby politicians from Paris, Athens, Rome and Madrid had precisely zero control over Europe's money. Any illusions that the glidepath to the new currency would be smooth were dashed immediately, despite the treaty's strict rules. Nine days after the treaty was drafted, before it was even signed, the Bundesbank dished out some pain to Paris, lest the French dared to imagine that they had co-opted Germany's central bank in accordance with Jacques Delors's original plan. Pushing a main interest rate to its highest level since the war, Frankfurt was signalling to the deficit nations that the single currency was being extended to them on condition of their constant readiness to be beaten back into their recessionary pen. If they failed to increase their interest rates too, at the cost of more unemployment and lower investment, their currencies would suffer and they would be knocked off the agreed glidepath. They could choose the path leading to the euro or they could opt for growth-oriented policies. They could not choose both.

Pierre Bérégovoy, France's prime minister, openly spoke of a 'victory of German selfishness over international solidarity';[25] Italian newspapers published condemnations of what they referred to as the Bundesbank's 'axe job'. In June 1992 Denmark, whose economy had suffered from a long recession as a result of the government's desperate attempts to keep its currency within the EMS-ERM band, held a referendum to ratify the Maastricht Treaty. When the Danes unexpectedly voted against it in a bid to maintain the relative independence from the Bundesbank that their national currency made possible,[26] Brussels officialdom was in disarray; the glidepath was called into question and markets began to turn against the currencies of the deficit nations. Italy, France and Spain reacted first by telling their central banks to spend all their reserves to keep the lira, the franc and the peseta on the glidepath. And when this proved insufficient in the face of the speculators' fervour, they turned to more austerity.

Meanwhile, at the Bundesbank President Schlesinger was planning further interest rate hikes fearing a rise in German inflation, while Chancellor Kohl used every trick in the book, and every possible threat against the Bundesbank, including the prospect of legislating less autonomy for Frankfurt, to prevent a fresh interest rate increase that would turn the glidepath into a free fall. On 16 July 1992 the Bundesbank reacted by increasing one, but not all, of its rates – a signal, albeit a dismal one, that it wanted peace with the federal government.

Margaret Thatcher made two errors regarding Europe. The first, a common one among British politicians and commentators, was to imagine that a single European market was possible without something resembling a single European state. Tariffs can be lowered and quotas abolished without affecting the sovereignty of national parliaments, but a single European market requires a lot more: it demands a single rulebook. This means that member states lose all power to set particular quality standards, environmental controls tailor-made for specific habitats or protections for workers and pensioners from cross-border races to the bottom. A single market may not need a single currency but it needs a single federal-like state to function properly. But, then again, if a single federal-like state is in place, then we might as well have a single currency too.

Margaret Thatcher was dazzlingly astute in her criticism of the idea of a single currency without a democratic state to back it. She correctly foresaw that the euro project would not lead to 'harmonious circumstances' when the common central bank behaved as if it were possible to depoliticize the most political of economic entities: money and its price (the rate of interest). But she was wrong to imagine that the euro was a Trojan horse for smuggling federation in through the back door.

Thatcher's second mistake was, in other words, to confuse the traditionalist Central European conservative tendency towards a Europe of states with the desire for actual federation. Mitterrand's mistake, however, was more of a moral and political failure in that he, like de Gaulle, Pompidou and Giscard before him, chose not to distinguish between 'We the government . . .' and 'We the people . . .' This is a crucial difference since only the latter can vest in institutions, like those in Brussels, the power to legislate on their behalf. Governments cannot.

A Europe of states provided the right foundation for the heavy industry cartel on which the European Union of the 1950s had been based. To Europe's elites and establishment politicians, therefore, the notion of a federal republic in which the sans-culottes of France, of Spain, heaven forbid of Greece, would have real influence upon Europe's collective decisions was anathema. It simply did not compute. So, unable to learn from history and unwilling to forget their petty agendas, Europe's ruling class set out to re-create the gold standard, demonstrating a grandiose failure to comprehend what they were doing.

Keynes described the gold standard as 'a dangerous and barbarous relic of a bygone era'. Little did he know that Europe would re-create it in the late 1990s, thus replicating the circumstances for another Great Depression in the 2010s, an economic crisis that ended up – as Nicholas Kaldor (another Cambridge economist) predicted in 1971 – preventing the very political union that was to have been its antidote.

5

The One That Got Away

I had a friend once who would attend parties only to whine about how boring they were. It is not difficult to draw a parallel with Britain's attitude to the European Union. Both major parties, Labour and the Tories, have for years been tearing themselves in shreds over the European question. To this day, the imperative of maintaining communications with Euroloyalists and Eurosceptics across Britain's political spectrum makes British officials visiting Brussels behave like my friend: they attend everything in order to declare their permanent dissatisfaction.

Margaret Thatcher, from the Right, and Tony Benn, from the Left, demonstrate why Britain's opposition to the European Union is founded on a great deal more than whimsical British snobbishness. Despite being at opposite ends of the political spectrum, both were opposed to further integration with Europe on the grounds that it would result in an undemocratic dilution of the powers of the British parliament.[1] Traditionally a trading nation, Britain needs to be part of the large marketplace on its doorstep. At the same time, a homogeneous single market requires rules, standards and regulations that cannot be decided at the level of the nation state.[2] The very sovereignty that Britain's political forces of both Left and Right want jealously to preserve within their cherished House of Commons is put under pressure by the exigencies of its most powerful social groups: traders, manufacturers and of course the City of London, for which Brexit is fraught with dangers.

This tug-of-war, between sovereignty on the one hand and the forces of financialized capital on the other, has led to a precarious halfway house: Britain is inside the European Union but constantly threatening to leave, maintaining its monetary independence but bamboozled by the sight of a eurozone whose crisis gives rise to developments outside London's control. Its institutionalized dithering on matters European notwithstanding, there is no doubt whatsoever that Britain was spared large-scale economic pain by getting away from the euro project in the nick of time. The nature of its escape from the euro and the reasons Britain remains permanently dissatisfied in its relationship with Brussels throw useful light on the state of Europe's union.

Major's folly, Lamont's bath

The 1980s were a terrible time for the Left. Trade unions were defeated; the working class began to shrink in numbers and in influence; inequality was seriously on the rise for the first time since the Great War; the Soviet Union was collapsing under the weight of its moral and economic decline, and social democratic parties the world over were being lured by the beast of financialization.[3] At the same time the 1980s struck a mighty blow at the simplistic monetarism that Margaret Thatcher and her New Right warriors had brought into vogue.

The monetarist mantra that London adopted in 1979, with Thatcher's elevation to power, was simple. Inflation, it insisted, was due to there being ever-increasing quantities of money available for the purchase of more or less the same quantity of commodities within a given economy. When this happens, the sum of money available to be spent per commodity – its price – increases, thus maintaining inflation at a high rate.[4] According to this logic, the monetarist remedy for inflation is to keep a lid on the rate at which the so-called money supply grows. To bring back the price stability that the Nixon Shock had destroyed in 1971, all that was necessary was to ensure that the pace at which the quantity of money grew was in sync with the growth rate in the production of goods and services.

Monetarism went hand in hand with legislative moves and economic policies that devastated British organized labour and its political agent, the Labour Party. But at the same time it devastated the labour market, depleted Britain's manufacturing base and put the country onto a trajectory of increasing social conflict. By 1983 it had become clear to Thatcher's economic team that simply targeting the quantity of money[5] would quicken their political demise. The period between 1983 and 1987 was an interregnum of sorts. Crude monetarism was abandoned, and the economy recovered. Only it recovered on the back of new bubbles in housing and finance – bubbles that soon spearheaded debt-fuelled growth utterly at odds with Thatcher's Victorian values.

Meanwhile, rising prices were beginning to put paid to the Tories' credentials as the party of sound money and low inflation. Some new target had to be discovered with which to replace the quantity of money in order to rein in inflation without returning Britain to the four million unemployed of 1981–3. It was at this time that the European Monetary System (EMS), with the Deutsche Mark at its heart, began to appeal to several members of Thatcher's government. From 1987 onwards, London targeted the pound's exchange rate with the Deutsche Mark, testing to see if sterling could be hitched to the EMS-ERM[6] bandwagon in a manner that kept inflation on a leash while allowing Britain's economy some breathing space. The problem with this strategy was that the interest rates necessary to keep sterling pegged to Germany's money were so high as to be politically toxic. And so the pound failed to keep up with the Deutsche Mark, the result being that by 1990 Britain's rate of inflation was three times Germany's.[7]

By the end of the 1980s Margaret Thatcher was on the wane politically, after more than a decade at the helm. In October 1990 she was hoodwinked into accepting Britain's membership of the EMS-ERM by John Major, her chancellor of the exchequer, who convinced her that this was the only available anti-inflationary device.[8] A month later she was ousted by Tory Euroloyalists (see the previous chapter) for refusing to take the next step – from acceptance of the EMS-ERM to embracing the euro project – and replaced by Major, who in turn appointed Norman Lamont in his place as chancellor. Lamont thus inherited Britain's place in the EMS-ERM fixed exchange system and tried to make the best of it, seeing it also as a bulwark for pushing down Britain's inflation rate from 12 per cent at the time he became chancellor to about 2 per cent in 1992.[9]

In April 1992 Major won the Tories' fourth successive general election. Buoyed by his largely unexpected victory and the pound's subsequent rise in response,[10] Major felt confident enough to make a proclamation he lived to regret: sterling was to become the EMS-ERM's strongest currency, its anchor maybe. Lamont must have bitten his tongue, knowing full well that such an outcome was just as unlikely as it was undesirable, and a few months later Britain's very place in the EMS-ERM was in jeopardy.

The early 1990s, like the early 1980s, were years of global recession. America's Federal Reserve, whose genes are happily free of the Bundesbank's deficit-phobia, responded by pushing interest rates down to less than half the level prevailing in Europe. As the dollar fell, British trade with the United States suffered and sterling struggled to keep up with a Deutsche Mark rising as the Bundesbank ratcheted up German interest rates to deal with the cost of German reunification.[11]

Everyone expected Chancellor Lamont to bump up British interest rates to keep sterling within its EMS-ERM band. Lamont's conundrum was that his loyalty to his prime minister clashed with his pessimism about Europe's monetary project. By August 1992 he thought that it was game over: the EMS-ERM had helped Britain rid itself of the high inflation that 1980s monetarism had bequeathed, but had nothing more to offer the United Kingdom except the unnecessary recession and social pain guaranteed by any attempt to push interest rates through the roof to keep up with the Deutsche Mark.

On 26 August 1992 pressure on the pound caused the City of London and all market players to expect from Lamont an interest rate increase that would keep sterling above its EMS-ERM floor, but the chancellor understood that there existed no interest rate level that could keep Britain in the EMS-ERM without crushing its real economy. Instead of making a clear-cut announcement that he would increase interest rates, Lamont made a strong but vague statement to the effect that he would do whatever was necessary to support sterling. The markets sensed a reluctance to push interest rates up and assumed that only the support of the Bundesbank could keep Britain inside Europe's problematic monetary system. But would the Bundesbank come to the party? Over the next week Britain's and Italy's currencies came under enormous pressure, at the edge of the glidepath only inches from a crash. On 3 September Lamont announced that, rather than push interest rates up, he would borrow more than £10 billion to prop up the pound. All eyes turned once more to the Bundesbank: would it climb off the fence and come to the Anglo-Italians' aid?

It was on the following day that the die was cast in response to a television debate in Paris. France was about to hold a referendum on the Maastricht Treaty. Unexpectedly and despite the 'yes' recommendation of the main parties, the 'no' vote was polling strongly, echoing the surprising result of the earlier Danish referendum. If the French too were to reject Maastricht, the euro would be dead in the water. Mitterrand knew this well and used that night's remarkable television debate to secure a victory for the 'yes' campaign.

The debate was extraordinary because alongside Mitterrand was Helmut Kohl, the German chancellor. On the opposite side was 'no' campaigner Philippe Séguin, who launched a tirade against Mitterrand's acquiescence to an unaccountable, anti-democratic European central bank. His arguments were not far from Margaret Thatcher's critique. Stung by the criticism and fearful that it might lose him the referendum, the president went a few steps beyond what the Bundesbank could stomach. His argument was that

> the technicians of the [European] Central Bank are charged with applying in the monetary domain the decisions of the European Council . . . One hears it said that the European Central Bank will be master of the decisions. It's not true! Economic policy belongs to the European Council and the application of monetary policy is the task of the [European] Central Bank, in the framework of the decisions of the European Council . . . The people who decide economic policy, of which monetary policy is no more than a means of implementation, are the politicians . . . [The members of the ECB would be like members of the Commission who] no doubt cannot help feeling a certain tenderness for the interests of their country.[12]

It was only a matter of moments before the good folk in Frankfurt pounced upon the insinuation that the European central bank they were about to defer to would be a plaything of France's politicians. Sensing that the Bundesbank was not keen to stand behind the existing exchange rates – yet another bid to teach politicians a lesson – money traders tested the system by immediately betting against the lira. As they had expected, the Bundesbank did not come to the Italian currency's rescue and the lira was pulverised. Nothing that the Italian central bank could do, not even raising interest rates from 1.75 to 15 per cent, helped restore the lira's Deutsche Mark value.

A few days later, at an informal meeting held in Bath involving Europe's central bankers and finance ministers, Lamont attempted to elicit from Schlesinger, the Bundesbank's head, a commitment to reducing German interest rates. That would have taken some of the pressure off sterling and the lira and perhaps kept the glidepath dream alive. To no avail. The Bundesbank was determined to humiliate the French by having Mitterrand's government request a formal devaluation of the franc within the EMS-ERM. It demanded a formal French concession in the form of a requested devaluation that would have ended the smooth, inescapable glidepath narrative.

For President Mitterrand, who had invested so much in the myth that the franc was already locked into the Deutsche Mark, this would probably spell defeat in the all-important referendum. For the Italian government, agreeing to devalue when France would not was equally poisonous. Britain also resisted the idea of devaluation, keen to keep Britain's interest rates at a level not far off Germany's. In the end, despite pressure from all quarters, Schlesinger conceded nothing and even gave an interview to announce the Bundesbank's intention to sit on its hands.

John Major, Britain's prime minister, then attempted to outdo King Canute with a speech in which he committed his government to shunning 'the soft option, the devaluer's option that would be a betrayal of our future and our children's future'.[13] It was the signal speculators needed, with George Soros famously ahead of the pack, to take the British government to the cleaner's: a once-in-a-century opportunity to profit from a commitment to an exchange rate with the Deutsche Mark that the Bundesbank had signalled it would not defend. In horse racing terms, it was as if he had known the name of the winning horse (the Deutsche Mark) while a very rich punter (the Bank of England) was committed to betting huge sums that another horse (the pound) would win: the more money Soros could beg, borrow and steal to bet against the rich punter, the greater his profit. To this effect, he led a syndicate of speculators with $10 billion at its disposal, with which he made his wager against the Bank of England and sterling. His estimated profit was in the vicinity of $1 billion for a few hours' 'work'.

Lamont knew that his prime minister's public commitment would end in disaster. Quite simply no interest rate below stratospheric levels existed that would do the trick. On 16 September 1992, at a cabinet meeting at 10 Downing Street, he recommended leaving the EMS-ERM forthwith.[14] His counsel was rejected and he was instead ordered to raise interest rates to 15 per cent. 'That was an expensive mistake by Major, but of course the blame was pinned on yours truly,' as Lamont put it to me recently in a private communication.

That same evening, also known as Black Wednesday, and after all attempts to stay the course had failed, Major was forced to make the announcement that Britain was exiting the EMS-ERM, with the media ridiculing his government's spectacular failure. A few days later the press reported that Lamont, instead of being downhearted, had sung in the shower. As always, the media had got it wrong: Lamont was taking a bath![15]

Fallout

Britain was the only nation whose finance minister sang in the bath when the EMS-ERM collapsed about his ears, but London did not succumb to the speculators alone. Rome followed and, very soon, the whole of Europe was forced to surrender to the impossibility of the EMS-ERM glidepath. London's open acceptance that it had all been a terrible mistake was also unique and largely due to Chancellor Lamont's determination to use Black Wednesday to nip in the bud any thought of Britain getting trapped again in Europe's monetary schemes. While some cabinet ministers, those at the forefront of overthrowing Thatcher, entertained hopes of returning to the EMS-ERM, Lamont would have none of it.[16]

Sweden and Finland, non-European Union countries not even meant to join the ERM-EMS but which tracked its currency settings, paid a hefty price for doing so,[17] followed Britain's lead and put clear blue water between themselves and Europe's monetary experiment. In contrast, Southern Europe, Rome and Madrid in particular, were loath to admit defeat. In the Mediterranean the EMS-ERM had become synonymous with the local elites' strategy to maintain their hold over their populations by promising eventually to forfeit that control and to transfer it to a competent technocracy of experts who would run Europe from Brussels.

France's establishment had a particular reason to pretend it was business as usual – that the EMS-ERM was alive and kicking. During Mitterrand's long presidency (1981–95) the dominant centre-left and centre-right parties alternated in government,[18] taking it in turns to impose austerity in pursuit of the *franc fort*, continuing Delors's original blueprint of 1983 in which austerity at home would capture the Bundesbank and thus end austerity at the continental level. A whole decade of political capital, based on this fanciful strategy, was at stake, and a fudge was better than outright admission of failure.

To avoid admitting to the debacle that was the EMS-ERM, a fig leaf was invented typical of European Union fabrications: the system would remain in place except that it would only be loosely binding, as the currencies within it would be allowed to fluctuate by up to a whopping plus or minus 15 per cent. In other words, if the currencies could not be made to stay within the original glidepath, then the glidepath's definition would be broadened to include anything – even falling out of the sky and crashing on a faraway hill would now be considered evidence that the glidepath remained operational.

The only European institution that saw the events of late 1992 as a vindication was Germany's Bundesbank. Hans Tietmeyer, who replaced Schlesinger as the head of the Bundesbank the following year, had a simple agenda: monetary union was to be given a go as long as any notion of symmetry between France and Germany was replaced by an ironclad commitment to the Bundesbank's unfettered domination of European economic policy. Paris and the riff-raff had to be taught whatever lessons were necessary to make them toe Frankfurt's line and bow to its authority.

France knew it had no option. While the 1992 referendum was won, even if only by a whisker,[19] its elites' grand plan was in tatters. For a decade they had played second fiddle to the Bundesbank and subjected their economy to a long slow-burning recession, thinking it a fair price to pay for the creation of a French-dominated European central bank that would ultimately defang the Bundesbank and render it obsolete once and for all. This plan had been stood on its head by Frankfurt's well-judged periodic backlashes, the intended captive turning into supreme schemer. The German central bank's *coup de grâce* was the way it had engineered the collapse of the EMS-ERM in 1992. It was the masterstroke with which the Bundesbank ensured the European Central Bank would be created in its image, that it would be located in Frankfurt and that it would be designed so as to impose periodic variable austerity upon weaker economies, including France.

After a stormy 1992, 1993 looked like a benign year. Recession in Germany, aggravated by the high interest rates with which the Bundesbank had undermined the EMS-ERM, opened the door to looser money from Frankfurt.[20] And looser German money worked like oil poured on the troubled waters of the normally tempestuous Franco-German canal. Except that every time calm returned, ambition got the better of some French official, who would issue a statement that the Bundesbank felt it had a duty to react to in its inimitable way. In April 1993 the governor of France's central bank thought it wise to repeat the outrageous – and not just to the Bundesbank – claim that the French and German currencies were equals and would provide comparable support to the single currency. It was as if France were demanding a few more smacks from the Bundesbank before Germany shared its money with the French. Sure enough, within hours German interest rates rose and the French central bank paid the price.

Financialization's helping hand

As France eventually learned the art of submission the hard way, the Minotaur was going berserk in the guts of the American economy, gobbling up enormous quantities of imported goods and foreign money. This helped stabilize Germany's economy by sucking out of it the oodles of idle cash that were accumulating there due to the country's large trade surplus.

The Clinton administration, and especially Robert Rubin and Larry Summers in the National Economic Council and the US Treasury respectively, were busily working to maintain the Minotaur's feeding frenzy. America's deficits kept global capitalism effervescent, creating the illusion of a Great Moderation when underneath the surface markets were increasingly addicted to America's growing imbalances. If the American Minotaur's frantic consumption of other people's products and money were to end, markets would take a hit, banks would go under and the global economy might keel over. Precisely as it did in 2008.

To prevent this, and to keep the Minotaur satiated, the Clinton administration felt the need to emancipate finance from the last remaining shackles tying it down since the New Deal. To sustain the illusion of a stable global equilibrium, constant injections of financial energy were necessary. But that meant unshackling the bankers and letting them loose to create gigantic paper 'value' out of capital moving in and out of Wall Street and the City of London.

In this brave new world of financialization, of bankers creating new 'products' that soon after their birth behaved like privately minted money, the world of finance and banking decoupled from planet Earth in ways that the world came painfully to grasp in late 2008. A world-wide spending and investment spree was powered by private money created within the private banks and financial institutions – Lehman Brothers, Goldman Sachs, AIG and the like – whose activities became increasingly distant from those which common folk, including German manufacturers, understood as banking.

In the mid-1990s European bankers and their political friends realized that something big was going on in the Anglosphere, and Europe ought either to embrace it or to reject it. Except that European officialdom lacks the political courage to do either and is bereft of the analytical capacity to take a stand on anything controversial. Their natural tendency is to fudge; to try to do both at once; to have their cake and eat it. So Brussels did nothing. Instead of regulating Europe's banks to stop them loading up with the toxic paper that they were buying wholesale, they whistled in the wind.

The Bundesbank, meanwhile, could also see financialization coming. Its spectre frightened the men and women in Frankfurt because they knew how primitive the German banks were. The Bundesbank liked them that way, loathing the all-singing, all-dancing Anglo-style banks that paid little heed to the needs of mid-sized manufacturers of the type constituting German's industrial backbone. German banking, even today, comprises a small number of Frankfurt-based global banks and a grid of numerous small banks, many of them regional and intimately connected to state governments and local manufacturers. The Bundesbank based its power on maintaining strong links with both types of bank.

Since the Nixon Shock, Germany's central bank had intervened ferociously in defence of small banks that foreign speculators tried to take over. Now the rise of financialization in the Anglosphere gave Frankfurt serious cause to worry about both the smaller banks, which were the blood vessels of German industry, and the multinational German banks, which ran the risk of decoupling from Germany's economy or doing silly things that jeopardized it. With these worries in mind, the Bundesbank found further reasons[21] to warm to the prospect of a European central bank located in Frankfurt with a charter copied from its own and Bundesbank genes determining its policies: greater German influence on the pace and nature of financialization throughout Europe and the maintenance of the Bundesbank's control over Germany's global banks.

By the end of 1993 the French authorities' capitulation to the Bundesbank was complete, and the road was open for the completion of a monetary union that Paris had first imagined as a means of capturing the Bundesbank but which Frankfurt eventually embraced after it shot the French stratagem out of the sky. Mitterrand, his government and officials in France's central bank knew they were defeated but decided to look on the bright side.

Once locked into the Bundesbank-dominated euro, France's ruling class, and the technocrats it was so good at producing, could at least look forward to maintaining their power within France and along the Paris–Brussels corridor. They might not have won Europe but at least they had not lost France – at least not yet.[22] Their government could also better resist pressures from organized labour, and its apparatchiks could take solace from exercising their skills in the European Commission, which Jacques Delors was beefing up into something resembling a European government. And despite France's failure to capture the Bundesbank, the European Union remained capable of promoting *planification*, code for looking after large French companies through bailouts, such as the rescue of Air France, and steps to help them expand across European borders, such as when a state-owned French company, aided and abetted by Brussels, purchased the largest part of Britain's privatized electricity industry.[23]

And so it was that, with a little help from Anglocentric financialization and the Bundesbank's successive victories against politicians both in Paris and in Berlin, the euro was permitted to be born. And even before the euro entered our wallets, pockets and ATMs, a glimpse of what Euroland would look and feel like (especially after its honeymoon period was over) was given to the people of Europe by the events of the 1990s. Lacking a political surplus recycling mechanism, Europe's monetary union meant that the weakest nations and their frailest citizens had to suffer a sharp contraction the moment Europe's capitalism went into a spasm in response to financialization's inescapable seizures. Only Mitterrand's original hope that a future global financial crisis would force upon the eurozone a federal solution offered any respite from the pitiless reality. By 2010, two years after the type of crisis Mitterrand had in mind, that hope had died too.

Entrance etiquette

The single European currency, the euro, can be thought of as a club whose rules of entry were meant to be violated and whose functions were designed as mind-boggling paradoxes.

Its entry rules, the so-called Maastricht Criteria of quantifiable thresholds – for example, the limit on a country's public debt of no more than 60 per cent of its national income, or a government annual budget deficit no greater than 3 per cent of national income – function as the members' book of rules. To be recited at regular intervals, the criteria are the eurozone's Ten Commandments, prescribing essential dos and don'ts and exuding a Protestant disdain for loose finances. They are texts of ritualistic incantations, promoting the worship of Europe's 'apolitical' money – the type of money that Margaret Thatcher had warned against. Of course, the Maastricht Criteria's real purpose was to allow into the eurozone countries that did not meet these criteria and then force them to do whatever it demanded to meet them. Greece is world famous for its statistics and the creative manner in which they were massaged to allow my country into the fold, but it is to Italy that we must turn to grasp best what happened.

Italy had to be admitted into the eurozone from the beginning – from 2000 – not least because German manufacturers were fed up with the falling lira, which periodically restored Fiat's competitiveness vis-à-vis Volkswagen et al. A eurozone without Italy but with France made no sense in view of northern Italy's strong trade links with France and Germany, its heavy industry's participation in the original cartel on which the European Union was founded as well as its full cultural integration into Central Europe.

But Italy's public debt was twice that specified by Maastricht as the maximum permissible level for an entrant, with its inflation rate languishing in the red zone too. Rome did its very best to push these numbers towards their Maastricht threshold. Smart officials, working with the best financial engineering Goldman Sachs could provide, indulged in creative accounting that shaved off some of the debt and a little of the government's budget deficit. However, the numbers budged very little even when Rome applied large doses of austerity to depress prices, suppress spending and generally give Italy the semblance of a nation in the process of acquiring Teutonic virtues.

So it was clear that the Maastricht rules had to be bent for Italy to trade its unloved, depreciating lira for the copper-plated euro. And bent they were. Brussels and Frankfurt offered a broad reinterpretation of their book of rules: as long as countries were moving in the direction of the Maastricht thresholds, Europe's authorities could decide that they had made the grade.

A year or so later Greece was also admitted into the euro. The financial press went crazy with stories of cunning Greek officials pulling the wool over the eyes of Northern European officials, with

'Greek statistics' as their weapon of subterfuge, but none of the stories was true. When I asked a friend who played a central role in Greece's induction talks how they had managed to convince Germany to let Greece into the eurozone, his answer was fantastically unassuming: 'We just copied everything the Italians had done, and a few tricks used by Germany itself. And when they threatened to veto our entry, we threatened them back that we would tell the world what Italy, and Germany, had been up to.'[24] Once bent to allow Italy through, the Maastricht rules could not have kept Greece out – at least not without exposing what the officials had done.

Common currency, uncommon flaws

The euro's design was built on three paradoxes and one fallacy.

The first two paradoxes were already embedded in the EMS-ERM system, Europe's attempted simulation of Bretton Woods. The first paradox dates to 1983, when France's socialist government espoused austerity as a means of ending . . . austerity at a pan-European level.[25] The second was the Greek–Spanish–Italian oligarchy's promise to their own peoples that the euro would rob them of power over their peoples![26] The third paradox was designed exclusively for the euro. The common currency was equipped with a European central bank lacking a state to support its decisions and comprising states lacking central banks to support them in difficult times.[27] To fill this institutional lacuna, the Maastricht Treaty and its successor treaties created a panoply of non-credible rules to constrain states. Of course noncredible rules end up as violated rules. Seeing its rules being violated, Brussels and Frankfurt made up new, even stricter, ones (see Chapter 6) that ended up suffocating those who tried to implement them.

As for the fallacy in the euro's foundations, it is one that humanity ought to have grasped between the wars, when it led unforgettably, one would have hoped, to depression and war. Encouraging free trade by removing tariffs and quotas may be combined profitably with attempts to fix exchange rates in order to make long-term prices more predictable for buyers and sellers, but to do this and at the same time allow for the free movement of money across borders is to ask for serious trouble. The reason for this is that when money is free to travel, during the good times it follows higher interest rates. Deficit countries offer higher rates and, given a fixed exchange rate, are very attractive for the excess money of surplus states. But this causes a build-up of debt in the deficit regions that goes bad at the first sign of an economic downturn. For this reason, one of the few things economists tend to agree on is that the freedom of goods and money to travel unimpeded cannot be combined with fixed exchange rates, unless a political surplus recycling mechanism is also part of the deal.[28]

Fixing exchange rates between disparate economic regions always brings benefits in the short term, but it resembles past invasions of Russia: a brisk beginning full of enthusiasm and hope, rapid progress that seems unstoppable, followed by a heart-wrenching slowdown as a cruel winter takes its toll, ending up with blood on the snow and ceaseless retributions thereafter. The Americans learned this lesson in the 1930s, with the 1920s gold standard, and applied it during the Bretton Woods era until they ran out of surpluses to recycle. The moment men like Paul Volcker saw that political surplus recycling was beyond the American economy's capacity, they brought the whole system down – with the 1971 Nixon Shock. For they understood the fallacy that Europe refuses to grasp: if you set up a free trade, free capital and single currency system without a political surplus recycling mechanism, you will end up with something like the 1920s gold standard.

After the Nixon Shock, European leaders set out to fix the exchange rates between their currencies, brushing aside the certainty of ensuing asymmetrical recessions – with the largest loss of income afflicting the weakest economies. In 1978 Chancellor Schmidt and President Giscard d'Estaing inaugurated Europe's monetary system. Then again in the early 1990s Chancellor Kohl and President Mitterrand oversaw the construction of their glidepath to the single currency. And finally, the euro – the mother of all fixed exchange rates – was inaugurated in 2000. Each one of these heart-rending attempts at monetary union led to the same pattern: a promising beginning that soon degenerated into tears and recriminations as economic warfare erupted and recession impoverished the weakest Europeans.

The reason Europe seemed to be prospering in the late 1990s and until 2008, despite having introduced an unsustainable gold standard, had little if anything to do with the design of its single currency and everything to do with the fact that there was no need for political surplus recycling, as the world of private finance was doing plenty of fair-weather recycling on the back of the American Minotaur.

In 2008, following Wall Street's collapse under the weight of its own hubris and the mountains of risk that financialization had amassed (while pretending that it was risk-free), America could no longer provide the European Union with the demand for its exports that had until then stabilized it. The Minotaur had been wounded mortally. Europe would soon discover that its private banks were replete with Wall Street-sourced toxic debt and that countries like Greece had insolvent states. The death embrace, or doom loop, between insolvent banks and insolvent European states had begun. The rest is history.

The eurozone's architecture was incapable of sustaining the shock waves of the 2008 earthquake. Since then it has been in a deep crisis reinforced largely by the European Union's denial that there is anything the matter with its currency's rules, as opposed to their enforcement.

Europhilia, Germanophobia and the French elites

Why did the Europeans create the euro? An analytically wrong but entertaining answer goes like this.[29]

The French feared the Germans.
The Irish wanted to escape Britain.
The Greeks were terrified of Turkey.
The Spanish wanted to become more like the French.
The southern Italians craved migratory rights to Germany.
The northern Italians wanted to become German.
The Dutch and the Austrians had all but become German.
The Belgians sought to heal their sharp divisions by merging into both Holland and France under the auspices of a reconfigured Deutsche Mark.

The Baltic states shivered at the thought of a resurgent Russia.

The Slovakians had nowhere else to go after separation from their Czech brethren.

Slovenia was escaping the Balkans.

Finland had to do something Sweden wouldn't.

And finally the Germans feared the Germans!

Like all big lies, this contains small but important truths. The corrupt ruling classes of Greece, Italy, Spain and their ilk were empowered by pledging to transfer their power to Brussels and Frankfurt. The French elites did indeed fear the Germans. And the German people had reason to fear that fear, as well as their own nation state's capacity to self-destruct through extreme belligerence.

It is almost an instinct of those who are critical of the euro to blame its adverse effects on Germany and the Germans. I have always opposed this tendency for two reasons. First, there is no such thing as 'the Germans'. Or 'the Greeks'. Or 'the French' for that matter. 'You are all individuals,' as Brian famously told his unwanted followers in Monty Python's classic comedy. The serious point here is that there is a great deal more divergence in character, virtue and opinion among Greeks and among Germans than there is between Germans and Greeks. The second reason I have always resisted the habitual censure of Germany is that, if the debate is allowed to stoop to this stereotypical level, Paris bears greater responsibility than Berlin for the euro's faults.

Recall the awful article in the French conservative daily *Le Figaro* which I first mentioned in Chapter 2. Published two days after Black Wednesday and two days before French voters were to deliver their verdict on the Maastricht Treaty, it said, 'The opponents of Maastricht fear that the common currency and the new Central Bank will fortify the superiority of the Deutsche Mark and the Bundesbank. But the exact opposite will happen. If it comes to Maastricht, Germany will have to share its financial might with others. "Germany will pay," they said in the 1920s. Today Germany does pay. Maastricht is the Treaty of Versailles without a war.'[30]

No German, indeed no European, could forgive such sentiments, and none would expect anything less from the Bundesbank than a plan for making France's conservative establishment, of which *Le Figaro* is a distinguished part, eat its words. The desperate struggle the French elites were caught in to persuade the sceptical French electorate to vote 'yes' in the Maastricht referendum (which almost produced a 'no') is no excuse. The 1919 Versailles Treaty condemned Germans to unspeakable misery, humiliated a proud nation and primed it to be taken over by Nazi thugs. The Nazis would have remained a historical footnote if it were not for the impossible reparations the victorious Allies had no right to impose and the German government no moral right to accept.

And this was not just the wayward editorial of a newspaper. President de Gaulle, as I mentioned in Chapter 2, saw monetary union with Germany as war by other means precisely in the spirit of *Le Figaro*'s article. Even Delors's 1983 U-turn was nothing less than a French plan to usurp an institution cherished by the German people – the Bundesbank – subsume it into a French-dominated central bank and extend into Germany and the rest of Europe policies close to Paris's heart. From a German perspective, Delors and *Le Figaro* were more or less on the same page. The fact that civilized Frenchmen like Delors and Mitterrand truly believed that their policies would prove good for Germany too is neither here nor there. After all, most Bundesbank officials also believe that their strict monetary posture is good for France, indeed for the Greeks too.

The fact that German politicians like Wolfgang Schäuble tend to speak incessantly about the sanctity of rules, whereas their French counterparts are prone to terminology more redolent of the French Enlightenment, is not evidence that Europe's problem is too much German power. When younger I would listen to well-bred representatives of the French ruling classes appeal to Europe's general will or common interest, and my Greek heart would flutter with joy. But the effect on me of such fine words changed once I learned to translate them into what they really meant. Before the euro was introduced, de Gaulle, Mitterrand, Delors and their kin would talk of Europe's common good when in reality they were demanding that the rest of Europe make sacrifices in support of the costly illusion that the franc was as hard a currency as the Deutsche Mark.[31] And whenever France's better-laid plans crashed on the shoals of reality, it was usual to blame it all on uncivilized foreigners who could not appreciate the finer aspects of France's plan.[32]

The euro changed all that. Locked into its steel embrace, France's sophisticated administrators imbibed sip by sip the bitter realization that monetary union would not deliver them Germany on a plate – indeed, that they were losing France. The latter was the natural and not unfair outcome of a monetary experiment egged on with vigour by Paris, with Germany a reluctant participant.

This chronicle of the journey towards the euro should have made clear to any reader that it was never going to be a smooth voyage across the high seas of the global economy. In the event, Europe's failure in the 1990s to understand that the value of money can never be depoliticized led to an agonizing struggle for dominance within the sinking ship of a monetary system.

Since the Nixon Shock the European currencies had stubbornly refused to move in sync, despite the authorities' best efforts. The euro was meant to deal with such stubbornness. Except that, instead of abolishing the headaches caused by exchange rate fluctuations, it engendered a series of real economy migraines. After an initial period of irrational optimism, which erected new mountain ranges of private and public debt, the new currency fed the old problems with steroids and let them loose upon unsuspecting Europeans.

In the 1990s, even as the American Minotaur was easing Europe's passage towards the euro, observing Europe's high officials at work was a little like watching *Macbeth* or *Othello* and wondering how supposedly smart people could be so gullible. After the American Minotaur's serious wounding in 2008, reality pulled the rug from under the euro's feet and Europe's leadership descended from tragic incompetence to a comedy of errors.

How could so many top journalists, academics, functionaries and politicians believe that they could sustainably bind together the French franc and the Deutsche Mark, let alone the Italian lira, the Spanish peseta and the Greek drachma, without a political mechanism for recycling German and Dutch surpluses and managing private and public sector deficits? Did they not see that German surpluses, left to

Frankfurt and Parisian bankers to scatter throughout Europe's periphery, would flood the deficit regions, causing massive bubbles? How did they expect the eurozone, bereft of any mechanism for coping, to handle the preordained bursting of these bubbles?

Much of the blame must be placed on the word 'union'. One puts 'monetary' and 'union' together and immediately imagines some prospect of convergence – of economies and peoples coming together. Except that the previous two chapters' take on the 1980s and 1990s reveals the opposite: forcing all the costs of adjustment on the deficit economies repeated the cardinal sin of the gold standard. But, unlike the gold standard, where states could just leave by severing the peg between their currency and gold overnight, once in the eurozone member states had entered a Hotel California they could never leave.

This is the beauty and the curse of the eurozone. Once in, you lack a currency to cut loose of the euro; you have only the euro. To get out of Europe's monetary union, Greece or Italy, for example, would have first to create a new drachma or a new lira and then unpeg it from the euro. But creating a new paper currency, distributing it around the country, recalibrating the banking and payment systems to function with it and doing everything else that would be required takes a minimum of twelve months. Given that the purpose of going through the palaver of re-creating a lost currency is to devalue it vis-à-vis the currency in people's hip pockets,[33] leaving the euro is tantamount to announcing a major devaluation a year before it happens. At the drop of a hint of a devaluation twelve months hence, a frightful race is on. Every Tom, Dick and Harriet will rush to liquidate whatever wealth they have, convert it to euros, take their euros out of the banking system and either stash them under the bed or carry them across the border to Germany or Switzerland for safekeeping. Before you can say 'panic', banks fail, the country is drained of all value, and the economy collapses.

The Hotel California clause embedded in the eurozone's design was therefore always going to prevent exit for the economies that needed to be out of the euro the most. Once in the euro, deficit countries are caught in the common currency's enormous gravity, condemned to ever-increasing depression the moment the global economy turns bad. At that point governments face three options:

death by a thousand austerity cuts, a lethal exit from the euro or a campaign of disobeying the edicts of Brussels and Frankfurt in order to force Europe either to reconsider its currency's architecture or violate its own laws by forcibly pushing a member state out of the eurozone. As Greece's minister of finance, I advocated the third option and resigned in July 2015 when my prime minister accepted the first in the belief that Brussels was about to impose upon Greece the second option – a forced exit.[34]

Seen from some emotional and historical distance, it is as if Europe had turned its own Balkanization into an objective, into an art form. What would have otherwise been relatively benign recessions ended up dividing Europeans and ruling over them, deepening divisions in living standards and causing different life prospects in different parts of the union. This was the consequence of attempting to keep currencies locked into one another before establishing any mechanism for recycling the surpluses of those who produced them by investing part of those surpluses into countries and regions in serious deficit.

Prior to the final lockdown of exchange rates in the late 1990s which preceded the euro's launch, Europe's fixed exchange rates had a tendency to unfix themselves regularly following political pressure from populations suffering as a result of their maladjustment. Instead of learning from this, the powers that be decided to up the ante: to fix the rates in an irreversible manner, to replace all currencies with a single one while doing nothing to provide the missing, the essential, political recycling mechanism.

Had Norman Lamont inherited not the EMS-ERM but the euro, he would not have had to worry about devaluation of his nation's currency. With the pound abolished, he would instead have faced a collapse of Britain's real economy, a build-up of unsustainable debt and demands from a ferocious European Central Bank for more austerity which would feed back endlessly to more recession. In short, the euro replaced the fear of devaluation with the certainty of depression.

During the late 1990s, as the euro loomed on the horizon, I remember heated debates with other economists internationally as well as with Athenian friends. However hard I tried to explain to them that the euro was badly designed, it was in vain. I used analogies from driving, from sailing, from any walk of life I could imagine, to warn that not only Greece, but also France, Italy, Spain and others had much to lose by entering a half-baked common currency. 'It's as if we removed the shock absorbers from a car and then drove it straight into the largest pothole,' I would say, my voice muffled by my inter-locutors' well upholstered certainties. 'It's like taking a fine riverboat out on a calm, majestic ocean, knowing that it's not designed for stormy weather' was another simile that produced the same degree of indifference. The lure of the euro was proving capable of over-powering the most rational of economic arguments.

Some argue that this idealism is evidence of Europe's virtue. They are wrong. Totalitarianism is underpinned by ideologies impervious to reason and capable of luring perfectly sensible people into its grasp. István Szabó's film *Mephisto* is perhaps the best depiction of a good mind's takeover by a sinister ideology. As the protagonist, played by Klaus Maria Brandauer, loses his critical faculties, he replaces them with an increasing hunger for power that he embellishes with the incantation of senseless certainties. My conversations with friends in the late 1990s revealed considerable evidence that Europe was in the grip of a similar trend.

In Europe's polite society, as well as among my friends and colleagues, doubts over the mechanics of the fledgling European System of Central Banks (comprising the ECB and the central banks of all the EU member states) were regarded as 'anti-European'. Subordination to the elites' agenda for squeezing wages and to Brussels's automatic right to dictate the answers to genuinely political questions was considered 'modern-ization'. 'Europeanism' became synonymous with the relegation of national parliaments to rubber-stamping agencies, and with the subju-gation of the weak to the superior opinion of the strong. Using self-defeating austerity as the sole macroeconomic policy instrument emerged as 'common sense'. And so on.

The common folk who liked the idea of sharing a currency with other Europeans as a first step to a mythical federation could not have known that they would be the first to be sacrificed on the altar of Europe's inane handling of the euro's inevitable crisis. But their elected representatives had no such excuse, except that they were too busy sharing in the immense discursive power and material rewards that the euro project distributed to the many thousands of bureaucrats and administrators who contributed to its genesis.

Margaret Thatcher feared that, under cover of the euro, a European federation was being sneaked in through the back door. If only she had been right! But if the euro was a Trojan horse it begat something far less heroic: a clueless, inefficient bureaucracy complete with its own mystical beliefs, working tirelessly for politicians with an infinite capacity to recite unenforceable rules. Democracy is too fragile a flower to survive such sadness.

6

The Reverse Alchemists

As the Iron Curtain was parting, one movie elegantly captured the emotional impact of Europe's postwar division, but also conveyed a brooding angst about the transforming European Union. It was Krzysztof Kieślowski's *The Double Life of Véronique* (1991).

Kieślowski's device was the overwhelming bond between two identical-looking strangers, Weronika in Poland and Véronique in France, both played by Irène Jacob. Their paths cross only once, as Europe is about to be reunited. Jubilant because she has just been invited to audition for a major singing part, Weronika is rushing home through Kraków's main piazza only to find herself in the midst of a demonstration. A protester accidentally knocks her bag, and her sheet music falls to the ground. As she is picking it up, she notices Véronique boarding a tourist bus. The two women's eyes meet for a fraction of a second. After a successful audition Weronika lands the part, but, while singing her heart out at the premiere, she collapses on stage and dies. At precisely the same moment, in Paris, Véronique is overwhelmed by deep, inexplicable grief.

Véronique's emotional and musical bond with her Polish double (they share a love of the same music) and the radical absence she feels upon Weronika's death symbolize the solidarity and cultural-cum-spiritual connection between Western Europeans and those left behind the Iron Curtain, and also with those in Southern Europe, in Greece, Spain and Portugal, who were not released from fascism until the mid-1970s. Films like *Véronique* epitomize a European cultural unity that not only survived but actually grew in the shadow of harsh divisions. It is also part of the cultural oeuvre that helped drive the idea of a single European currency.

As borders receded and the single market triumphed, deeper unification became synonymous with the monetary union that began life in 1972 with the ill-fated snake, begat the EMS agreement between Giscard and Schmidt in 1978 and took its final shape in 1993 under the firm guidance of Mitterrand and Kohl. The bitter irony, as the present demonstrates, is that the push towards European unification backfired, producing unprecedented discontent.

Today Weronika might get a recording contract in Paris or in London, but her music would be homogenized within a European marketplace for music and art that knows no boundaries and lacks a heartland. Instead of being bonded by melody, emotion, guilt and culture, Véronique and Weronika would be bound by a contract drawn up by some global legal firm. Indeed, Véronique would probably be worried that Weronika will move to Paris and take her job. In this harsh world there is no longer room for films like Kieślowski's *Véronique* to romanticize Europe's unity.

In centuries past alchemy was the expression of an infinite optimism that lead could somehow be turned to gold – that something precious could be made out of the mundane. Before the single currency glidepath, the European Union was a precious source of hope, a gleaming attractor of dreams. But then came the reverse alchemists. Committed to exploiting the magnificent opportunities for profit and power made available by the folly of depoliticizing Europe's money, they set out systematically, even if unwittingly, to turn Europe's gold into lead.

Frenzy

Franz worked for a major German bank for twenty-five years. In November 2011 we sat next to each other on a long-haul flight from Frankfurt to New York. After the first few hours, in which we exchanged a couple of nods and sat in silence, as is typical between strangers, we struck up a conversation about the euro crisis that had begun, in Greece, a year earlier. Within minutes Franz had confided to me that the euro's 'good' years, by which he meant from the late 1990s to just before 2008, had been the worst of his life.

Before 1998 his job had entailed flying around European capitals, assessing the creditworthiness of governments, local authorities, utilities, developers, local banks and large businesses. Prospective borrowers would take him to the nicest restaurants, give long presentations of their business plans, caress his ego, take him to the opera, put on a mixed display of subservience and superiority and, most importantly, make an effort to prove their creditworthiness. Franz would remain non-committal, fly back to Frankfurt and, at his leisure, pore over the data and the documents he had brought back in order to reach a decision as to who got how much of his bank's money. 'Before the euro,' he told me, 'I felt like royalty.'

Things changed abruptly the moment the markets realized that the euro was going to happen and that even Greece would be joining. Around 1998 Franz's charmed life was suddenly transformed into a nightmare. The pressure from his bosses became relentless. 'Lend, lend, lend!' was their new creed. From a relaxed purveyor of scarce money he was transformed into an angst-ridden overpaid proletarian. A weekly quota of loans that he had to make regardless of the creditworthiness of his clients robbed him of the discretion that had previously made him feel important.

The tremendous bonuses he earned for exceeding his lending targets were no compensation, he insisted, for his clients soon realized he was no longer the boss. They were. When Spanish businessmen, Irish developers, Greek bankers, Italian industrialists caught on to the pressure Franz was under to lend to them, their attitude changed. The more strident HQ's orders to unload more of the money sloshing around in their Frankfurt lair became, the cockier they grew. For a time Franz tried to caution the bank's board against the tide of iffy customers the bank would not have touched with a bargepole a little while back. His reports were ignored, and he felt the cold draught of disapproval emanating from his superiors on the odd occasion he spent time in Frankfurt. Soon he realized that his reports clashed with senior management's business plan. He was running a serious risk of being labelled disloyal and an unsafe pair of hands.

In strategic sessions organized to galvanize the workforce around senior management's new logic Franz and his colleagues found that their job descriptions had changed dramatically. They were no longer there to pass judgement on clients. Risk assessment and management had been taken away from them altogether. They were there to peddle loans, to reach their quotas in a manner not dissimilar to encyclopedia salesmen whose salaries depended on how many units they shifted.

'But what about the risk involved?' Franz told me he had once asked. Unlike encyclopedias, which can be ignored by the seller once transferred to the customer, loans have a nasty habit of biting the supplier back. Bankers like Franz had felt important because they were responsible for assessing the riskiness of every loan they granted. It was what gave them their kudos, their sense of self-importance, their mojo. Alas, a new division of labour within banking had brought all this to an end.

People like Franz were now instructed to turn a blind eye to risk. 'Leave risk to our risk managers,' they were told. 'Your job is to chase yield[1] and maximize the sums you lend.' Once the client signed up and received their loan from Franz, the contract was turned over to the risk managers, who would begin a process first developed on Wall Street. Just as in the United States, Franz's loans would be sliced up into small pieces, mixed and matched with slices of other loans, then bundled together into new products, known as derivatives, and sold on to other financial institutions in the four corners of the planet. And so the risk that Franz had created by lending to dodgy Europeans was supposedly dissipated on the vast archipelago of 'riskless' global risk.[2]

Franz's new circumstances were clearly not specific to the eurozone's banks. They were born on Wall Street as a result of the financialization built on the American Minotaur's back, then they made their way to the City of London and to Frankfurt and Paris. What was different about Franz's experience, compared to his colleagues in the Anglosphere, was a particular folly to do exclusively with the form that chasing yield took in the euro area.

Maastricht had declared that monetary union was for ever. To cement this thought, the 1993 treaty specified conditions for entering the single currency but made no provision for exiting. Thus the Hotel California doctrine was enshrined in European law. Once markets had come to believe that no one would ever leave the eurozone, German and French bankers began to look at an Irish or a Greek borrower as equivalent to a German customer of the same creditworthiness. It made sense. If Portuguese, Austrian and Maltese borrowers all made their income in euros, why should they be treated differently? And if the risk involved in lending to particular individuals, firms or governments did not matter, as the loans were dispersed throughout the known universe immediately after being granted, why not treat prospective debtors across the eurozone all the same?

Now that the Greeks and the Italians earned money that could never again be devalued vis-à-vis German money, lending to them appeared to the German and French banks as advantageous as lending to a Dutch or German entity. Indeed, once the euro was invented, it was more lucrative to lend to persons, companies and banks of deficit member states than to German or Austrian customers. This was because in places like Greece, Spain and southern Italy private indebtedness was extremely low. The people were of course generally poorer than Northern Europeans, lived in humbler homes, drove older cars and so on, but they owned their homes outright, had no car loan and usually displayed the deep-seated aversion to debt that recent memories of poverty engender. Bankers love customers with a low level of indebtedness and some collateral in the form of a farmhouse or an apartment in Naples, Athens or Andalusia. Once the fear of devaluation of the lira, the drachma or the peseta in their pocket passed, these became the customers that bankers like Franz were instructed to target.

Franz went to some lengths to impress upon me the suddenness and force with which his bank targeted the European periphery. Its new business plan was straightforward: to secure a higher share of the eurozone market than other banks, the French banks in particular, which were also on a lending spree. This meant one thing: lend to the deficit countries, which offered the bankers a triptych of advantages.

First, the low levels of private indebtedness left enormous room for a lot more lending. Back-of-the-envelope calculations made French and German bankers salivate at the scope for loans in the Mediterranean, in Portugal and in Ireland. In contrast to British or Dutch clients, who were mortgaged up to their ears and in a position to borrow little or nothing more, Greek and Spanish customers could quadruple their borrowing, given that they had so little debt to begin with. Second, the surplus nations' exports to deficit countries welcomed into the euro were now immune to devaluations of the defunct, weaker currencies.

In what the bankers considered a virtuous circle, their increasing loans to deficit nations foreshadowed more domestic growth, which in turn justified the loans they were extending to them. Third, German bankers drooled over the difference between the interest rate they could charge to German customers and the going rate in places like Greece. The chasm between the two was a direct consequence of the countries' trade imbalance. A large trade surplus means that cars and washing machines flow from the surplus to the deficit country with cash flowing the opposite way. The surplus country becomes awash with 'liquidity' – with cash accumulating in proportion to the net exports pouring into its trading partner. As the supply of cash increases within the surplus nation's banks – in Frankfurt to be precise – it becomes more readily available and therefore cheaper to borrow. In other words, its price drops. And what is the price of money? The interest rate! Thus interest rates in Germany were much lower than in Greece, Spain and their equivalents, where the outflow of cash as the Greeks and the Spanish purchased more and more Volkswagens maintained the price of euros in Europe's south above its equivalent in Germany.[3]

It was this burgeoning chasm of lending interest rates between the eurozone's core and the periphery countries that wrecked Franz's life, for his task was to lend wherever he could charge the highest interest rate – chasing yield. The euro's creation had inadvertently saturated the German banks with liquidity that men like Franz were then forced by their bosses to re-export to every nook and cranny of the deficit nations – nations typified by a hitherto low level of indebtedness. Franz's mission was to boost debt in the deficit countries for the purpose of reaping the huge rewards that were springing from the chasm between interest rates in the weaker and stronger eurozone nations.

Towering above all other lending, courtesy of the larger sums involved, was public debt – the borrowing of governments. Even a small difference between the interest rates bankers charged the Greek state relative to the German government was a licence to print money. As long as the assumption held that the monetary union was for ever, these differences in interest rates – known as spreads – ensured that a banker taking money out of Germany or France (at a rate of, say, 3.5 per cent) and lending it to the Greek state (at, say 4 per cent) would make a risk-free profit. How much? The difference between the two rates (0.5 per cent) multiplied by the amount lent to the Greek govern-ment. But the more money lent to the Greek government (or the Irish banks for that matter) the lower the spread[4] and therefore the more loans the banker had to shift in order to maintain his profits. 'Frenzy' is probably too mild a word to convey what was going on.

'I lived the life of a predator lender' were Franz's words as the plane touched down. Picking up our hand luggage we headed for the customs area. Franz shook my hand, adding, 'Greece was our sub-prime market. Good luck, mate.' Little did either of us know that four years later I would be struggling to explain to my fellow finance ministers that Greece's unpayable debt was a symptom of collective eurozone folly.

Nein cubed

It is September 2008. Dick Fuld, Lehman Brothers' last CEO, begs Hank Paulson, the US treasury secretary, for a gigantic credit line to keep Lehman afloat. Paulson famously turns him down. The best he can do, he tells Fuld, is to ask other investment bankers to help shoulder some of Lehman's bad trades. But that's all: no bailout. 'File for bankruptcy, if you must.'

Imagine a slightly different, entirely fictional, exchange in which the US treasury secretary were to say to Fuld, 'No bailout for you and you are not allowed to file for bankruptcy!' What? Surely a figure of authority cannot demand of a bankrupted entity that it refrain from insolvency while at the same time denying it a bailout. It couldn't happen. Except that it did happen. Not in the United States, of course, but in Europe eighteen months later.

Towards the end of 2009 George Papandreou, the newly elected Greek prime minister, had all the indications that Greece was another Lehman Brothers. By January 2010 there was no doubt left: the Greek state stood no chance of servicing its gigantic debt of more than €300 billion. Locked into the eurozone, there was no drachma to devalue and no Greek central bank to assist. Desperate for a bailout before markets and citizens became fully aware of the situation, he contacted Greece's European partners for help. There were two key people with the capacity to answer his distress call: Chancellor Angela Merkel of Germany and Jean-Claude Trichet, a Frenchman presiding over the European Central Bank who was terribly keen to maintain the French elites' pretence that France and Germany spoke with one voice and shared a single agenda on matters monetary.

Merkel's answers, enthusiastically seconded by Trichet, will go down in history: *nein* to a bailout for Greece, *nein* to interest rate relief[5] and, stupefyingly, *nein* to Greece defaulting on its debts Lehman-style. Denial has never appeared more vividly nor been delivered with greater aplomb. The leader of a bankrupt country, whose currency was issued in Frankfurt and controlled by Mr Trichet, was instructed by the German chancellor not even to think of declaring bankruptcy, even as he was being denied assistance.

The Greece–Lehman analogy is justified in a number of ways, despite the fact that one is a country and the other a defunct merchant bank. Both Lehman and Greece were bound to collapse as soon as financialization got into trouble. Tasked with feeding the American Minotaur's enormous appetite for the surplus nations' exports and money, financialization was certain to experience a sharp reversal once the mountain of derivatives it had built reached a tipping point. Like a vicious tide that turns without warning, credit and money disappeared from America's and Europe's financial circuits. Deprived of the piles of private money the financiers conjured up daily, the entities with the greatest burden of debt would be the first ones to crash. Lehman and Greece were the most famous of them, but behind the headlines, and beyond the tragic figures of Mr Fuld and Mr Papandreou, something larger and more terrible was unfolding: the certainties upon which the eurozone had been erected were about to be revealed as illusions. The German chancellor's triple *nein* to Mr Papandreou summed up the determination with which Europe's establishment denied the truth about the eurozone: that it was the one globally significant macro-economy least prepared to sustain the shock waves of this most violent *fin de siècle*.

Subterfuge

Financialization's house of cards (or derivatives, to be precise) began to collapse in 2007, under the weight of its hubris. With private money minting winding down, as the bankers no longer trusted each other's paper products, liquidity dried up fast everywhere. The first bank run hit Britain's Northern Rock, and the first taxpayer-funded bailout – of US investment bank Bear Stearns – followed. American officials like Paulson, Fed chairman Ben Bernanke and New York Fed chief Timothy Geithner began frantically trying to contain the contagion. In the course of the next twelve months they authorized the manufacture of as much public money as they deemed necessary with which to replace the private money disappearing from the system. But how many of their banker friends should they rescue, and whom should they abandon to the raging market forces? In September 2008 they opted for a nuanced response.

They would allow one bank, Lehman, to fail as a morality tale for the rest of the bankers and as a signal to the American people that their public officials were not entirely under the banks' spell. Meanwhile, they were preparing to bail out all other financial institutions if Lehman's insolvency got out of hand. The result was the largest ever transfer of private losses from banks' books onto the public debt ledger.

Wall Street's troubles instantly infected the City of London, and the Anglosphere went from financial supremacy to global basket case. Officials in Brussels, Paris, Frankfurt and Berlin rejoiced, confident that the Anglos, who had been lecturing them on the flimsiness of Europe's monetary union and social market model, had got their comeuppance. Until, that is, they realized that Germany's and France's banks were in a state worse than Lehman, with their asset books weighed down with US-sourced derivatives that had lost 99 per cent of their value.

Germany's federal government panicked. In 2009 the Bundestag, Germany's federal parliament, was bamboozled into setting aside €500 billion of credits and transfers to save German bankers. Similar action was taken in France, where the top four financial institutions faced immediate obliteration. Parliamentarians in both nations were told in no uncertain terms: cough up ridiculous sums for the banks or the world as you know it comes to an end.

And so it was that politicians used to quibbling over a few million euros to be spent on pensioners, health or education gave their governments carte blanche to transfer hundreds of billions to bankers hitherto awash with liquidity. This helped Germany and France's banks survive the collapse of their foolish derivative trades. However, another calamity beckoned: the loans that bankers, like Franz, had granted to the deficit regions of the eurozone were sizeable enough to bankrupt those nations if stressed Irish, Spanish, Greek banks were to default. Before the ink of the first agreements had dried, a second bank bailout was in progress: a bailout for the bankers of deficit countries whose governments could not afford to rescue them.

France and Germany's governments were loath to go back to their parliaments to ask for fresh money for Irish, Italian, Spanish and Greek banks, so the task was passed on to the European Central Bank. Lacking the powers that a proper central bank ought to have, the ECB allowed the eurozone's banks to do something remarkably dicey: issue IOUs that no one would want to buy[6] (given that the banks were insolvent), take these IOUs to their government's finance minister, have the minister stamp on the IOUs a state guarantee (which everyone knew the state could not honour) and finally have the banks deposit these IOUs back with the ECB as collateral in exchange for money that the ECB created to lend to them.

In effect, the eurozone's central bank, whose Maastricht-era charter bans it from lending to member-state governments or to insolvent banks, was lending indirectly to the government of each deficit nation the money its insolvent banks required to pretend they were not insolvent.[7] The banks thus pretended to be solvent; the deficit states pretended they had the money to guarantee that the banks were solvent; and the ECB stood by, pretending that these sad pairs of insolvent banks and insolvent states were perfectly solvent and thus eligible under the ECB's charter for ECB liquidity.

The strangest ritual I had to endure during my five months as Greece's minister of finance in the first half of 2015 concerned this shenanigan almost eight years after it was first invented. My most trusted aide and good friend Wasily Kafouros would come to my office bearing the contracts according to which my ministry, and by extension the Greek state, was guaranteeing IOUs on behalf of Greece's bankers. Mindful of my contempt for this arrangement, Wasily would approach me with the utmost care and only at times he deemed relatively stress free. Both of us shook with rage at the sad fact that my signatures were guaranteeing more than €50 billion of private bank debt while our state could not rub together a few hundred million euros to pay for our public hospitals, our schools or Greece's old-age pensioners.

Placing my signature on these pieces of paper, week in and week out, was probably the oddest and at once the ugliest thing I had to do. The closest rival for the title of Most Disagreeable Ministerial Chore was the obligatory repetition of the lie that Greece's banks were solvent and that the government would honour all its commitments to every one of its creditors, including the guarantees that I was signing in the full knowledge that I could not honour them if the need arose. My only solace was that I was not alone: eurozone finance ministers and central bankers all over the continent had been engaged in this type of gross subterfuge since the heady days of the fall of 2008.[8]

Denial

The reason Greece became the first eurozone country to go manifestly bankrupt was simple. From the moment it looked likely that the drachma was history and Greece's place in the euro was safe, bankers like Franz had gone into a frenzy of lending for the reasons he explained to me so eloquently as we were flying to New York.

The part of the story that Franz left out, probably because he had missed its significance, was the labour market measures – known as the Hartz reforms[9] – that the German Federal Republic enacted as soon as euro notes began to circulate. Implemented at a time of US-led growth, these reforms aimed at enhancing German exports and their competitiveness by making them cheaper through reducing German workers' average take-home pay significantly, both by cutting hourly wage rates and pushing large numbers of workers into so-called mini-jobs.[10]

The result was that German workers, as their share of their employers' profits fell, could not afford the goods they produced. Deprived of domestic demand, surplus German products thus flowed to places like Ireland, Greece and Spain, where demand for them was supported by the loans Franz and his Frankfurt banker colleagues, dipping into the

German corporate profit glut, had shifted to Europe's periphery. The export of German goods and German profits to the rest of the eurozone created debt-fuelled annual growth of 5 per cent in Greece and Ireland, making these fragile deficit-ridden societies look like miracle economies, in contrast to Germany growing at a feeble 1 per cent.

Is it any wonder that financially stressed German workers visiting Greece in the summer months rubbed their eyes at the sight of rising living standards they could only dream of? And is it surprising that when the German loan-driven bubble burst in Europe's south, this bewilderment turned into hostility towards Greece, Spain and Italy's grasshoppers? Of course what the German tourists never saw was that Greece was full of hard-working ants struggling to survive during those years of miraculous growth. Low-wage workers and pensioners were being told that they'd never had it so good – that their real wages and living standards were rising – only they did not feel that way. And they were right.[11] Whereas richer Greeks, who lived well off the back of German and French bank loans, prospered, poorer Greeks fell increasingly into a poverty trap. In the good times! And when the bad times came in 2010 they were told that they had been profligate grasshoppers who had caused the crisis and now had to pay the price.

Many ask: did the authorities in Brussels, Berlin and Athens not recognize that Greek public debt (and the rich Greeks' lifestyle) was unsustainable? The startling answer is that they did not, and here is why. If you think of a nation's public debt and its national income as two growing mountains, debt appears manageable as long as the income mountain grows at a greater pace than the debt mountain. The debt mountain grows automatically as interest piles up on top of it at a rate equal to the interest rate. In Greece that rate had fallen to 3 per cent, courtesy of the foreign-sourced lending spree. At the same time, the national income mountain (measured in euros) was growing much faster, at 8 per cent – 3 per cent of this growth due to rising prices and 5 per cent resulting from higher production. Thus it seemed that Greece's public debt, while large, was serviceable owing to much faster rising incomes. But when the events of 2008 spread the credit crunch, two terrible things happened at once that put paid to this illusion.

First, the almost complete cessation of new credit meant that the Greek state could no longer refinance its debt unless it was prepared to pay the few risk-loving investors left in the money markets interest rates exceeding 10 per cent. Second, Greek national income went into reverse growth, falling because of a global recession that depressed tourism and the incomes of the countless Greeks trading in debt-financed imports. When the debt mountain's growth rate – the interest rate – shot up from 3 to 10 per cent and the income mountain instead of growing started shrinking (first by –3 per cent, then by –5 per cent), Greece's debt sustainability became a contradiction in terms.

Against these brutal facts, the triple *nein* in reply to George Papandreou's request for help in early 2010 was devastating in its inanity. It was as realistic as suggesting to him that he ought to beam Greece up to another galaxy where it was possible to avoid declaring bankruptcy without devaluation, without debt relief and without new loans. The triple *nein* was a knee-jerk expression of Europe's denial that it was facing a structural crisis. It had created a monetary union featuring states without a central bank to back them at a time of global crisis and a European Central Bank without a state watching its back. The Maastricht rules were impossible to abide by.

The triple *nein* held from January 2010 until May of that year, when at last Berlin and Frankfurt could no longer avoid the fact that Greece was about to default on its debts to German and French banks. At that point Europe's denial mutated into another form: into Greece's so-called bailout, which was to become the blueprint for equivalent action in Dublin, Lisbon and Madrid and which left its mark on Rome, even on the Netherlands and on France, pushing the whole continent into a new recessionary phase.[12] The gist of the deal offered to Greece was simple: as you are now insolvent, we shall grant you the largest loan in history on condition that you shrink your national income by an amount never seen since the grapes of wrath. It would take a smart eight-year-old to see that such a bailout could not end well.

But this was not a bailout. Greece was never bailed out. Nor were the rest of Europe's swine – or the PIIGS, as Portugal, Ireland, Italy, Greece and Spain became collectively branded. Greece's bailout, then Ireland's, then Portugal's, then Spain's were primarily rescue packages for French and German banks.

In bending its rules to rescue the PIIGS's private banks with the issue of the aforementioned IOUs, the ECB had given Chancellor

Merkel and France's President Nicolas Sarkozy some respite from having to go back to their parliaments for more taxpayers' money for French and German bankers. But much more was now needed. By May 2010 Greek government bonds had lost 82 per cent of their value. Put differently, a bank or private investor owed 100 euros by the Greek state could only sell this debt on for 18 euros. This was a disaster for those French and German banks that were owed up to €200 billion by Greece. It was also only the tip of a huge iceberg. In 2009 the exposure of German banks to Greek, Irish, Spanish, Portuguese and Italian debt amounted to a dizzying €704 billion.[13] Much, much more than the total capital base of Germany's banking system. If Greece went under, and contagion brought down some of the other peripheral banks, Germany's banking system would be toast.

Suddenly it became imperative to save Greece. But with the Greek state cut off from money markets, as no sane investor would lend to the Athens government, the German and French banks feared the worst: Greece would have to default, and the banks would be at the mercy of regulators whose rules said they had to declare the insolvency of venerable banks like BNP Paribas or Finanz Bank. Another German and French bank bailout had become unavoidable. The second one in less than two years.

The problem was that Chancellor Merkel and President Sarkozy could not imagine going back to their parliaments for more money for their banker chums, so they did the next best thing: they went to their parliaments invoking the cherished principle of solidarity with Greece, then with Ireland, then Portugal and finally Spain. Thus Mr Papandreou was pushed into accepting the largest loan in history, of which the bulk, more than 91 per cent, went to prop up the French and German banks by buying back from them at a hundred euros bonds whose market value had declined to less than twenty euros.

A cynical ploy that transferred hundreds of billions of losses from the books of French and German banks to Europe's taxpayers was presented to the world as the manifestation of European solidarity. What makes this transfer sinister rather than just cynical was that the Greek loan came not only from French and German taxpayers but also from the Portuguese, the Slovaks, the Irish – from taxpayers whose banks had nothing to gain. In essence, the private losses of French and German banks were spread throughout the eurozone, forcing even the weakest citizens of the weakest of member states to chip in.

The Greek bailout did not go down well in the sixteen parliaments where it was discussed. Nationalists and anti-Europeans grabbed the opportunity to lambast their governments for daring to ask the people to cough up money for the worst of the Mediterranean's grasshoppers when they themselves were suffering from the post-2008 recession. Behind the scenes the governments would inform them that the Greek bailout was all about saving their own banks, but the opportunity for putting on a show of patriotism was too tempting to ignore. So they demanded to see some Greek blood before signing off on the deal.

The Greek loan thus came with vicious strings attached – strings designed to cause visible pain to the weakest Greeks. The conditionalities, as the strings were called, boiled down to the dismantling of basic social welfare provisions, this to be supervised by officials representing the ECB, the European Commission and the International Monetary Fund.[14] Thus the troika –the triumvirate of the ECB, the EC and the IMF – was born. It comprised a small group of bailiffs, disguised as technocrats, who acquired powers that Europe's governments cannot dream of. With every visitation of the troika, the dream of shared European prosperity was dealt another blow.

Fiscal waterboarding

My use of the term fiscal waterboarding back in 2010 was, after I became finance minister in 2015, used as evidence that I was a provocateur. In fact it was a perfectly apt and reasonable term by which to describe the troika's practices in Athens and elsewhere. What does waterboarding involve? You take a subject, lay him on his back and engulf his head with water so that he suffocates. Just before he dies, you stop, you allow the subject to take a few agonizing breaths, and then you start again. You repeat until he confesses.

Fiscal waterboarding is obviously not physical, it's fiscal. But the idea is the same, and it is exactly what happened to successive Greek governments from 2010 onwards. Instead of air, Greek governments nursing unsustainable debts were starved of liquidity. At the same time they were banned from defaulting to creditors. Facing payments they were being forced to make, they were denied liquidity till the very last moment, just before formal bankruptcy. Instead of confessions, they were forced to sign further loan agreements, which they knew would add new impetus to the crisis. The troika would provide just enough liquidity in order to repay its own members. Exactly like waterboarding, the liquidity provided was calculated to be just enough to keep the subject going without defaulting formally, but never more than that. And so the torture continued with the government kept completely under the troika's control.

This is fiscal waterboarding, and I cannot imagine a better and more accurate term to describe what has been going on since 2010. During my five months in the finance ministry I came to know this most interesting process at first hand. Such as, for instance, when the European Central Bank connived to reduce our government's access to liquidity by preventing Greece's banks from purchasing our treasury bills.

Of course the problem with waterboarding is that it is a poor method of eliciting the truth, as subjects will confess to anything the interrogator wants to hear to stop the torture. So it was with the troika's fiscal waterboarding. Successive governments of indebted eurozone member states agreed to the troika's programmes even though they knew they would deepen the crises.

Ponzi austerity

Franz and his banker colleagues had been, in effect, running a huge Ponzi scheme in the deficit nations of Europe's monetary union. This is what Franz meant with his sad admission, 'I lived the life of a predator lender.' And when the pyramid crumbled, as Ponzi schemes inevitably do, Ponzi growth metamorphosed into what I once called Ponzi austerity.

Standard Ponzi schemes are based on a sleight of hand that creates the appearance of a fund whose overall value is growing faster than the value of the investments made in it. In reality the opposite is true. The fraudster behind a Ponzi scheme usually helps himself to some of the incoming capital, but the fund is not creating any new capital with which to replenish these leakages, let alone pay the returns it has promised. Any dividends paid to maintain the illusion of growth come from new investments. And this appearance of growth that does not really exist is, of course, the lure that brings into the scheme new participants, whose capital is utilized by the Ponzi scheme's operator to maintain that facade.

Ponzi austerity is the inverse of Ponzi growth. Whereas Ponzi growth schemes are based on the lure of a growing fund, in the case of Ponzi austerity the attraction is the promise of debt reduction for the purposes of defeating insolvency through a combination of austerity belt-tightening and new loans that provide the bankrupt with necessary funds to repay maturing debts, such as bonds. As it is impossible to escape insolvency in this way, given austerity's depressing effect on income, Ponzi austerity schemes, just like Ponzi growth schemes, necessitate a constant influx of new loans to maintain the illusion that bankruptcy has been averted. But to attract these loans, the Ponzi austerity's operators must do their utmost to maintain the facade of deficit reduction.

Ponzi growth has been around for ages. But it took the collective wisdom of Europe's great and good to create history's first Ponzi austerity scheme. The Greek, Portuguese, Irish, Spanish and Cypriot loan agreements are splendid examples. Bankrupted states, in a death embrace with bankrupted banking sectors, were forced to take on ever-increasing loans (mainly from European taxpayers) on condition of belt-tightening austerity. As the scheme progressed and more loans were agreed, public debt as a proportion of national income only rose. Again, as in Ponzi growth schemes, where more and more investments are required to maintain the pretence of growth, in the case of Greece, Portugal, Ireland, Spain and Cyprus more and more loans were necessary in order to maintain the pretence of debt reduction.

Here is an example of eurozone-style Ponzi austerity at its worst. It is spring 2012. The Greek government that signed up to the country's second bailout[15] has collapsed under popular anger at the nation's sad state. A fresh election is due in May 2012, and Syriza, a radical left-wing party that advocates rescinding the bailout agreement, is rising fast in the polls. Horrified at the prospect of an anti-troika party in government, the troika suspends the disbursement of loan payments to the interim Greek government.[16] The administration is left with no alternative other than to suspend its own payments to institutions and individuals. Hospitals, schools, wages, pensions all suffer. But the concern of the great and the good is about Greece's debt to the European Central Bank – the ECB.

You see, dear reader, in 2010 an ill-fated attempt to shore up Greek government bonds by the ECB's president, Monsieur Jean-Claude Trichet, involved the purchase by the ECB of a tranche of Greek bonds at low, low prices. The stated objective was to prop up their value and thus help prevent the Greek state from losing its market access – its capacity to borrow from private investors.[17] Trichet's ploy failed, as did Greece.[18] Regardless, the ECB holds these bonds, which start maturing. Had they not been purchased by the ECB in 2010, they would have been 'given a haircut' (written down) together with the rest of the Greek government's bonds in private hands a few months earlier, in early 2012. But no, the ECB cannot accept write-downs from member states because it is against its charter, which prohibits it from doing anything that resembles financing member states – except, of course, when it bends its own rules in order to rescue assorted bankers, as we saw earlier.[19]

This means that the caretaker Greek government, while putting Greece's social economy through the wringer, has to find €5 billion in a few days to repay the ECB for one of these maturing bonds. Where will the money come from? The troika has suspended loan payments and no privateer is ready to go where even the troika refuses to tread.

The obvious thing to do under the circumstances is for Athens to default on the bonds that the ECB owns or for the ECB to offer the Greek government longer maturities, a debt swap or something of the sort. But this is something that Frankfurt and Berlin reject with venom. When it comes to countries like Germany and France, the rules are meant to be broken.[20] But for countries like Greece the rules are the rules are the rules! Even if they are unworkable and unenforceable. The Greek state can default against the weakest of Greek and non-Greek citizens, against pension funds and the like, but its debts to the ECB are sacrosanct. They have to be paid come what may. But how?

This is what they come up with in lieu of a solution: the ECB allows the Greek government to issue worthless IOUs – short-term treasury bills – that no private investor will touch, and pass them on to the insolvent Greek banks.[21] The Greek banks then hand over these IOUs to the European System of Central Banks[22] as collateral in exchange for loans that the banks give back to the Greek government so that Athens could repay the ECB.

If this sounds like a Ponzi scheme it is because it is the mother of all Ponzi schemes, a merry-go-round of Ponzi austerity which left both the insolvent banks and the insolvent Greek state a little more insolvent while the Greek population sank deeper and deeper into despair. And all so the European Union could pretend that its inane rules had been respected.

This is but one example of the vicious cycle of Ponzi austerity replicated incessantly throughout the eurozone. Its stated purpose was to reduce debt. But debt rose everywhere.[23] Is this a failure? Yes and no. It is a failure in terms of Brussels's stated objectives but not in terms of the underlying motives. For the true purpose of the bailout loans was to effect a transfer of the periphery's bad debts from the books of the (mainly) Northern European banks to the shoulders of Europe's taxpayers at the cost of increasing debts and a recession caused by the conditions attached to the new loans.

These toxic transfers, effected in the name of European solidarity, led to a death dance of insolvent banks and bankrupt states, sad couples sequentially marched off the cliff of competitive austerity. Deflation, ultra-low investment, social fragmentation and rising poverty ensured that large sections of proud European populations, mostly the weakest of their citizenry, were dragged into the contemporary equivalent of the Victorian poorhouse.

Impotence

It is 2011. The contagion of default and collapse is spreading via the common currency from country to country. The minister of finance of a major European nation with an economy that dwarfs Greece's is keen for ideas on how to stop the domino effect taking his country down. He agrees to see a friend of mine who wishes to convey to the minister a proposal on how the eurozone debt juggernaut could be stopped in its tracks.

The minister hears the idea and likes it a lot. Immediately he asks his aides to organize meetings between his visitor and Brussels officials, members of the European Parliament and the like with a view to helping his visitor lobby these important European policymakers in favour of this interesting proposal. At that point his visitor turns and says, 'Minister, what is the point? Why should I try to convince all these officials if I have convinced you? You are the finance minister of a major European nation. You sit on the Eurogroup and Ecofin [the European Union's council of finance ministers]. If you like my proposal, why don't you table it as your own at the next meeting?'

The minister smiles. He sits back in his plush armchair and responds in a manner that, tragically, makes perfect sense.

'Do you know what will happen if I table your splendid proposal? SMSs will stream out of the room while I am talking. The press will shortly be reporting that I am tabling a proposal for the central management of a part of the debt of every eurozone member state. Seconds later the money markets will refuse to lend to my government, except at usurious interest rates, as the rumour spreads that, for me to be proposing such ideas, my government cannot refinance its debt. My friend, I shall cease to be minister the next day. How exactly will that help promote your proposal?'

A year later that minister was gone anyway, and so was his government. What never went away, judging by my own more recent experiences, is the terrible disconnect between the eminently sensible things some ministers say behind closed doors and the inanity of their statements in the Eurogroup, other official bodies and when the television cameras are switched on.

Falling dominoes or tumbling mountaineers?

As the Greek disease spread, infecting Ireland, Portugal and Spain, before reaching Italy and threatening to bring the whole house of cards down, the metaphor of falling dominoes became rather oversubscribed in the media. A better analogy would be that of a mountaineering club.

Imagine a group of disparate mountaineers perched on some steep cliff face, some of them more agile, others less fit, all bound together in a forced state of solidarity by a single rope. Unbelievably, the members of our mountaineering club abide by an irrevocable rule: the common rope is never pinned to the rock face they are climbing. Suddenly an earthquake hits (such as the collapse of Wall Street), and one of them (of, let's say, a Hellenic disposition) is dislodged, her fall arrested only by the rope. Under the strain of the stricken member's weight, dangling in midair, and with some especially loose rocks falling from above, the next-weakest mountaineer (Irish perhaps?) struggles to hang on but eventually has to let go too.

The strain on the remaining mountaineers greatly increases, and the new next-weakest member is now teetering on the verge of a fall that will cause another hideous tug on the remaining line of saviours. Will the stronger members hold on? Will they manage to reach the peak, carrying the hangers-on with them, before the ruthless pull of gravity plunges the whole group into the ravine below? Or will the strongest members cut themselves loose with their knives (and revert to something akin to the Deutsche Mark)?

The reason why the mountaineering analogy is far better than the domino metaphor has to do with the eurozone's architecture and in particular the Maastricht rule that no member state should count on financial aid from other member states or from the union – the so-called 'no bailout' clause that was meant to deter governments from getting into trouble in the first place.[24] Could this rule (the equivalent of not pinning the common rope to the cliff) be respected while at the same time prohibiting countries like Greece from declaring bankruptcy and defaulting on the bankers? Ordinary minds would answer in the negative. But Brussels functionaries are not ordinary people.

Aided ably by financial consultants who had made a fortune out of bending logic to their advantage, they came up with an ingenious alternative. They created a new fund, which they called the European Financial Stability Facility (EFSF), to bail out the fallen member states, lending them the money necessary to make the bankers whole. It was the financial equivalent of binding our mountaineers more tightly together but still without pinning the common rope to the cliff face.

The trick that allowed member states to lend to other stricken members while still apparently respecting the 'no bailout' clause was hidden in the devilish structure of the bonds that the EFSF would issue. At the beginning, when only Greece needed bailout money of, say, €1 billion, the EFSF would issue a bond with a face value of €1 billion, sell it to the money markets and pass the money on to the Greek government, which would promptly pass it on to Europe's bankers. The €1 billion liability now fell upon Greece but was backed by the eurozone member states that remained solvent, which had suddenly become Greece's creditors, each one of them bearing a proportion of this new debt equal to its relative national income.[25] To preserve the 'no bailout' clause and to ensure that there was no common debt whatsoever – that every euro of debt belonged to one and only one member state – the slice of that €1 billion bond belonging to, say, France would bear a rate of interest payable to the bond's owner (the investor that purchased it) equal to the interest rate France paid to borrow for its own purposes. The Spanish slice would bear a different interest rate, so too the Italian, and so on.

So each nation participating in Greece's rescue, or later in Portugal's, Ireland's and the rest, paid market interest rates depending on its own creditworthiness, which reflected its country-specific risk of bankruptcy. This meant that the member state with the highest probability of going Greece's way paid most interest for the slice of the EFSF bond it guaranteed so that Greece could receive the €1 billion of new debt.

Those familiar with the structured derivatives that brought down Lehman Brothers and Wall Street along with it – so-called collateralized debt obligations, or CDOs – will recognize in the EFSF bailout bonds the same form of synthesized risk. Except that the EFSF bonds were even more toxic than Wall Street's noxious derivatives! To see this, consider what happened when Ireland went bankrupt and needed an EFSF-funded bailout.

The EFSF had to issue new debt to lend to Ireland on behalf of all the eurozone countries except Greece, which had already fallen into insolvency, and of course Ireland. This meant that, with Greece and Ireland out of the group of creditor nations, a greater burden had to be shared by the remaining EFSF members. The markets immediately focused on the next marginal country, the one currently borrowing at the highest interest rates within the EFSF in order to loan money to the fallen Greece and Ireland: Portugal. Immediately, Portugal's own interest rates shot up, pushing it over the edge.

This would continue until the band of nations within the EFSF became so small it was either unable or unwilling to bear the burden of the fallen states' combined debt. At that point, led by Germany, the remaining solvent nations would have to signal the euro's bitter end and withdraw. Or the ECB would have to invent another trick to violate its impossible rulebook.

Ignorance

Europe's finance ministers traditionally gather at least once a month in the context of the Eurogroup. During the worst of the eurozone crisis their meetings produced one calamitous decision after the next. By 2011, as the markets learned to ignore the Eurogroup's upbeat communiqués, the half-life of their positive impact on market sentiment dropped to a few hours at best.

In the fall of 2011 the Eurogroup met in Poland. Timothy Geithner, the US secretary of the treasury, was in attendance with some solid advice for the Europeans on how to prise apart the death embrace linking insolvent banks and bankrupt states. Geithner's chief recommendation was that the European Central Bank should somehow signal its readiness to underwrite part of the debt of key countries, such as Italy, to show the markets that Europe was ready to halt the domino effect threatening to topple the eurozone. He was not just ignored; he was attacked. As the meeting ended, Ms Maria Fekter, the Austrian finance minister, speaking on behalf of her European colleagues, opined that the Americans had no business telling them how to deal with the debt crisis when America's debt was higher than the eurozone's. 'We need no lectures from the United States,' she said defiantly.[26]

When I saw her on television speaking those words I must admit I despaired. I despaired because her words revealed the deep ignorance of European leaders and their unwillingness to understand the simple, useful advice that the US treasury secretary had brought. She and the other eurozone finance ministers seemed on a mission to misunderstand their problem. To believe that Europe's problem was debt. Not the architectural design of the eurozone. Not its unenforceable rules. But debt. Debt was never Europe's problem. It was a symptom of an awful institutional design. Our finance ministers resembled doctors who misdiagnose a cancer patient in severe pain as afflicted with a pain crisis. No wonder the medicine they prescribed was worse than the disease.

Ponzi austerity spreads

At the end of 2011 ECB president Jean-Claude Trichet, arguably the world's worst central banker, was replaced by Mario Draghi, a frightfully smart former chair of Italy's treasury and central bank and, not insignificantly, a former Goldman Sachs International vice president. Draghi could see that his own country had only a few months left before falling into the same rut as Greece, leading to Spain and France's incapacity to service their multi-trillion-euro debts. In effect, the euro was about to dissolve as the eurozone's mountaineering club members toppled sequentially, and in slow motion, into the abyss. So Draghi decided to take immediate action.

His first move, a couple of weeks after taking over the ECB's helm, was to 'print' a trillion euros and lend them to the eurozone's stricken banks. As long as the bankers could find some sheets of paper lying around, Draghi would accept them as collateral and hand over the cash.[27] As is Europe's habit, this simple operation was given a complex name, Long Term Refinancing Operations. Draghi's real intention with the LTRO was to lend to the banks for next to no interest so that the banks would, in turn, do what the ECB's charter did not allow him to do: lend to the faltering states, in particular to the Italian government, which was on its way to the poorhouse.

Meanwhile the concept of a democracy-free zone, which had begun life in Brussels in the 1950s, had just been given a new twist in Rome, and indeed Athens. Two prime ministers, George Papandreou in Greece and the inimitable Silvio Berlusconi in Italy, had been deemed by

Chancellor Merkel (with France's President Sarkozy in tow) unfit to maintain the pace of austerity necessary to justify in the Bundestag the propping up of Italy's and Greece's unsustainable debts either via the EFSF or the ECB. It is hard to believe that prime ministers of European nations can be pushed aside or selected at the whim of another European leader, but this is exactly what happened when Papandreou was replaced by the ECB's former vice president, a certain Mr Loukas Papademos, and Silvio Berlusconi by Mario Monti, a former European commissioner.[28]

Monti's mission was to set Italy's public finances in some kind of order. He knew that Berlin was keen to put Italy through the same ordeal as Greece, with the hated troika invading Rome's ministries and imposing hyper-austerity. So he tried to prevent this by introducing a milder form of austerity himself, hoping to contain Italy's debt before going to the Eurogroup cap in hand. In this latter task, he looked to the other Mario, the ECB's Mr Draghi, for badly needed help. It was to arrive in the form of the aforementioned LTRO trick.

At the time all Europe's banks were on the verge of collapse, while front-line states like Italy were faring just as badly. The ECB hoped that its LTRO loans, at almost zero interest, would net the borrowing banks a nice little profit from lending the money on to the states at higher interest rates which would nevertheless be far, far lower than the usurious rates private investors were demanding from those same governments. Both banks and states would thus be reprieved, at least for a while.

One morning in February 2012 the CEO of one of Italy's largest banks informed Monti's government that his bank would fail unless it received €40 billion there and then. A state that was about to collapse under its own debt burden, Greek style, was thus put in an awful dilemma: fork out a sum it could not afford or sit idly by as the nation's banks closed their doors one after the other. Thankfully Draghi's LTRO was at hand. So this is what happened: the failing bank issued IOUs worth €40 billion on that very morning that no investor would buy, given the bank's parlous state. The Italian minister of finance guaranteed this private debt by committing future taxes to it, thereby adding €40 billion to Italy's public debt. Finally, the bank took these IOUs to the ECB and received cash from Mr Draghi's generous LTRO programme.

So, at the end of the proverbial day, Draghi's plan to prop up the Italian banks and the Italian state had failed. Instead, his scheme was supporting the banks but had plunged the Italian state deeper into unsustainable debt.

Despotism

Mr Klaus Masuch was until recently the ECB's representative in the troika delegation that spreads panic everywhere it goes. In early 2012 the troika passed through Dublin. At the press conference after his meeting with Irish officials Mr Masuch felt comfortable enough among mostly sycophantic journalists to relate his view that the Irish people were sophisticated because they understood that the troika's endeavours were tough but necessary. His precise words were: 'The attitude [of the Irish people] as far as I can see, and I have a limited perspective, is very good. I am impressed by the depth of the discussion in Ireland and by the understanding of complex financial and economic arguments . . . When I come from the airport by taxi the taxi drivers are very well informed, so I think this is a very good sign that here we have an open discussion. It's a difficult adjustment process but there is an economic debate and this is how it should be.'

At which point Vincent Browne, a seasoned Irish journalist, asked a killer question that set off a fascinating exchange.

> BROWNE: Klaus, did your taxi driver tell you how the Irish
> people are bewildered that we are required to pay unguar-
> anteed bond holders billions of euros for debts that the
> Irish people have no relation to, or no bearing with,
> primarily to bail out or to ensure the sovereignty of
> European banks? And if your taxi driver were to ask you
> that question what would have been your response?
>
> MASUCH: I would say I can understand that this is a difficult
> decision that was made by the government but there are a
> number of different issues to be balanced against each other
> and I understand that the government came to the view
> that the cost for the Irish people, for the stability of the

banking system, the confidence in the banking system, would have been much greater for the taxpayer than the action you mentioned . . . So the financial sector would have been affected, the confidence in the financial sector would have been negatively affected, and I can understand that it was a difficult decision which was taken in that direction.

BROWNE: That does not address the issue! We are required to pay on behalf of this defunct bank, in a way that has no bearing on the benefit of the Irish people at all, billions on unguaranteed bonds in order to ensure the health of the European banks. How would you explain that situation to the taxi driver that you referred to earlier?

MASUCH: I think I have addressed the question.

BROWNE: No, you have not addressed the question. You referred to the viability of the financial institutions. This institution that I am talking about is defunct. It's over. It's finished. Now, why are the Irish people required, under threat from the ECB, why are the Irish people required to pay billions to unguaranteed bond holders under the threat of the ECB?[29]

MASUCH: . . . [Inaudible]

BROWNE: You did not answer the question the last time, maybe you will answer it this time.

MASUCH: . . .

BROWNE: This is not good enough! You people are intervening in this society, causing huge damage by requiring us to make payments not for the benefit of the people here in Ireland but for the benefit of European financial institutions. You must answer the question. Why are the Irish people inflicted with this burden?

MASUCH: I think I have addressed the question . . .

BROWNE: You have nothing to say? There is no answer, is that right? Is that it? No answer?

MASUCH: I have given an answer . . .

BROWNE: You have given an answer to a different question.

MODERATOR: This is your view.

BROWNE: This is my view and it will be the view of the taxi driver!

Unable to silence the indefatigable journalist, Masuch gathered his papers and left the room with his tail between his legs. If anyone wants a visual depiction of Europe's democratic deficit or an explanation of why its citizens increasingly have no confidence in European institutions, put 'Vincent Browne versus ECB official' in your search engine, watch the clip and weep.

Through one of his characters Berthold Brecht once quipped, 'Brute force is out of date – why send out murderers when you can employ bailiffs?'[30] In the era of the troika Europe gave his quip another spin, employing well-groomed technocrats like Mr Masuch in that capacity. Three years later, in February 2015, I was to come face to face with Mr Masuch, he in the same role, as the ECB's troika point man, me as the finance minister of a Greek government elected to say no to the irrational misanthropy that passed as official European policy.[31]

As I sat opposite Klaus in a drab Brussels office, exchanging niceties prior to beginning a tough negotiation, those images from the YouTube clip featuring the gutsy Vincent Browne came back into my mind. Our meeting led to an impasse because, unlike the Irish government in 2009, I had authorization from my cabinet, our parliament and the prime minister to say no to him. Vincent Browne would have been pleased, I like to think.[32]

Monti's mutiny

Meanwhile, as the winter of 2012 was passing the baton to a troubled spring, Italy was on its knees, a short step away from ruin, and a struggling Mario Monti was feeling the strain of collapsing state finances and banks with burgeoning black holes on their books. Most Italians saw Monti as a safe pair of hands, courtesy of a successful tenure in Brussels, a strong academic background and basic human decency. However, he was unelected and owed his meteoric rise to Italy's highest office to Chancellor Merkel's insistence that he replace the elected albeit obnoxious Silvio Berlusconi – not the best of credentials for endearing him to an Italian public sceptical of the German leader's right to decide who ruled their nation.

Chancellor Merkel had charged Monti with the impossible task of reining in Italy's burgeoning debt at a time when the interest rates the state was paying were going through the roof owing to the contagion that had begun in Greece. Monti's own priorities were different. Having observed the ignominy that Greece had suffered at the hands of the troika, his patriotic duty, as he saw it, was to exploit his good relationship with the German government to implement a type of austerity-lite that would keep Mrs Merkel at bay and thus avoid a troika-administered takeover of his country.

Soon after his appointment Mario Monti could see that his task was becoming increasingly difficult. Italy's banks were reaping all the benefits of Mario Draghi's efforts without even getting out of the woods themselves. But the bond markets, where Italy had to borrow daily to service its €2 trillion debt, were going feral, asking for extortionate interest rates and thereby pushing Italy's total debt into the stratosphere. Monti now believed that, as long as investors saw Italy's problematic banks relying on his problematic government, there was no level of mild austerity that would placate them. Sensing the impossibility of his situation, his critics, both those on the Left, who disdained his austerity policy, and those fuming at his predecessor Berlusconi's ousting, were sharpening their knives, while his few admirers were losing faith in his magic.

Monti knew he had to act. And act he did!

At the June 2012 European Union summit, as the meeting was drawing to a close and Chancellor Merkel was preparing to exit the room, Monti demanded the floor. In his mild voice he articulated possibly the most jagged statement of his life. The chancellor sat down again, realizing that for Mario Monti to be taking such a stance something of significance must be up.

Monti's message was simple: unless a radical agreement was reached there and then on the financing of eurozone banks, he would veto the summit's communiqué. His point was that it was absurd to expect stressed states like Italy to borrow money on behalf of insolvent banks while expecting the same banks to fund the state through loans from the ECB.[33] Things had to change. In particular, Monti demanded that banks in need of further capital injections should borrow directly from Europe's bailout fund, the European Stability Mechanism (ESM), which had in the meantime succeeded the temporary EFSF. Monti's key point was that these loans, from the ESM to the banks, should totally bypass national governments and not count as part of the member states' national debt. A commercial bank in Italy, in Spain or in Greece that needed taxpayers' money to stay afloat should, Monti insisted, get it from Europe's bailout fund and not from the stressed governments of Italy, Spain or Greece.

Monti had broken protocol by doing something dreadfully radical by European standards that happened also to be radically sensible: he had demanded a proper banking union, like the one in the United States. If his key point was approved, Italian banks that got into trouble would be Europeanized – managed and funded directly by the euro-zone exactly as a Nevadan bank in trouble is recapitalized, resolved and handled by Washington, without asking the state government of Nevada to borrow on the bank's behalf on Wall Street or in the City of London.[34]

For a few moments Monti's statement was met with an eerie silence. Then, moved by his own yearning for a similar solution for Spain's failing banks, Prime Minister Rajoy of Spain dared second Monti's proposal. And then perhaps the meekest of leaders, President Hollande of France, in his first summit intervention, joined in. Faced with a united Latin front, Chancellor Merkel relented but added a precondition: OK to direct bank recapitalizations for Italy and Spain's banks, but only after member states agreed to form a formal banking union within Europe's monetary union.

Who could disagree with such a sensible suggestion? I, for one, would have agreed enthusiastically. The idea that all banks should be under the same regulatory regime, overseen by a single supervisor sitting in the ECB's Frankfurt offices, answerable to Europe as a whole and with a union-wide common recapitalization fund – the ESM, according to Monti's proposal – was a rare display of rationality by the standards of European Union summit meetings. So had Mario Monti managed to push the German chancellor into taking the first, and possibly most significant, step towards a proper economic union?

To a union willing and able to treat a bank failure in Italy or in Greece or in Germany as a European financial sector insolvency to be addressed by a European institution, without referring the failed banker to a member state's stressed government?

For a moment it looked that way. Except that it was an all-too-fleeting moment.

In the breach

When the June 2012 summit meeting ended, the press rightly hailed Mario Monti as the hero who had saved the eurozone or at least succeeded in imposing upon the German chancellor and her finance minister a policy that created the first all-important shock absorber in the system.[35] It was also the first time that, as a commentator on the euro crisis, I had gone on television to praise a European leader and say good things about an EU summit decision.

Except that a few weeks later Monti's triumph dematerialized. The first signs of what was to come appeared in a letter Germany's finance minister, Wolfgang Schäuble, published in the *Financial Times* in August 2011. In this letter[36] Dr Schäuble hailed the decision to form a banking union but added ominously that he could not imagine how such a union of more than six thousand banks could be effected in practice. This was the beginning of a process, directed from Berlin, which instituted a banking union in name only in order to pay lip service to the June 2012 agreement when in reality the Monti proposal was being defanged.

This process required several careful steps. First, Berlin insisted that banking union concerned only 'systemically significant' financial institutions, meaning 124 banks. Its purpose? To leave out the many smaller, state-based German regional banks whose network of political and corporate vested interests the German government and the Bundesbank wanted to keep to themselves and outside any European supervision. The second step was to limit the banking union to common supervision of large banks by the ECB, leaving most of the costs of resolving failed banks at the national level.[37] The third step was to create a collective insurance fund to which everyone would contribute, to be drawn on in the event of another meltdown, but which would in fact be hopelessly inadequate if another crisis like that of 2010 were to hit.

Taken together, the second and the third steps meant one thing: the nexus of failed banks and bankrupt member states – the hideous embrace – was to be preserved intact. When crisis threatened a German or a Dutch bank, depositors would be safe. If it hit a Greek or Portuguese bank, depositors with more than €100,000 in the bank would probably take a large hit,[38] and insured deposits (less than that sum) would burden the stressed state's finances.

In short, Monti's excellent idea was to be honoured in the breach, not in the observance. Europe's celebrated banking union lives in name only, while in reality and in practice its banking disunion is as toxic as ever. Ultimate proof of this came in my last weeks in office as Greece's finance minister, when the ECB closed down the Greek banks even though, in its capacity as the banking union's sole supervisor, it considered them to be solvent. What sort of banking union allows the closure of banks it considers solvent in order to pressurize a member state government to accept more fiscal austerity, more pension cuts, higher sales taxes and the like?

With Monti's last-ditch effort in tatters, his days were numbered. That same summer, in 2012, the burden of Italy's salvation – tantamount to the euro's own survival – was to be passed on to the other Mario, the one presiding over the European Central Bank.

Whatever it takes?

As the summer heat of 2012 built up, the euro's fault lines widened to breaking point. Italy and Spain were the front-line states, their defences buckling under bets taken out by emboldened bond dealers against Rome and Madrid's ability to avoid fates similar to those of Greece, Portugal and Ireland. Berlin recognized it was facing a simple dilemma: exit the monetary union itself or allow the ECB to save the euro by violating the spirit, possibly even the letter, of its Bundesbank-imposed charter.

In mid-July Christian Noyer, representing France's central bank, made a hitherto unthinkable admission in an interview with the

German financial daily *Handelsblatt*: 'We are currently observing a failure of the transmission mechanism of monetary policy. From the markets' perspective, the interest rate facing individual private banks depends on the funding costs of the state where they are domiciled and not on the ECB overnight interest rate . . . Hence the monetary policy transmission mechanism does not work.'[39] This was equivalent to an airline pilot picking up the intercom and saying to the passengers, 'The landing gear has failed and the wings are about to crack.'

On 26 July 2012 Mario Draghi took matters into his own hands with an elegant speech in London, addressing frazzled investors: 'The euro is like a bumblebee. This is a mystery of nature because it shouldn't fly but instead it does. So the euro was a bumblebee that flew very well for several years. And now – and I think people ask, "How come?" Probably there was something in the atmosphere, in the air, that made the bumblebee fly – now something must have changed in the air, and we know what after the financial crisis. The bumblebee would have to graduate to a real bee. And that's what it's doing.'

Undoubtedly Draghi wanted to see the euro graduate into a proper currency, complete with surplus recycling mechanism and the kind of political legitimacy that only liberal democracy can yield – the very liberal democracy that the eurozone was designed to lack. His hopes rested on a political investment from all involved in not allowing the single currency to die, in the way that the EMS-ERM had died in the early 1990s, and he said so in no uncertain terms: 'When people talk about the fragility of the euro and the increasing fragility of the euro, and perhaps the crisis of the euro, very often non-euro-area member states or leaders underestimate the amount of political capital that is being invested in the euro.'

Having reiterated that the euro was a political project, albeit a paradoxical one in that it was erected as a politics-free zone, Draghi came to the one sentence that did more to save the euro in the summer of 2012 than all the hundreds of billions the ECB had poured into stabilizing it put together: 'Within our mandate, the ECB is ready to do whatever it takes to preserve the euro. And believe me, it will be enough.'[40] What did he mean by 'whatever it takes' and 'within our mandate'? In the next few weeks an official ECB announcement explicated Draghi's commitment: Spain, Italy and indeed France would not be allowed to go Greece's way. 'Whatever it takes' meant that Spain and Italy, the front-line states in the battle to save the euro, would not have to borrow from other European taxpayers; their debt would be bolstered by money printed by the ECB. But how could that be done within Draghi's 'mandate'? His answer came in the form of announcing the Outright Monetary Transactions programme.

The simple idea of the OMT was that at a time of the ECB's choosing – in other words, when the going in Italy and Spain got really tough – the ECB would step into the money markets to buy unlimited numbers of Italian and Spanish bonds in order to stabilise their value – and with them the interest rates that the Italian and Spanish governments paid to refinance their public debt. And how would the ECB finance these purchases? By creating digital euros from nothing. But was this member state debt support permissible under the ECB's charter? Did it not violate the 'no bailout' clause that the Bundesbank had insisted would be the centrepiece of the ECB?

Draghi's ingenious argument was that the OMT had nothing to do with propping up Italy and Spain's state finances; it was all about restoring the broken circuits through which the ECB's monetary policy was transmitted throughout the eurozone.[41] True enough, even though the ECB's interest rates had fallen to less than 1 per cent, companies in Italy and in Spain were having to borrow at 9 per cent, while equivalent companies in Germany or Holland were borrowing at less than half that rate. So Draghi's argument was that the OMT did not aim at helping monetarily the governments of Spain and Italy, since such an intention was explicitly banned by the ECB's charter. No, the purpose of buying Italian and Spanish public debt (government bonds), claimed Draghi, was to restore ECB control over the interest rates businesses paid throughout the eurozone; to recover the ECB's capacity to do that which its charter asked of it: maintain full control over the interest rates that businesses and households paid. Except that, as Draghi explained, to do this, the ECB had first to push down the interest rates the states paid in the hope of a therapeutic spillover that would bring down commercial interest rates too.[42] In other words, Draghi presented the OMT as a mechanism for restoring the central bank's control over interest rates, with any assistance to the state finances of Italy and Spain a secondary consequence of his policy – merely a means, not an end in itself.

While it was true that the transmission mechanism of the ECB's monetary policy was broken and needed fixing, it was also true that Draghi's real intention was to prevent the Italian and Spanish governments from going bankrupt Greek-style. And the only way of doing this was to do that which the ECB's charter banned: 'monetizing' member states' public debts.[43]

With the Bundesbank waiting in the wings to denounce Mario Draghi as an apostate and a violator of the Maastricht Treaty, the ECB president had to take an important legal precaution: he had to make any purchase of Italian and Spanish public debt conditional on the acceptance by Rome and Madrid respectively of a programme of harsh Greek-style austerity, to be administered by the hated troika. It was the price Mrs Merkel made Mr Draghi pay to be allowed to save the euro by announcing his OMT programme.

Even before the OMT was announced, Draghi's London speech and 'whatever it takes' had worked. Interest rates fell sharply, giving Italy and Spain a welcome reprieve. So thirsty were the money dealers for a good news story from Europe that they lapped up Draghi's commitment, ignoring all evidence that it was a non-credible commitment – a threat, or a promise, that the ECB president would not be allowed to carry out if it became necessary to do so.[44]

Draghi, however, knew better. He knew precisely that which those of us with a sense of the euro's faulty architecture had been fearing all along: the OMT programme was based on a non-credible threat by the ECB against bond dealers planning to 'short' Italian and Spanish debt – that is, to bet serious money that their value would fall. As Mario Monti and Luis de Guindos, Spain's minister of finance, confirmed in conversations we held years later during my tenure as finance minister, neither Rome nor Madrid was prepared to sign a Greek-style memorandum of understanding with the European Commission, the European Central Bank and the International Monetary Fund. For if they did a deal with the troika, the Italian and Spanish governments would not have lasted more than a few weeks.

The OMT will go down in history as an unlikely success story. It quelled the market for the bonds of Italy and Spain, later on of Portugal and Ireland too, based on the ECB's non-credible promise to buy these bonds in large numbers. The reason it worked was that, like a winning bluff, the ECB was never tested. Draghi's word was taken on trust – or fear, to be more precise. Bond dealers began purchasing Italian and Spanish debt in order to lock in the gains from rising bond prices following Draghi's speech, and so he never had to put his money where his mouth was, the result being that Rome and Madrid never had to sign memoranda of understanding with the troika.

Thus Mario Draghi bought precious time for the euro. Rome and Madrid imposed upon themselves mild austerity to exorcize the troika's much harsher version, and interest rates fell steeply, but so did average prices and nominal incomes, making those countries' debts as unsustainable as ever. Italy, in particular, found itself in a rare bind: the country exported more than it imported, and its government reported a healthy surplus, not including interest and debt repayments, of more than 2 per cent of national income. And yet its public debt was increasing considerably as a proportion of national income. Why? Because overall national income was still falling, while debt was still rising – even if slowly as a result of the ECB's OMT programme.

Draghi knew that the OMT had bought him at most a year. He would have to do a lot more monetizing of member states' debt if the illusion behind the euro's salvation were to be maintained. Unfortunately for Draghi, Jens Weidmann, the Bundesbank president, knew that too. In the OMT he saw a violation of the rules the Bundesbank had dictated as a condition for giving up the Deutsche Mark. And he also foresaw that this violation would have to get far, far worse if Draghi's quest to save the euro were to succeed.

North and south

The Irish and the Greeks are in many ways very different people. And yet the euro crisis merged their fortunes significantly as the weakest of the Greeks and the weakest of the Irish were forced to cover the private losses of German and French bankers.[45]

Vincent Browne's pounding of Klaus Masuch at that press conference put the hapless ECB official in the impossible position of having to defend the ECB's indefensible behaviour towards the people of Ireland. In his questioning Browne alluded repeatedly to the ECB's blackmail of the Dublin government, forcing it to transfer private debts to the public purse of a bank that was dead and buried and thus posed no threat to Ireland's financial stability. Little did Browne know, however, that the ECB's dirty work was not fully done.

To begin at the beginning, when the Anglo-Irish Bank and other such financial time bombs exploded in 2009, the ECB forced the then Irish government, without the consent of its electorate, to offer the bankrupt bankers so-called promissory notes – another type of IOU – which, as every Irishman and -woman knows, bankrupted the nation, brought mass emigration back and condemned the majority to untold hardship. The promissory notes specified regular payments by the Irish treasury to the bearer of the notes that were steep and payable in a few years, thus causing both a liquidity crisis in the public sector and the insolvency of the Irish state. The defunct Irish banks took these promissory notes and deposited them as collateral with Ireland's central bank, drawing liquidity to repay their (mostly German) uninsured bond holders.

That government collapsed under the weight of its hubris, but the new Irish government bowed too to the ECB's pressure not to haircut or restructure the promissory notes. Instead Dublin adopted the 'model prisoner' strategy: 'We shall do as we are told in the hope of a later reprieve.' From then on the promissory notes sat on the books of Ireland's central bank and the Dublin government struggled to pay them as they matured. For two years the Irish government petitioned Brussels and Frankfurt to elongate the promissory note repayment schedule while subjecting the weakest of Irish citizens to the worst cuts Northern Europe had seen since Ireland's potato famine.

Alas, the ECB was adamant: the Irish central bank was not allowed to give better terms to its own government because that would be considered a violation of the 'no bailout' clause of the Maastricht Treaty. In other words, uninsured private bankers had to be bailed out illegally[46] and utterly unethically, but the taxpayers who were forced to carry that can could not even be given better terms for repaying the odious private debt they were forced to acquire in order to bail the bankers out.

Only in 2014 did the ECB relent, accepting that the notes could be swapped for new, longer-term, interest-bearing Irish government bonds. The ECB in effect accepted that this repulsive debt should be restructured, lessening a little the strain on the Irish state. Thus Ireland's central bank swapped the hated promissory notes[47] it was holding for fresh Irish government bonds that promised their bearer significant interest payments in the long term. And, as long as the bearer was the Irish central bank, which kept these bonds to maturity, the government would pay this interest to its own central bank, which would in turn pay it back to the government as dividends. In a sense the long-term beneficiary would be Irish taxpayers, small compensation for the pain the ECB and the bankers had put them through.

But the ECB would have none of that. *What?* its Frankfurt functionaries thought. *The Irish state benefiting from the swap of the promissory notes for government bonds? We can't have that! This would be a gift to Ireland's taxpayers. Monetary financing by the ECB of the Irish state. What will the Bundesbank think?* And so the good people of Frankfurt pressured Ireland's central bank to unload the government bonds, to sell them to private bankers who would then, in the fullness of time, collect the interest from the Irish taxpayers. If anyone was to benefit, it ought to be the bankers and the hedge funds again. Never the citizens.

Something similar was happening at the same time in Greece. In the spring of 2012 Greece's public debt did eventually get a haircut, confirming that an unpayable debt will receive a haircut whatever the dogmas of European officials. The question was, who would lose and who would gain from the haircut's timing and features? In this case it was the bonds held mostly by Greek banks, Greek smallholders and pension funds that took a hit. The troika insisted that the Greek government do nothing to compensate the smallholders or the pension funds but that it fully reimburse the bankers.

Greek banks had indeed lost €38 billion from the haircut and were, to all intents and purposes, bankrupt.[48] So Greece's second bailout, which accompanied the haircut in the spring of 2012, set aside

€50 billion that the government would borrow from the EFSF-ESM to recapitalize the banks – a sum that would, in contrast to Mario Monti's insistence, further increase Greece's public debt. In effect, the bankrupt Greek state was forced by Europe to borrow from Europe on behalf of bankrupt Greek bankers and ensure that the latter received capital injections without losing control of their banks – without being nationalized. To allow the bankers to keep control of the banks, the Greek parliament legislated that, if the bankers showed that they could raise 10 per cent of the additional capital, the Greek state would put in the remaining 90 per cent required – the money that the taxpayer would borrow from Europe – but have no control over the running of the banks.[49]

And as if that were not enough, the same piece of legislation specified that private buyers of bank shares would receive with their shares something called warrants. Warrants are essentially options to buy more shares at the original low share price. Put differently, the state was not only allowing the bankers to remain in control of the banks they had bankrupted but was also committing itself to passing on to them whatever benefit there was from an increase in bank share prices. Heads the state lost, tails the bankers won. Simple!

Naturally, these insanely generous terms, especially the warrants, caused a whirlpool of speculative interest in Greece's banks. To seal the bankers' gains, in April 2014 a change in the bank recapitalization rules was slipped through Greece's parliament in such a manner that almost no parliamentarian noticed. An apparently innocent amendment to a bill prevented the Greek state from buying the new shares the banks were about to issue. By allowing for new shares to be issued at prices well below those that the Greek state had paid during the injection of almost €40 billion into the banks and at the same time banning the state from buying these shares, the state's shares lost value and its equity in the banks was diluted substantially. In short, the Greek public was short-changed in a way not dissimilar to what transpired in Ireland that very same week – when the Irish central bank was forced to unload the government bonds it had received for its promissory notes.

And what is the common thread between these fresh assaults on the Irish and the Greek people? The presence of Europe's custodian of the euro, the defender of the monetary realm, the pursuer of Europe's common interest: the European Central Bank.

The empire strikes back

In December 2012, at the country's constitutional court, Germany's central bank, the unyielding Bundesbank, struck back against the ECB and Mr Draghi's OMT programme with a deposition by the bank's president, Jens Weidmann.[50] Three statements made this a bombshell. The first openly questioned whether the ECB had a mandate to prevent the euro's collapse. The second questioned the joint decision of Chancellor Merkel and ECB president Draghi in the summer of 2012 to keep Greece in the eurozone. And the third challenged Mr Draghi's oft-stated conviction that the ECB's broken monetary transmission mechanism should be mended as quickly as possible.

Taken together, these three statements constituted an act of war against the euro as a coherent currency, especially in view of the fact that these were official depositions made by the Bundesbank to the German Constitutional Court for the purpose of invoking a constitutional ban on Mr Draghi's last remaining monetary instruments, with which he was trying to keep the eurozone together.

But if it is not the ECB's job to keep the euro together, as Mr Weidmann suggested, then whose is it? By challenging the notion that the euro's survival was the ECB's remit, the Bundesbank adopted an interesting new position: the eurozone's salvation was not paramount, even if Europe's political leadership thought it was. The Bundesbank's tendency to be a backseat driver in Europe's evolution had evidently not been laid to rest with the passing of its cherished Deutsche Mark. Even if it had gone to sleep for a while, with Jens Weidmann it had now woken up.

Reading the Bundesbank president's deposition more closely, though, it acquires an eerily plausible rationale. The deposition attempted to blast out of the water the credibility of the OMT programme, with which Mr Draghi was striving for the euro's irreversibility, using Greece as its artillery. Weidmann argued that the ECB's determination to keep Greece in the eurozone could not be squared with its charter. If preventing sequential fragmentation of the monetary union necessitated a willingness to do 'whatever it takes' to keep Greek banks open, then the ECB was declaring to the world its determination to buy debt owned by Greek banks even after they had lost any genuine claim to being solvent. But such a declaration was equivalent to an ECB statement that it was prepared to violate its charter to save the euro!

Weidmann was of course correct. To keep the eurozone intact, the ECB repeatedly had to find shrewd excuses for bending its own ridiculous Maastricht-era rules. No one has done this better, or with more panache, than Mario Draghi. If the euro is alive today, for better or for worse, it is down to the ECB president's dexterous handling of this potentially explosive game: subverting the ECB's rulebook in a manner neither obvious nor excessively coy.

Jens Weidmann could see this and knew that Draghi would have to up the ante. That once OMT was established as a bona fide policy, he would have to go further in order to keep ahead of the bond dealers. Livid at the prospect of further violations of the charter it had so painstakingly imposed upon the ECB, the Bundesbank was, and remains, prepared to do 'whatever it takes' to stop Mario Draghi in his tracks.

The fact that Herr Weidmann has so far failed is testimony to Chancellor Merkel's determination not to have the euro crumble on her watch. But, as Draghi knows too well, neither he nor Berlin can afford to ignore either the Bundesbank's wrath or its preference for a smaller euro area.

Uneasy easing

Mr Draghi's OMT was the perfect weapon in that it worked because it was never fired. The ECB president nevertheless knew that if his bluff was called by bond dealers and he had to fire it, the result would be underwhelming.[51] He could also see that the austerity that had first been imposed upon Greece before being exported to most of the rest of the eurozone was causing a vicious deflation that threatened to push the whole of the eurozone into a postmodern version of the

Great Depression of the 1930s. In this sense, OMT had merely bought him time to bring out the big guns: quantitative easing.[52]

QE was invented in Japan in the 1990s and adopted in the United States after the 2008 disaster. Once a crisis proves so large that everyone is trying, against all hope, to pay off debt in conditions of shrinking incomes, no one wants to borrow even if interest rates come down to zero. At that point central banks run out of means to stimulate the economy in their usual way – by reducing interest rates. Zero is, indeed, a radical number, and any interest rate below it means that depositors, who must now pay for the banks to hold their money, will rush to withdraw every penny, causing the banking sector's collapse.

John Maynard Keynes, back in 1936, had to quote Ibsen's *Wild Duck* in order to convey to his readers the problem that a central bank faces when interest rates fall to zero but the economy is still in the doldrums: 'The wild duck has dived down to the bottom – as deep as she can get – and bitten fast hold of the weed and tangle and all the rubbish that is down there, and it would need an extraordinarily clever dog to dive after and fish her up again.'[53] QE was meant to be Keynes's 'extraordinarily clever dog' – an alternative way by which central banks could stimulate the economy.

The idea is simple: the central bank buys from commercial banks other people's debts. Who are these 'other people'? They can be families that owe mortgages to the bank, corporations, or even a government that has sold bonds to the bank. In exchange for these debts and the stream of income they produce, the central bank deposits dollars or euros in an account the commercial bank keeps at the central bank. Where does the central bank find the money? From thin air, is the answer: they are just numbers that the central bank conjures up and adds to the commercial bank's account. Why do this? In the hope that the commercial bank will use this money by lending it to businesses wishing to invest and to families wanting to buy houses, cars, gadgets and so on. If this happens, economic activity will rise again as liquidity rushes in. At least this is the theory of how QE stimulates a flagging economy.

QE works but even under the best possible circumstances works neither very well nor in the manner it is intended to. The reason is that, for QE's virtuous wheel to start spinning, a multiple coincidence of impossible beliefs must occur.

Jack and Jill, who are Bank Y's customers, must trust that the property market has bottomed out in the medium term and that their jobs are secure enough to dare ask the bank for a mortgage. Bank Y must be willing to take the risk of stretching its already large assets column (list of income-generating loans) by lending Jack and Jill the money to buy a house in the hope that Bank X will buy that mortgage from it using its QE-funded reserve account at the central bank. Companies thinking of employing people like Jack and Jill in the medium to long term must believe that Bank X will indeed buy Jack and Jill's mortgage from Bank Y and, moreover, that this sort of transaction will increase demand for their products, thus justifying hiring more staff.

To cut a long story short, a great deal of believing must occur before QE delivers on its promise to boost the real economy. But given the state of self-confirming pessimism that prevails in the depths of a severe crisis, to expect that these beliefs will flood into the different agents' minds simultaneously is to believe in miracles. More likely, as we witnessed in Japan and in America, where QE was tried out with a vengeance, banks tend to lend the money conjured up by the central bank not to other banks or to Jack and Jill but to companies. Except that these companies do not invest the borrowed money in machinery and workers, fearful that the demand will not be there for extra output produced. What they do is to buy back their own shares in the stock market in order to increase their price and collect a nice bonus for having 'added value to the company'. While this process does boost, to some extent, upmarket house prices and demand for luxuries, the only genuine beneficiary is gross inequality.

In Japan and in the United States QE failed to bring about recovery[54] but at least it ensured that the recession was not allowed to turn into depression. In Europe QE was always going to prove more problematic as a result of the eurozone's shoddy architecture, reflected in the Maastricht Treaty's incongruities. President Draghi knew this but felt he had no alternative except to implement QE. He had two main reasons: first, because he knew his OMT bluff would sooner or later be called and, second, because he expected that, once the Federal Reserve and the Bank of Japan began to curtail their own QE some time in 2014, volatility would return and his OMT ploy would need bolstering.

The ECB, as the Bundesbank keeps reminding Mario Draghi, does not have the right to monetize member-state debt. It cannot thus buy

Italian bonds at will from Italian or Spanish banks in the way that the Fed buys treasury bills.[55] To stay as much as possible within the strictures of its charter, the Draghi-led ECB governing board came up with the following plan: bonds would be purchased from every member state in proportion to its shares in the ECB – that is, in proportion to the size of its economy. Draghi was clearly banking on the excuse that, if everyone's debt was monetized by the ECB in proportion to its economy's relative size, no one was being bailed out. Further, to counter Jens Weidmann's claim that by buying the bonds of insolvent states the ECB was edging towards buying debt from insolvent banks connected to them, Draghi accepted that nations that had fallen into the arms of the troika would have to be omitted from QE. This meant that the country with the greatest need of ECB quantitative easing, Greece, was to be excluded from it, and that the states that least needed QE, indeed economies that might be damaged by it, would get the largest dose.

The German case illustrates this well. The ECB's economists calculated that, for the ECB's eurozone-wide QE programme to work, in other words for the deflationary spiral that threatened the euro to stop, the ECB ought to purchase €60 billion worth of bonds – public debt – per month. To stick to its rulebook, the ECB was obliged to ensure that 27 per cent of these bonds were German *Bunds* (as German bonds are called), as Germany owns 27 per cent of the ECB, reflecting the fact that Germany's national income is about 27 per cent of the eurozone's aggregate national income.

The problems created by these negative interest rates were legion. German savers and pension funds, who rely on decent interest rates to survive, faced ruin. Additionally, speculators taking advantage of rock-bottom rates in Germany borrowed money to buy shares on the stock exchange, pushing the value of stocks up and thus creating financial profits for already rich Europeans at a time when working men and women were suffering low wages in Germany and devastation in places like Greece and Spain.

If Mario Draghi had been allowed to act as a properly independent central banker, he would have been able to buy only Spanish and Italian bonds, and no German *Bunds*, reflecting the fact that deflation afflicts Spain and Italy but is virtually non-existent in Germany. But no, the ECB must buy German *Bunds* in order to maintain the fiction that the ECB's silly charter is respected.

A very European coup

Mr Draghi's QE caused the price of shares and upmarket property in surplus countries like Germany and Holland to go up, but it did not help mobilize idle savings in those countries by turning them into productive investments, and it especially failed to do this in the crisis countries. And yet the financial press seems convinced that QE has worked.

In fact, what happened was that, as the quantity of euros manufactured by the ECB increased, a portion of those euros was exchanged for other currencies, and as more euros were sold in the foreign exchange markets for other currencies, the international value of the euro – its exchange rate – fell. For some countries like Spain this created a small export bonanza. But one look at Spain's devastated labour market, where wages were at rock bottom, confirms that the only jobs created by this boost were at the expense of jobs in France, where wages had not yet fallen. European corporations simply took advantage of the beleaguered Spanish, while the net effect on employment in the eurozone was negligible. The non-negligible reality is that Europe is devaluing its own labour through internal competition just as it devalued its own currencies through competition in the 1930s. In this context, Mr Draghi's QE stabilized the eurozone's deflationary forces only to allow this form of fruitless and integrity-busting beggar-thy-neighbour to take hold without actually helping to overcome the crisis.

Ironically, the greatest success of the ECB's QE policy from the perspective of Brussels, Frankfurt and Berlin was that it allowed the troika to defeat the Greek government's effort to renegotiate the failed programme that condemned our people to a never-ending depression. How did it do that?

By the end of 2012, Greece's two bailouts had completed the transfer of potential private losses onto Europe's taxpayers, thus shielding Europe's banks from the Greek drama. With the arrival of QE, the knowledge that Mr Draghi could print up to €60 or €70 billion monthly to purchase the bonds of fiscally stressed nations (except Greece's) acted as a further shock absorber in the financial markets. This allowed the Eurogroup and the ECB to close down Greece's banks without any ensuing panic in the bond markets. A policy that was meant to curb deflation across Europe first excluded the one country that needed such treatment the most – Greece – and then strangled its newly elected government for daring to question the austerity programme and unsustainable debt that had caused the depression in the first place. Only the eurozone could have created such a despicable role for a monetary policy meant to ease its citizens' pain.

Wickedness

A few years ago, long before a political career loomed, I found myself in Brussels discussing the latest twists and turns of the crisis with one of the European Commission's high priests. It was my first discussion with anyone so high and mighty in Brussels's self-regarding technocracy, and I asked a couple of almost impertinent questions to which I was surprised to receive an honest answer.

'Why is the commission pushing Portugal to increase indirect taxes at a time of collapsing demand?' (Would such tax hikes not push sales and, by extension, the state's sales tax revenues down? So too with the doubling of taxes on heating fuel in Greece.) 'Why are you pushing for this?' I asked. 'Don't you see that people will simply not heat their homes and that government revenues from the fuel tax will fall?'

'Of course. But we are only pushing for higher sales and fuel taxes as a deterrent. The point is to demonstrate to Rome what it has coming its way if they do not comply with our demands for greater austerity there.'

More recently, when I was negotiating on the Greek government's behalf with the commission, the ECB and the IMF, I came up against exactly the same rationale. When I asked an interlocutor whether he thought that the exorbitant sales tax rates he was trying to push down my throat would improve our state's tax revenue, he freely admitted that they would not. 'So, why do you insist upon them?' I asked. His answer? 'Someone whose views matter here wants to demonstrate to Paris what is in store for France if they refuse to enact structural reforms.'

It is not therefore without justification that when I address Italian or French audiences on the subject of my recent experiences with the troika I tell them, 'I have not come here to seek your sympathy or help. I am here to warn you that there is no such thing as a Greek or Irish or Portuguese crisis. We are in it together. Greece is just a huge laboratory where failed policies are tried before being transplanted to your backyard.'

This is what the euro crisis has been doing to Europe. A clueless political elite, in denial of the nature and history of a crisis whose roots go back to at least 1971, is pursuing policies akin to carpet-bombing the economies of proud European nations in order to save them. Greece, Portugal, Ireland and Spain were beaten to a pulp in order to keep Italy and France in awe and the ECB in business. Meanwhile, these misanthropic policies are presented in the name of community, solidarity, efficiency, responsibility and, of course, heart-felt concern about the loss of the so-called credibility of European institutions.

Reverse alchemy is no easier than alchemy. The transmutation of lead into gold, the alchemist's Holy Grail, proved impossibly difficult to achieve; turning gold into lead is no easier.

Europe's reverse alchemists – the bureaucrats, politicians, commentators and academics whose accomplishments this chapter has recounted – have worked diligently and over many years to achieve something that ought to be just as impossible: the replacement of decades of continental integration with a leaden disunion that weighs heavily upon Europeans' hearts and minds. But they have achieved this – by means of a single currency.

Looking down from the heights of the famous Ferris wheel at the Prater amusement park in Vienna, Harry Lime – as played by Orson Welles in *The Third Man* – advances a provocative theory of European civilization. Under the Borgias, he says, three decades of bloodshed gave us the Renaissance. In contrast, five centuries of Swiss democracy and peaceful coexistence produced nothing more spectacular than the cuckoo clock.[56]

Facetious though Lime's theory certainly was (not to mention grossly unfair to Swiss history), European history and culture is drenched in blood and underpinned by conflict. It is the reason

Europeans cherished the thought of a union. Art and music, realms in which Europe has contributed greatly to humanity, offer further evidence of our darker side. Picasso once said that a painting is not meant to decorate but to act as 'a weapon against the enemy'. Beethoven dedicated his Third Symphony to Napoleon and then tore up the dedication in anger when Napoleon declared himself an emperor. D. H. Lawrence displayed a raging contempt for democracy, with a sprinkling of virulent anti-Semitism thrown in for good measure. Ezra Pound's poetry celebrated his immense love of European culture, which alas proved no impediment to his glorification of fascism.

Against such a rich and discontented cultural background, a common currency that works to dissolve European unity seems less of a paradox. From the moment Europe was expelled from America's comforting postwar dollar zone, its elites struggled to re-create the zone within Europe. Never having grasped the lessons that the New Dealers learned during the 1930s and 1940s, European officialdom repeated the mistakes of the 1920s, creating an ill-designed currency resembling the gold standard in the heart of Europe.

From the late 1990s onwards, Europe's banks copied the practices of the Anglosphere's all-singing, all-dancing financial sector without having the safety net of a Federal Reserve, a Bank of England or even a Bank of Japan to catch them when the inevitable fall from grace occurred. The combination of the eurozone's flimsy monetary architecture and the imperatives of Anglo-Saxon financialization, which infected the Parisian and Frankfurt banks under the noses of Brussels and the ECB, produced a reliance on money markets that Europe's monetary union could not withstand.

While the American Minotaur roared and kept German, Dutch and Chinese factories humming nicely, Europe followed Britain and the United States in subordinating its industry to finance and converting society to the new creed that markets are ends in themselves, totems to be worshipped in their own right, temples whose sanctity is beyond rational scrutiny.

There was nothing wrong with the idea of a single market from the Atlantic to the Ukraine and from the Shetlands to Crete. Borders are scars on the planet and the sooner we dispose of them the better, as the recent Syrian refugee crisis confirms. And there is nothing wrong with a single currency either. What was dangerously wrong-headed was the idea that we could create a single market and a common currency without a powerful Demos to counterbalance, to stabilize, to civilize them.

Forget the mind-boggling economics of it all. A glance at the euro's aesthetic speaks volumes. Take a look at any euro banknote. What do you see? Pleasing arches and bridges. But these are fictitious arches and non-existent bridges. A continent replete with cultural treasures has unbelievably chosen to adorn its freshly minted common currency with none of them. Why? Because bureaucrats wanted nothing contentious on the new money. They wanted to remove culture from our currency in the same way they craved the depoliticization of politics and the technocratization of money. Even if one knew nothing of economics and the eurozone's hideous financial architecture, a glimpse of the cultural desert displayed on the euro notes might suffice for one to guess what would transpire. In place of a sovereign European people with a shared culture that it proudly displays on its money, Europe continued along the path of the 1950s, transferring immense political power to a colossal nominally technocratic bureaucracy that ensured democracy and solidarity were more honoured in the breach than in the observance.[57]

And here is the irony. Before the border fences were torn down between Poland, Germany, France and Britain a film like *The Double Life of Véronique* resonated perfectly in Warsaw, in Paris, in London and in Stuttgart. Today a similar film would not. Véronique and Weronika would have no bond, no mystical connection. They would be pitted against each other in the context of a ruthless European Union where solidarity has been reduced to predatory 'bailouts' that increase debt, 'reforms' that translate into savage cuts in the poorest Europeans' wages and pensions, and 'credibility' synonymous with following failed economic recipes.

The Brussels-centric commentariat keeps pointing out that the demand for European Union membership has never been stronger. Is this not proof that Europe is working? They forget that the Roman empire imploded when its inner core became too brittle while its borders were expanding eastward. A cultural degeneration known as the Middle Ages was the result. Today the European Union is also seeing its core disintegrate at a time of eastward expansion. With one proud nation being subjected to fiscal waterboarding after the other; with one people turning against another, with Ponzi growth being replaced seamlessly by Ponzi austerity, with no serious discussion of how to create a rational economic architecture and with some Europeans increasingly convinced they are more deserving Europeans than others, Europe's core is weakening perilously and the bonds of authentic solidarity are breaking.

Meanwhile, across the Atlantic, the Americans are watching in disbelief as the continent they helped save from itself all those years ago is now at it again: turning against itself, sowing the seeds of conflict in its midst and in the process jeopardizing America and China's efforts to stabilize the global economy.

Is there anything that can be done to stop Europe's frightful reverse alchemy?

Can Europe snatch a democratic future from the jaws of a postmodern Dark Ages?

Or do Europeans, once again, need a helping hand from across the Atlantic, even if they do not want it?

One thing is certain: Europe is too important to be left to its clueless rulers.

7

Back to the Future

Every time I sat on the ministerial benches in Greece's parliament, immediately opposite me sat the democratically elected thugs of the Nazi party Golden Dawn.[1] Each time I failed to avoid their gaze, or when friends from the United States, Britain, Australia, Thailand or China asked me to explain the Golden Dawn phenomenon, I was reminded of the figure of Kapnias.

The first time I met Kapnias was in December 1991, at the southern Peloponnese farm he shared with Grandma Georgia, his wife, whom I was visiting and whose life story deserves to be the centrepiece of some talented tragedian's labour of love.[2] Having driven from Athens to spend a weekend with them, I caught my first glimpse of him standing next to his goats, a hawk hovering motionless overhead against the backdrop of an electric-blue sky. A dishevelled yet not undistinguished figure dressed in the work clothes poor Mediterranean farmers think of as their uniform, his octogenarian weather-beaten face, covered in white stubble, smiled at me. A friendly and at once ominous smile packed with the promise of disturbing yarns and indecipherable truths. 'We meet at last! Welcome to my humble abode,' he cried, spreading his arms.

Although Kapnias's reputation had preceded him, I was not prepared for the quiet ferocity of that night's welcome. After settling into the bedroom that Grandma Georgia had adoringly prepared and having broken bread with them, I excused myself and drove to the nearby town to meet local friends. Upon returning to the farmhouse, well after midnight, I could hear Kapnias's distant snoring and an array of excited cats. Exhausted, I was ready for a night's rest in the lap of the Peloponnese countryside. Then I saw the two books resting on my pillow.

One was entitled *Memoirs of a Prime Minister*. Its author was Adamantios Androutsopoulos, the last prime minister of the military dictatorship that had darkened my youth and the puppet of Dimitrios Ioannidis, the brigadier who took the neo-fascist junta further into neo-Nazi territory after the student massacre of 17 November 1973. The second book was a small leather-bound volume in an advanced state of disrepair. Incredulous even after I had read the title, *Mein Kampf*, I opened it. It was an original German edition, published somewhere in Germany in 1934. Bedtime material to shock the visiting leftie with, I surmised. Courtesy of a semi-illiterate farmer who clearly wanted to make a point.

Upon waking in the morning, I took my time getting out of bed, hoping that Kapnias had headed out to tend to his animals and crops in the meantime. To no avail. He was never going to miss my emergence, overflowing with eagerness to gauge my reaction to his late-night offerings. And so we started talking.

Kapnias was once an 'untouchable' farmhand bonded to Grandma Georgia's father, who before the war was something of a nobleman in the mountainous village of their origin – a beautiful village that was virtually depopulated by the 1944–9 civil war. During the Nazi occupation (1941–4) Georgia's father liaised between British intelligence and the local left-wing partisans, sabotaging in unison the nearby *Wehrmacht* brigade and several platoons of Italian soldiers. Georgia, the local beauty, fell in love and secretly married George Xenos, one of the partisans. Against the background of a harsh war, two young children were born to the defiantly happy couple.

Meanwhile, Kapnias, the teenage menial, decided to throw his lot in with the other side: he joined a paramilitary unit assembled by the local Gestapo and was sent to Crete for training in the art of interrogation and counter-subversion. It was there that Hans, his instructor, gave him the leather-bound copy of *Mein Kampf*, like those preachers who hand out copies of the Bible to illiterate natives before moving on to proselytize others.

The Second World War ended, but the conflict in Greece intensified as the country sank into the mire of a nightmarish civil war. Allies turned against one another, brother against brother, daughter against father. Xenos, Georgia's partisan husband, found himself fighting the national army put together by the British of which her father was a local stalwart. Within two years a modern Greek tragedy had unfolded. Xenos was injured in battle against the national army and finished off by an American officer during the interrogation that followed his capture.[3] Georgia's father was killed soon after by her husband's partisan comrades for having also finished off an injured partisan who had sought refuge in his home. Thus Georgia was widowed by her father's nationalists and orphaned by her husband's partisans.

These events were Kapnias's cue. Having made the transition from Gestapo-organized paramilitary to local gendarmerie, he was now in a position to exact revenge on the upper class of his small quasi-feudal universe. He approached Georgia with a proposal: 'You marry me, and I shall stop my ilk from ridding the land of you and your communist seed,' referring to her two young orphans. Georgia acquiesced, hoping that Kapnias's uniform would provide safety for herself and her children, whose origins she shrouded in the convenient lie that their partisan father had been murdered by the partisans. Alas, not long after their bleak wedding, Kapnias was dismissed from the gendarmes for using excessive force during an interrogation – a little like being fired by Mephistopheles for excessive malice. His wrath and associated brutality then turned against his new wife, her seed and the whole world. Thus Georgia bought her family's survival at the price of a life of abuse, poverty, tears and terror under Kapnias's permanently cruel regime. She was never to find respite until her death in 2012.

Back then I had assumed that figures like Kapnias were a dying breed whose like would fade from the land of our parents. It was not to be, as the sight of the Golden Dawn deputies in the Athens Parliament House confirmed some years later.

Serpent DNA

Nothing prepares a people for authoritarianism better than defeat followed closely by national humiliation and an economic implosion.[4] Germany's defeat in the Great War and its submission to the Versailles Treaty, coupled with the middle class's economic calamity a little later, played a well-documented role in the rise of the Nazis. Greece suffered a comparable defeat and humiliation in 1922 at the hands of Mustafa Kemal as a result of its own government's hubris.[5] The political instability that followed this military and economic catastrophe, coupled with the intensification of poverty after the 1929 global crisis, gave rise to our own variety of fascism, the regime of Ioannis Metaxas installed by a coup on 4 August 1936.

Of course none of this was out of the ordinary. Only a few days before Greece's fascist regime was born, Spain was falling into the same crevasse with Generalissimo Franco's assault on the Republicans. Italy had turned to fascism ten years earlier under Mussolini, as had Portugal under Salazar. Hungary, Serbia, Romania, Bulgaria and the Baltic states all fell to some variant of the serpent.[6] Even Britain had its brush with Oswald Mosley's blackshirts, not to mention several royals of a pro-Nazi disposition. Today we tend to forget that the spectre of fascism haunted most of Europe well before Hitler's first cannon shots, air raids and Panzer divisions kick-started the Second World War.

We also forget that the dream of European union predated the war. The spirit of Charlemagne, which French president Valéry Giscard d'Estaing and Chancellor Helmut Schmidt invoked decades later in support of Europe's monetary union, had a sordid history of earlier invocations. In late 1944, when it was evident to all with eyes to see and ears to hear that Hitler had lost the war, between seven and eleven thousand Frenchmen enlisted in a new SS division named after Charlemagne – to give it its full name, the 33rd Waffen Grenadier Division of the SS Charlemagne (1st French). In the months that followed they fought doggedly and were the last SS unit to defend the Führer's bunker, fighting to the bitter end.[7] Something motivated those Frenchmen to fight, and that something had to do with the idea of a *Paneuropa* worthy of Charlemagne's legacy, which Hitler represented in their deluded minds. This is a potent reminder that the symbols of European unity, having fallen prey to our continent's dark side once, may easily do so again.

Today Europeans assume that our continent's dark side has been eradicated. That the European Economic Community, which evolved with the Maastricht Treaty of 1993 into the European Union, constitutes a bulwark against totalitarianism. While it is true that after the war Europeans imagined the continent's new European institutions were defences against another war and another totalitarianism, it is not at all evident that the actual institutions we created were entirely consistent with this aspiration. If a grasp of history is a prerequisite for averting the resurrection of various forms of evil, this assumption must be interrogated. The task below may help in doing so.

Take a look at the following two quotations and guess who, and in what context, might have uttered such stirring words.

> Above and beyond the concept of the nation state, the idea of a new community will transform the living space given us all by history into a new spiritual realm . . . The new Europe of solidarity and cooperation among all its peoples, a Europe without unemployment, without monetary crises . . . will find an assured foundation and rapidly increasing prosperity once national economic barriers are removed.

> The people of Europe understand increasingly that the great issues dividing us, when compared with those which will emerge and will be resolved between continents, are nothing but trivial family feuds . . . I am convinced that in fifty years Europeans will not be thinking in terms of separate countries.

The first of the two speakers was Arthur Seyss-Inquart, a Nazi who, as Austria's newly appointed chancellor, signed the Anschluss before becoming minister of security and the interior in the post-Anschluss Nazi government. Later he was anointed prefect of occupied Holland. In the quote above he was addressing his Dutch subjects in 1940.[8] Seyss-Inquart was sentenced to death at the Nuremberg trials in 1946. The second is Joseph Goebbels, speaking in 1940.[9]

Does the fact that the Nazis were the first to plan a European economic and monetary union – one perhaps too close for comfort to today's European Union – imply that the latter was founded on fascist principles? No, of course it does not. The important point is not that the European Union was spawned by the serpent but, rather more constructively, that Europeans have a moral duty to dispel the dangerous illusion that the notion of a European union within which nationalisms and the nation state are supposed gradually to dissolve is inherently incompatible with the autocratic, misanthropic, racist, inhuman warmongers who rose to prominence as a result of the interwar European crisis. However, a united Europe based on free trade, free capital movements, common labour laws and a single currency is unfortunately as compatible with a Nazi agenda as it is with a progressive, humanist, internationalist one. A sobering thought which Europe today has an obligation to keep in its collective mind.

Conferences on European integration, common agricultural policies, coordinated industrial policies, joint schemes to promote technological progress, monetary union and so on are not in themselves moves in the direction of a brighter European future. The first such conference, with the full participation of academics, government ministers and officials, to discuss (and I quote from the official programme) 'the formation of a European Economic Community' took place in Berlin in 1942 under the auspices of Walther Funk, Hitler's finance minister. What this means is that a European union very much like the one now administered by the Brussels technocracy is not incompatible with totalitarianism.

A multitude of evils can hide behind the ideological veil of top-down European integration, especially when it is accomplished in the midst of (even by means of) a vicious asymmetrical recession. Europeanists craving to imagine Europe as our common home, but who also sensibly fear that Europe is sliding into authoritarianism, threatening to turn our common home into a shared concentration camp, better beware. The slide into totalitarianism is not to be prevented by technical means applied by faceless bureaucrats primarily concerned with their own banal careers. It can be prevented only by a functioning, healthy democracy. By precisely the political process that Brussels and Frankfurt officials disdain so deeply and which every twist of the troika's screw depletes. With every toxic bailout, with each triumph of the Eurogroup over a democratically elected government, Europe is pushed further into a dark and arid future consistent with the serpent's plans.

The evidence is all around us. Today, as of this writing, France's National Front, with its roots deeply buried in a racist Holocaustdenying mythology, is predicted to top the first round of the next presidential election. Hungary has a government with ultra-right-wing credentials. In the Baltics memorial services commemorating local Nazis who joined the SS and fought alongside the Charlemagne Division are held frequently, often attended by democratically elected government ministers. Political parties and paramilitary groups with allegiances to the memory of the Nazis' wartime collaborators remain influential in Ukraine, Serbia, Croatia and Albania.

Be that as it may, Greece remains a puzzling outlier. Only in my home country did an unashamedly Nazi party, Golden Dawn, manage to register impressive electoral results. Why are the Nazis back in Greece's parliament? The Spaniards, the Irish, the Portuguese and the Italians have also felt the impact of the eurozone crisis in their bones. So why is it that only Greece has an out-and-out Nazi party in parliament with its storm troopers terrorizing the streets?

The main reason is that the economic collapse in Greece was far more serious than those which took place in the other eurozone countries. Having fallen first, after the 2008 global crash, Greece became the troika's laboratory. The most unsustainable public debt was dealt with by means of the largest bailout loans accompanied by the harshest austerity. The experiment failed disastrously, with almost a third of all incomes and jobs lost and debt casting an increasingly long shadow over Greece within which nothing flourishes but fear and loathing. So, when it turned its attention to the other failed eurozone member states, the troika was already fearful of the zone's survival. To make some amends for the wasteland it had created in Greece, it applied much lighter versions of austerity to Ireland, Portugal, Spain and Italy. Less austerity, shallower recessions, less room for Nazism to grow roots.

Another reason for the re-emergence of fascism in Greece is hidden in Kapnias's story. In Greece the occupying Nazis attempted to create a local SS-like body of marginalized men disaffected with both the local bourgeoisie and the Left and living under a permanent cloud of collective disgrace brought on by a previous national humiliation. 'Kapnias' was a nickname (his real name was George) derived from the Greek words for tobacco (*kapnos*) and for soot (*kapnia*), words whose destructive bitterness Kapnias embraced as representative of his image: a bitter, angry man perpetually seeking revenge on a world that had never given him a chance. Until, that is, the Gestapo offered him one; a chance that he grabbed with both hands and which he savoured to the bitter end, surrounded by his innocent, unsuspecting goats.

During our long conversations Kapnias appeared intoxicated with the power that his Nazi instructors had given him. Attuned to his own empowerment from an alliance with the dark side, he revelled in the retreat from decency that was to mark his life thereafter. 'The Germans were above God,' he told me. 'Unlike the Italians or our own mob, they could use any means to get the job done. Without wincing! With no fear! No passion! . . . You had to see them with your own eyes.' 'They were magnificent' was his last utterance on the matter, his face lighting up like a Christmas tree, his heart filled with extra pleasure from noticing that my stomach was turning with every one of his words.

And yet I understood where he was coming from. Being handed that little leather-bound book, which Kapnias did not have the German to read, was for him like induction into a European brotherhood – an evil one, undoubtedly, but one that was also vastly more technologically advanced than his own community, giving a marginalized cowardly man like Kapnias a priceless sense of belonging to some circle of the select. A sense that can elicit a hideous outpouring of violent sentiments, words, acts.

The influence of Kapnias-like misanthropes faded but did not die out after the left-wing partisans were crushed in 1949. Men of his ilk higher up in the state's hierarchy remained central to the postwar Greek state, murdering left-wing parliamentarian Grigoris Lambrakis in 1963,[10] taking power in 1967 with a military coup[11] and remaining present in various state institutions after that regime's collapse in 1974.

Kapnias died in 2009, as did around that period most of his wartime brethren. However, the serpent's DNA did not perish with them; it remained dormant, awaiting the next crisis to sprout again.

Migrant dreams, Ponzi growth, mounting discontent

When Greece managed to enter the eurozone in 2001, it was largely due to the influx into the country of migrant labour in the 1990s from across the collapsed Iron Curtain. Spain and Italy also benefited greatly from undocumented foreign workers, who boosted their competitiveness indices and helped them put on a display of convergence towards the Maastricht criteria. But while Europe's periphery, from Greece to Iberia and from there to Ireland, was abuzz with the sound of bulldozers and drills funded by stressed bankers like my travelling companion Franz, the gigantic struggle to get these countries into the eurozone had in fact condemned a large segment of their poorer citizens to a slow-burning unseen recession.

Economic activity was booming but, beneath the surface, good jobs were disappearing: while most investment in the periphery was being pumped into building bubbles, traditional manufacturing centres were actually dying out, drowned by waves of manufactures imported from the more advanced surplus economies. Bubbles offer great opportunities for spivs but create very little meaningful, sustainable employment, especially when large German, Dutch and French conglomerates rush in to purchase local firms, wind down their manufacturing activities and use their premises as warehouses to stock goods imported from their own plants.[12] Boom times in Europe's periphery coincided paradoxically with falling living standards for the weak. Even as they bought new cars and refrigerators on credit, they knew the tide of liquidity might one day turn into torrents of liquidations.

True, wages rose during the eurozone's golden decade, from 1998, when official interest rates were equalized, to 2008. In some cases, such as in Greece, Ireland, France and Spain, we were told that they were rising too fast, making these economies less competitive in relation to Germany, Finland, Holland and the rest, where labour costs per unit of output were either falling or rising more slowly. And yet discontent was rising too. In Germany the reason was obvious: workers worked harder, their companies were generating unprecedented profits, but wages weren't keeping up and their living standards were stagnant. But why was there even more discontent in countries such as France, Spain and Greece, when official statistics, television presenters, newspaper reports and politicians were telling us that we had never had it so good, that our purchasing power was on the rise, that prosperity was engulfing us?

A close look at the official statistics suffices to dispel the superficial paradox. Wages were indeed rising in the deficit nations a little faster than the average speed with which prices grew, so it was true that the 'average' Greek, Irish person, Spaniard was indeed doing better. Except that there is no such thing as an average Greek, Irish person or Spaniard. In fact, the prices of basic goods – the things that everyone must buy, however poor – were actually rising much faster than average. Meanwhile, the prices of luxury goods, such as those purchased by the top 10 per cent, were falling dramatically.[13] On average, wages were rising, except that the majority of working people were doing far worse than average – not least because that average was heavily skewed by the huge salaries of the oligarchs' managers and by falling prices for goods that only privileged folk could afford.[14]

Alongside this burgeoning division between rich and poor, another insidious fault line was growing: between native workers and migrant workers. The latter were more mobile, willing to suffer humiliations that locals would reject, and therefore willing to work for less and take advantage of jobs in places that natives, wedded to immobile families and heavy housing costs, could not move to. The weak were thus getting weaker, divided and discontented, while the strong grew more affluent and cockier than ever. And all this during the largest Ponzi growth scheme in history, during which Spain was inundated with white elephants such as motorways to nowhere, Greece became one huge construction site, spewing out highways, metro systems and the 2004 Olympic venues, and the Celtic Tiger was either building endless rows of apartment blocks in the middle of nowhere or littering Dublin's skyline with commercial 'spaces'.

Concealed by the cacophony of so much moneymaking, the serpent's egg was incubating nicely, kept warm by a hidden recession felt only by the weak and unacknowledged by the champagne-popping commentariat; blue-collar workers were increasingly abandoned to the sirens of racist misanthropy. With Europe's Left nursing its wounds from the historic defeat of 1991, when the Soviet empire collapsed, and with social democratic parties scrambling to jump on financialization's bandwagon, the only political parties that fed on the growing discontent were racist, ultra-nationalist organizations like France's

National Front, Italy's Northern League and of course Greece's Golden Dawn.

By 2005 the rate at which Wall Street, the City of London and Frankfurt's banks were minting private money had slowed a little. That minor reduction in the rate of Ponzi growth made it harder for paperless migrant workers to find jobs. To offer an example, as the 2004 Olympics in Athens drew closer, the migrants who had been labouring like ants to get the stadia ready in time for the athletes and dignitaries suddenly had no jobs. They became more visible but simultaneously less lucrative. Not only were they 'bloody foreigners', they now had less money to spend too. Similarly, in France and elsewhere throughout Europe the serpent's hatchlings were ready to break from their shells, blaming the immigrants for the hidden recession afflicting weaker locals actually caused by the eurozone's inherent design faults.

France's electoral map showed a stark shift in votes from left-wing parties traditionally associated with defending the weak to the National Front; socialist president Mitterrand's chickens were coming home to roost. So too in Greece, Italy, Ireland and Spain, where centre-left parties, having played a central role in bringing about monetary union, had now lost moral authority and saw many of their voters turning to the intransigent, nationalist Right.

Around the same time Greece's Nazis shifted up a gear, planning a campaign of 'cleansing' neighbourhoods that brought despair to survivors of the 1930s. Copying a strategy pioneered by the German ultra-rightist National Democratic Party in eastern Germany in the 1990s, Golden Dawn aimed at 'liberating' the suburbs in which many of the migrants lived. They called them 'brown scum' and soon set up 'citizens' committees' which were effectively supremacist vigilante groups, tolerated and in many cases aided by the police.[15]

Before long certain areas like Attiki Square (not far from the centre of Athens) became dangerous for anyone who dared look different. Migrant-owned shops were repeatedly targeted Kristallnacht-style, and the victims learned the hard way that it was pointless to take the matter to the police. Property developers saw in Golden Dawn a nice little earner – buy properties at low prices, have the migrants removed forcibly by Golden Dawn and then cash in. Even mainstream television stations gave a platform to 'incensed locals' describing migrants as rabies-infected animals that had to be quarantined, if not put down. Before long, the list of those who had it coming included prostitutes, gays, lesbians, transsexuals and, of course, left-wing migrant lovers.

Then came the American Minotaur's demise and the subsequent economic tsunami that bankrupted Greece in late 2009 and led to the so-called bailout of May 2010. The steel strings of austerity that accompanied the massive loan agreement then demolished Greece's social economy. With Golden Dawn in place and the political centre going down the drain along with the country's economy, a Nazi revival was on the cards. The figure of Kapnias suddenly turned from a reminder of a terrible past to a very contemporary presence.

While Greece is an outlier, and the swastika is not being waved by crowds in the rest of Europe, racism and the whiff of evil are spreading throughout the continent. This was made hideously apparent during the summer of 2015, when the leaders of supposedly civilized European countries seemed to compete with each other as to who would offer sanctuary to the fewest refugees arriving from war-torn Syria. But this should not surprise us. While the unimpeded movement of goods, money and moneyed executives has always been a sacred cow of globalized finance and the founding principle of free trade zones such as the European Union, the North American Free Trade Agreement or the Transatlantic Trade and Investment Partnership, the equivalent freedom of movement for ordinary people has always been severely circumscribed. No wonder then that racism grows in proportion to our free trade zones' economic crises.

Nazis in power, even though not in government

Many will rightly point out the great differences between Europe now and the Europe of the 1930s: for example, today no Nazi party is close to taking control of a government in Europe. However, ultra-rightist movements do not need to be in government in order to be in power. Not only has France's National Front legitimized an openly xenophobic nationalist narrative, it has heavily influenced the policies of mainstream parties: a large part of France's political spectrum has shifted rightward in a reactive move to prevent the loss of more formerly left-leaning working-class votes to them.

Greece's Golden Dawn got its first taste of real power just *before* the election of May 2012, when it would score its first electoral success. It came in the form of a despicable decree issued by the then minister of public order, Michalis Chrysohoidis, a long-time socialist party minister. Chrysohoidis and his colleague Andreas Loverdos, then minister of health, mounted a campaign against the weakest women in Greece. Loverdos even addressed a United Nations conference, informing his flabbergasted audience that Greek 'family men' were being put at risk by HIV-infected African prostitutes.[16] The two ministers ordered the police to arrest prostitutes in central Athens, many of them undocumented migrants, forcibly subject them to HIV tests and post their photographs and names on the ministry's website so as to warn potential Greek clients.

Over several weeks the police swept central Athens, arresting with no warrant any woman who did not seem to them sufficiently respectable, shoving her in a van and taking her to a police station, where officers restrained her while a blood sample was extracted. If the HIV test came back positive, they would throw the hapless woman into a police cell without any counselling whatsoever, charged with endangering public health. In one fell swoop, a swathe of liberal democracy's cherished principles were torn up. For what? So that two embattled socialist politicians could profit electorally from a moral panic based on xenophobic narratives that were grist to the mill of organizations like Golden Dawn.[17]

It is in this sense that Golden Dawn found itself in power even before it entered parliament. Why should its thugs care about being elected if its policies were being implemented by mainstream politicians occupying ministries under the command of the troika of Greece's lenders? True ideologues, the Golden Dawn brutes celebrated the conversion of their sinister agenda into Bailoutistan's public policy.

A few weeks later, in June 2012, two consecutive elections delivered a new Greek government under the leadership of conservative Antonis Samaras. The government lost no time in passing an extraordinary piece of legislation clarifying that Greek citizenship and good grades in college entrance examinations were not sufficient for a young person to enter Greece's police or military academies. What else was needed? Proof of *ithageneia* – Greek blood lineage – which naturalized migrants of course lacked. Why? To play to Golden Dawn voters, who like all fascists have a penchant for blood and land, hoping to entice them back to the fold of the right-wing mainstream.

Thus, for the first time since the Nazi laws of the 1930s, a European country introduced legislation that classified its citizens (not just its residents) according to who had the 'right blood' and who didn't. A terrifying chill ought to travel through our spines at the very thought, and a deep shame ought to fill our hearts that this should be allowed to occur in the world today.

Lotus eaters

One hot June afternoon in 1968, a little more than a year after the colonels had come to power and cast a shadow over our lives, my mother and I were walking just outside the ancient stadium where the first modern-era Olympics had been staged in 1896. A newsboy announced at the top of his voice that someone called Bobby Kennedy was dead. My mother's eyes filled with tears. I vividly recall her first words after regaining her composure: 'He was our last chance.'

In my red blanket days two German-speaking politicians and an American featured as figures of hope. The chancellors of Germany and Austria, Willy Brandt and Bruno Kreisky, were social democrats who had stood up to Greek fascism and created pockets of authentic solidarity in which we could take shelter. The American was Senator Bobby Kennedy, the renowned champion of the Civil Rights Movement and in 1968 a popular Democrat candidate for the presidency. To my mother, Bobby Kennedy represented hope that the United States would regret their support for our neo-fascist dictators and facilitate a return to democratic rule. Her grief at the news of his murder was motivated by her despair that a powerful defender of the weak had been lost.

With hindsight, Bobby Kennedy represented something else too: perhaps the last American who could have kept the spirit of the New Deal alive in the White House. With his death and with Lyndon Baines Johnson gone from the scene, there was no one to stand in the way of the Nixon Shock which would irreversibly unleash forces that unhinged Europe.

Once upon a time, Europe's social democrats and American New Dealers understood what their role ought to be. They knew that civilizing capitalism required the deployment of a portion of the industrialists' profits to fund projects such as hospitals, schools, unemployment insurance and the arts. Bruno Kreisky, Willy Brandt, Swedish social democrat Olof Palme,[18] Britain's Labour Party all understood that this was their task. Some were more successful than others but they all shared that same basic conviction. But when financialization rode into town on the Minotaur's back, some time after 1980, all this changed.

In the 1980s and 1990s Europe's social democrats and America's Democrats abandoned the idea that capitalism had to be civilized by driving a hard bargain with the captains of industry, supporting organized labour and containing the bankers' natural instincts. They forgot that unregulated labour and financial and property markets are profoundly inefficient. They ignored inequality created as a by-product of that inefficiency. They lost sight of the fact that inequality destabilizes financial markets and reinforces capitalism's tendency to fall on its face.

What possessed the Clinton administration to dismantle the New Deal's last remaining constraints on Wall Street? After all, it was not Reaganites or neocons but bona fide democrats like Robert Rubin, Larry Summers and Tim Geithner who in the 1990s took apart the Glass-Steagall Act and its related legal constraints on finance, thus unleashing turbocharged financialization on an unsuspecting planet. And why did Europe's social democrats abandon the cherished principles of Bruno Kreisky, Willy Brandt and Olof Palme?

One answer lies in the transformation of global economics and finance in the aftermath of the Nixon Shock under the guidance of men like Paul Volcker.[19] As we have seen, the birth of America's Global Minotaur needed finance to be liberated so that the beast could do its work, supplying German, Japanese, Swedish and, later, Chinese factories with sufficient demand while also being nourished by the profits of the German, Japanese, Swedish and, later, Chinese factory owners, who poured them into Wall Street.[20]

With paper profits mounting, European social democrats and American Democrats in government were lured into a Faustian bargain with the bankers of Wall Street, the City of London, Frankfurt and Paris, who were only too pleased to let reformist politicians take a small cut of their loot as long as the politicians consented to the complete deregulation of financial markets. Franz and his mates had lending quotas to fill and no alternative other than to strike opportunistic bargains with the greatest opportunists among the politicians.[21]

It seemed like the kind of situation that is annoyingly – at least to me – labelled 'win-win'.[22] Bankers were unshackled and centre-left politicians no longer had to wrestle the captains of industry to fund their social programmes. Financiers only had to feign displeasure at handing over some crumbs from their substantial table for the politicians to acquiesce in the logic and the ethics of financialization, suspend their critical attitude to capitalism and believe deeply that the financial sector knows best how to regulate itself.

In Homeric terms Europe's social democrats became our era's lotus eaters.[23] The lotus that made them soft and complicit with the awful practices of runaway finance was the private money-minting that Wall Street inaugurated and its international copiers scrupulously replicated. Its honeyed juice lulled them into a haze of faith where they could have their cake and eat it, where risk was riskless and where a mystery goose would lay increasing quantities of golden eggs from which the welfare state, the sole surviving connection with their conscience, could be financed.

And so, when in 2008 the vast pyramids of financial capital came crashing down, Europe's social democrats did not have the mental tools or the moral values with which to combat the bankers or to subject the collapsing system to critical scrutiny. And unlike their American counterparts, back in power after Barack Obama's victory in November 2008, Europe's social democrats did not even have the backing of a functional central bank, given the European Central Bank's straitjacket of a rulebook. President Obama, from his first day in office, had a Fed willing and able to stand by him every step of the way as his administration attempted to refloat Wall Street and clean up its mess. Undoubtedly the result of these efforts left a great deal to be desired, but imagine how much worse things would have been in the United States, and in the world at large, if the Fed had had to labour under the European Central Bank's mandate and use its tools.

Lacking the ethical, intellectual and financial weapons that they and their predecessors had willingly retired or refused to create some years before, satisfied instead with a steady supply of financialization's lotus, Europe's social democrats were ready to fall. Ready to retreat. To bow their heads to the bankers' demands for bailouts to be purchased with self-defeating austerity for the weakest. To shut their eyes to the transfer of the costs of the crisis from those responsible for it to the majority of citizens, Germans and Greeks alike, the very people that social democrats were supposed to represent.

Unsurprisingly, European social democracy went to ground, leaving the way open to racist ultra-rightist thugs all too happy to act as the protectors of the weak – as long as the latter had the right blood, skin colour and prejudices.

Metternich's echo

In 1993, with the Maastricht Treaty fully operational, the dominant storyline was that German reunification, following the fall of the Berlin Wall, was just one part of a pan-European unification project that was to begin in the realm of money: the eurozone. Concerns about German dominance, which President de Gaulle, Margaret Thatcher and others had harboured and which had hung in the air in France and elsewhere for years, were now dismissed on the basis that East and West Germans wanted to be reunited only while losing themselves in a broader European Union.

Jacques Delors, the former French finance minister and driver of the eurozone in his capacity as president of the European Commission, made a big song and dance about the need to limit the influence of large countries through the principle of subsidiarity: the idea that realms of policy that could be dealt with reasonably competently at the level of the nation state should be delegated to the national governments to design and implement for themselves. Decentralization was to be the brake on German and French domin-ance of the union.

At the same time, plenty of commentators, historians and polit-icians were drawing parallels between European monetary union and the manner in which Germany itself had unified – not in 1991 but over the course of the nineteenth century. Prior to 1833, what is Germany today encompassed a multitude of different states, city-states and jurisdictions, each with its own standards, time zone and currency. Trading across these multiple borders was nightmarish and the reason that Germany was so far behind Britain in terms of industrialization, innovation and governance. German unification began with a customs union known as the Zollverein, an 1833 agreement between the various territories promoted as a first step towards freer trade and much needed economic integration.

One shrewd observer at the time was deeply concerned with the Zollverein. Chancellor Klemens von Metternich of the Austro-Hungarian empire was the key figure in the so-called Holy Alliance, the league of Austrian, Prussian and Russian monarchies whose common purpose was to impede any political movement and prevent any change that might jeopardize the established scheme of things. Metternich could not fail to notice that the Zollverein treaty had been driven by Prussia, the dominant German kingdom, and excluded the Austro-Hungarian empire. Just as Beijing today sees as a major threat the American drive to forge a Pacific Basin free trade zone that excludes China in the form of the Trans-Pacific Partnership (TPP), Metternich too felt that Prussia was up to mischief. In a letter to his emperor he wrote:

> Within the great Confederation, a smaller union is being formed, a status *in statu* in the full sense of the term, which will only too soon accustom itself to achieving its ends by its own machinery and will pay attention to the objectives and machinery of the Confederation only when convenient . . . [O]n every question that comes before the Diet [the Confederation's parliament] (and not only commercial affairs) [it] will act and vote as one according to prior arrangements. Then there will no longer be any useful discussion in the Diet; debates will be replaced by votes agreed in advance and inspired not by the interests of the Confederation but by the exclusive interest of Prussia . . . Even now it is unfortunately easy to determine

in advance how these votes will be cast on all the questions where the interest of Prussia conflicts with that of
the federal body.[24]

This description could have been written, with very few emendations,
to describe my experience of the Eurogroup deliberations as finance
minister of a small European nation in 2015. Metternich could have
been writing about the manner in which matters of crucial importance
for various eurozone member states, especially those with large deficits and unbearable debts, were settled on the basis of modern Prussia's
'exclusive interest'.[25]

In modern times we imagine that nineteenth-century politicians
primarily used the sword to expand their empires, rather than appealing
to the self-interest of prospective subjects. That was not true of the
German Confederation. The idea of voluntary accession on the basis
of the self-interest of the smaller states was indeed central to the
Zollverein. Prussia persuaded the smaller German states to enter into
the new arrangements by insisting that they would be better off
inside the union, where they would be well positioned to influence
matters, than outside, where they could only react to decisions the
confederation reached.

Even the notion of subsidiarity, or something close to it, was
employed. The promise of decentralized power worked miracles in
convincing the German states that feared a Prussian-dominated
union to enter it. However, some argue that this was a well-laid trap.
The German constitutionalist Heinrich Triepel observed that 'a
looser association of states encourages hegemony more than a tight
one . . . the more unitary elements predominate in a federation the
more inner firmness there is, and the greater are the obstacles to
the creation of a hegemony'.[26] Indeed, a surplus state that seeks to
dominate a confederacy may achieve this precisely by weakening its
central institutions: the absence of a central political surplus recycling
mechanism, which is necessary to avert crises and to subdue them
when they occur, increases the likelihood of a severe economic
downturn; by that stage, with the various member-states now highly
integrated, tackling the downturn demands systemic solutions – in
other words, centralization. At that point, in the absence of well-

defined federal processes for doing so, the centralization proceeds on autopilot and the central institutions are created on the most powerful state's terms.

This is what happened in Germany after 1833. It is also what happened in the eurozone after the Maastricht Treaty begat the 2010 euro crisis: every incantation of the merits of subsidiarity and decentralization precipitated a wave of authoritarian, unaccountable rule from the centre. In the nineteenth century a swathe of harmonizing legislation emanated from Prussia to establish industrial standards and legislation favourable to Berlin. In the eurozone all the institutional changes effected since 2010 were done in accordance with the priorities of the Federal Republic.

In 1871 the centralizing process that Metternich had so feared gave rise to the German empire, complete with a central bank (the Reichsbank), a single currency (the Reichsmark) linked to the gold standard and a common parliament (the Bundesrat) dominated by the Iron Chancellor, Otto von Bismarck. Prussia had only seventeen votes out of fifty-eight in the Bundesrat but by that stage enjoyed full control with the assistance of the votes of the representatives of the smaller states that since 1833 had fallen within the Prussian zone of influence.[27] However, as of this writing, it is highly unlikely that history will repeat itself in precisely the same manner. The eurozone may indeed resemble Germany of, say, the 1860s, with a swathe of smaller states competing as to which one will be picked as Prussia's best pupil, but the circumstances are quite different. France is important in that, despite rapid decline after its ill-fated attempt to capture the Bundesbank, it remains difficult to subdue and almost impossible to absorb into a modern-day version of Bismarck's unitary empire.

Nevertheless, the combination of two impossibilities leaves a huge question mark hanging in mid-air regarding Europe's future. On the one hand, there is the impossibility of the eurozone continuing with its present terrible architecture, constantly spewing out different versions of Greece's tragedy. On the other hand, there is the impossibility of forming a unitary, centralized state with Berlin and Frankfurt at the centre and Paris taking its impotence on the chin, accepting vassal status once and for all.

This leaves us with two possibilities: a break-up or a proper federation. The problem is that too much political capital has been invested to allow for a velvet divorce, while at the same time the euro crisis is creating so many animosities between the peoples of Europe that a real federation could not be more utopian than at present.

Back to the USA

Few progressive Europeans would argue against a democratic United States of Europe, with a proper government elected on a pan-European ticket and answerable to a proper parliament vested with complete sovereignty over all decisions and matters. But this is wishful thinking. The sobering reality is that it is not in the European Union's DNA to evolve into a federation.

The reason the eurozone is experiencing a never-ending existential crisis that tears Europeans apart is, as we have seen, because of its initial reliance on fair-weather surplus recycling instead of a proper political surplus recycling mechanism. Even more importantly, its political institutions and the vested interests behind them – in particular, Frankfurt's and Paris's commercial banks – displayed a resilient commitment to not creating such a mechanism even after the crisis erupted. The big question here is: why? Why reject the political surplus recycling that is, as the United States realized in the 1940s, essential to maintaining an asymmetric monetary union?

One reason is that European elites took it for granted that European business could for ever freeload on US-directed surplus recycling. They assumed that America would play this stabilizing role perpetually on behalf of Europe. Indeed, this assumption was one of the eurozone's founding principles, laid out in Maastricht, which I like to refer to as the 'principle of perfectly separable debts and banking sectors'. The idea behind it is simple: each euro of debt, whether private or public, stops at the borders of the nation state. No euro owed should end up being owed by more than one state, whether it is a euro owed by the Greek government to a French bank or an Irish bank's debt to some private creditor. There should be no pooling of debt between European nations, no sharing of the burden of insuring bank depositors, no common fund by which to fight a crisis of the common monetary system.

In an important sense, this principle is a ban on having a political surplus recycling mechanism. Importantly, the lack of such a mechanism is not due to neglect on the part of the euro's designers; it was intentional. As a result, the euro could only function as a stable currency if someone else was stabilizing it. That someone else was the United States economy and its Minotaur.

During the era of Bretton Woods, which ended in 1971, and the subsequent era of the Minotaur, Europe's process of integrating markets and bureaucracies, with Brussels as the pivot, proceeded rather smoothly. And as long as the rivers of private fair-weather liquidity continued to flow from the Anglosphere, they allowed Brussels and Frankfurt to maintain the illusion that there was no need to centralize fiscal policies – that fair-weather recycling was all their ramshackle eurozone needed; that there was no need for the European Demos to keep in check the Brussels-based technocracy and a lawmaking process unconstrained by anything resembling a sovereign parliament. With national parliaments supposedly exercising democratic control over fiscal policy, the European Union's institutions worked in the interests of an unholy alliance between the original cartel of Central European heavy industry, high-output (mainly French) farmers and a burgeoning financial sector.

However, in 2008 the United States lost its capacity to stabilize the global economy through the operation of Wall Street and America's trade and federal government budget deficits. And so the eurozone began to unravel. The more Europe maintained that the events of 2008 could be accommodated within its rules, the greater the crisis afflicting Europeans. The deeper into the crisis Europe descended, the more difficult it became for the Fed and the US Treasury to reignite the stalled engine of America's economy.

At that critical juncture there was no alternative to the centralization of the management of Europe's public debt and thus of fiscal policies. But how could fiscal policies be centralized when in principle they remained in the remit of national parliaments and governments that were essentially bankrupt and in a death embrace with insolvent banking sectors? The answer Europe opted for was not, even now, to create the federal political union it so badly lacked. Instead, it chose centralization of a different sort: by means of large loans to the insolvent nations, which to win the approval of the surplus countries' parliaments came with punitive strings attached.

Thus the centralization of eurozone fiscal policy was achieved through the creation of an austerity union that magnified the crisis, caused it almost to dissolve the euro and, finally, when the European Central Bank acted in the summer of 2012 to save the common currency,[28] transferred the crisis from the money markets to the realm of Europe's real economy. Europe's crisis migrated from the debt (or bond) markets to its industry, shops and benevolent societies, while the bureaucrats and the politicians behind the new austerity union celebrated its resolution.

Throughout, Washington's officials looked on, wondering what if anything they could do to help Europe's decision makers get it.

As the fault lines between the surplus and the deficit eurozone member states deepen, the whole edifice is losing coherence and sliding towards fragmentation. Even the most ardent defenders of the original European design, who tell American officials to mind their own business, now understand this. At last they have even begun to advocate a political union to save the eurozone.

Be that as it may, the rest of us should beware: it is a cardinal error to mistake talk of a political union for a move towards federal democracy.

Schäuble's plan

'Ideally, Europe would be a political union . . . Consider two proposals. Why not have a European budget commissioner with powers to reject national budgets if they do not correspond to the rules we jointly agreed? . . . We also favor a "eurozone parliament" comprising the members of European Parliament of eurozone countries to strengthen the democratic legitimacy of decisions affecting the single currency bloc.'[29]

The above was penned by two influential German politicians who were thought of as true-blue federalists in the early 1990s, thanks to their articles arguing in favour of political union: Wolfgang Schäuble, Germany's current finance minister, and Karl Lamers, a member of the federal parliament responsible for foreign affairs policy in Germany's conservative Christian Democratic Union.[30] In it Schäuble returned to his favourite theme: a particular form of political union that he advocates, offering two examples of how it would work. Casual readers might think that Germany's powerful finance minister was advocating two proposals that would take Europe towards a federal democracy. He was not.

Currently, the Brussels-based European Commission looks at a member state's budget and makes recommendations. If the budget goes into a deficit exceeding the Maastricht Treaty maximum of 3 per cent, the commission issues warnings that can eventually lead to sanctions. Usually this process triggers long negotiations between the member state and the commission which become the subject of lengthy Eurogroup meetings, leading to some additional austerity for the country in question plus a great deal of creative fiddling with its macroeconomic accounting. Schäuble's first radical proposal was for a fiscal overlord to end national sovereignty over budgets. To have the right, and duty, to take a look at, say, France's national budget and either deem it fit to pass or declare it unacceptable.

This would mark a significant departure from the present practice. A national budget that had been approved by a national parliament could be thrown out, at the stroke of a pen, by a Brussels-based overlord. Naturally, Schäuble's idea has provoked sharp reactions, especially in Paris. But we need to grant him this: he is the only German politician to have taken the eurozone's current philosophy and architecture to its logical conclusion. Demonstrating remarkable consistency over the years, Dr Schäuble was repeating, perhaps somewhat more mildly, views that he had outlined twenty years before. For instance, on 8 June 2000, in the *Frankfurter Allgemeine Zeitung* he took a swipe at the notion of national sovereignty, calling it nonsensical, expressing scorn for the 'academic debate over whether Europe is a federation or an alliance of states'.[31]

If Dr Schäuble was right, that there is no noteworthy difference between a federation and an alliance of states, then the idea that the eurozone should establish a fiscal overlord with the power to veto national budgets makes perfect sense. The creation of such a position of great central power would indeed signal closer political union and a move towards federation. But is there really no difference between a federation and an alliance of states or a Europe of nations? Of course there is. And it is the difference between democracy and despotism.

No sovereignty, no democracy

One often forgotten fact about liberal democracies is that a constitution's legitimacy is determined by politics, not by its legal niceties. As Tony Benn, the British Labour politician, once suggested, we should constantly ask those who govern us five questions. What power have you got? Where did you get it from? In whose interests do you exercise it? To whom are you accountable? And how can we get rid of you?[32]

Ever since Sophocles' *Antigone* we have known that all good women and men have a duty to violate laws lacking political and moral legitimacy. Political authority is the cement that keeps legislation together, and the sovereignty of the body politic that engenders the legislation is its foundation. To claim, as Dr Schäuble did in 2000, and as he implied again in 2014, that it makes no difference whether the eurozone is an alliance of independently sovereign states or itself a sovereign federation of states is to purposely ignore the fact that only a sovereign people can create political authority, whereas an alliance of states cannot.

Dr Schäuble's alliance of states can of course come to mutually beneficial arrangements, such as a defensive military alliance against a common aggressor, or agree to common industry standards or even the creation of a free trade zone. But it can never legitimately install an overlord with the right to strike down or overrule a member state's sovereignty, since there is no collective, alliance-wide sovereignty from which to draw the necessary political authority to do so.

This is why the difference between a federation and an alliance of states matters. For while a federation replaces sovereignty forfeited at the national or state level with sovereignty at the unitary, federal level, centralizing power within an alliance of states is, by definition, illegitimate, for there is no body politic that can legitimize it.

One may retort that the European Union's democratic credentials are beyond reproach, as the commission is appointed by elected heads of state who also form the European Council that legislates on behalf of Dr Schäuble's alliance of states. Moreover, there is the European Parliament, which has the power to throw out parts of this legislation. To round off this rejoinder, it is often added that sovereignty is in any case highly overrated and profoundly meaningless in an interdependent, globalized world. In the global village the French, the Germans – all Europeans, even the Greeks – enjoy more sovereignty when they pool their national sovereignties together into one common European realm. And if this means that we have to create a fiscal overlord with the remit to keep us all in fiscal awe, and in line with the eurozone's rules, so be it.

But these arguments demonstrate how badly European appreciation of the founding principles of liberal democracy has been degraded. The critical error of such a defence is to confuse political authority with power. A parliament is sovereign, even if it is not particularly powerful, when it can dismiss the executive for having failed to fulfil the tasks assigned to it within the constraints of whatever power the executive and the parliament possess. Nothing like this exists in the eurozone today.

While the members of the European Council and the Eurogroup are elected politicians answerable, theoretically, to their respective national parliaments, the council and the Eurogroup are themselves not answerable to any parliament, nor indeed to any body politic whatsoever. Moreover, the Eurogroup, where all the important economic decisions are taken, is a body that does not even exist in European law, that operates on the basis that the 'strong do as they please while the weak suffer what they must', that keeps no minutes of its proceedings and whose only rule is that its deliberations are confidential – that is, not to be shared with Europe's citizenry. It is a set-up designed to preclude any sovereignty traceable back to the people of Europe.

One may argue that a European country is more powerful within the eurozone than outside, but what about its sovereignty? Prussia, as Metternich had predicted, convinced smaller German states that their sovereignty was better protected inside the Zollverein than outside – only to dismantle it in short order soon after. This is precisely what is taking place in Europe today, except that it is happening faster and with less resistance because it is happening in the midst of crisis. The fact that it will ultimately cause the dismantling of Europe – when the people of France, Italy and elsewhere at some point say, 'Enough!' – does not slow this devastating process.

'Surely there is no room for small sovereign countries in this globalized world,' I was told by another finance minister during a break in a Eurogroup meeting. 'Iceland can never truly be sovereign,' he concluded, satisfied that he had made his point. Except that his point was hollow. To claim that Iceland's sovereignty is illusory because it is too small to have much power is like arguing that a poor person with next to no political clout might as well give up her vote. To put it slightly differently, small sovereign nations like Iceland have choices to make within the broader constraints created for them by nature and by the rest of humanity. However limited these choices might be, Iceland's body politic retains absolute authority to hold its elected officials accountable for the decisions they have reached within the nation's exogenous constraints and to strike down every piece of legislation that it has decided upon in the past.

In sharp contrast, when the eurozone's finance ministers return home from Brussels – or wherever it is that the Eurogroup and Ecofin has just met – they immediately decry the decisions that they have just signed up to, using the standard excuses: 'It was the best we could negotiate' or 'I was outvoted.' My insistence, as Greece's finance minister, on agreements that I could take back to Athens and defend as consistent with Greece and Europe's interests was attacked as obstinacy, as a form of stubborn unreasonableness. The satisfaction of Europe's powers that be at my resignation on 6 July 2015 was due precisely to my peculiar commitment not to sign any agreement that I could not defend as an economist, a politician, an intellectual and as a Greek. It was considered unacceptable behaviour in an institution created to treat sovereignty and accountability as nuisances that impede the smooth running of Europe's monetary union.

The euro crisis caused this lacuna at the centre of Europe to grow hideously larger. Brussels functionaries, German and French officials, representatives of the European Central Bank all learned to expect smaller member-state representatives to toe the line, just as the representatives of the soviets were expected to raise their cards during meetings of the Central Committee of the Communist Party of the Soviet Union. And they expected us to return home and tell our national parliaments that, while we disagreed with the Eurogroup's or the council's decision, we had been too 'responsible' to resist. At the same time, it became not uncommon for officials of the more powerful states to blame other representatives for bad decisions that they had consented to under duress so as not to undermine European solidarity. So even if a majority of Eurogroup members rejected the logic of, say, Greece's bailouts, the Eurogroup adopted it and the troika then took over, ramming the bailout agreements through national parliaments scared of being branded 'unreasonable' or 'un-European'.

No forum or assembly of European citizens including the so-called European Parliament could, after that point, strike down these decisions or censure those who had reached them, even if it became clear that they had been atrocious blunders. In this sense, small, powerless Iceland continues to enjoy full sovereignty while the comparatively omnipotent European Union has been stripped of all forms of sovereignty.

Would any of this be ameliorated if Wolfgang Schäuble's second proposal, that of a chamber exclusively for members of the eurozone within the European Parliament, were implemented?[33] The European Parliament is indeed the only European Union institution that remotely resembles a federal body. Elected directly in pan-European elections, it seems, to the untrained eye, equivalent to the US House of Representatives or Britain's House of Commons. However, upon closer inspection, the European Parliament is nothing like any assembly consistent with liberal democracy. In the latter all legislative power is vested in the parliament or congress, with clear demarcation between executive and legislature. In the European Union the main legislative organ remains the Council of Ministers, which meets and votes behind closed doors and is composed not of legislators but of members of the member states' executives. Moreover, the eurozone is ruled by an informal group – the Eurogroup – meeting in secrecy, which because it is informal never reports to the European Parliament.

These revolving doors between legislative power at the centre and executive power in the member states were designed purposely to ensure that laws could be passed without any serious scrutiny by any sovereign parliament vested with the authority of democracy's final arbiter, the people. While the European Parliament has over the years acquired new powers alongside the council, it is still not a proper parliament. The fact that it shares legislative power with the European Council and, remarkably, lacks the authority to initiate any legislation, means that it lacks the political authority required to legitimize the transfer of sovereignty from the national level to any euro chamber within the European Parliament. Such a transfer would be the equivalent of transporting water from a local pond to a faraway central reservoir using a sieve.

Wolfgang Schäuble likes the idea of a euro chamber because he assumes that it would legitimize the actions and authority of his fiscal overlord; that it would provide the 'democratic legitimacy of decisions affecting the single currency bloc'.[34] However, the only way one can agree with him is by deleting from one's faculties all understanding of what parliaments are meant to be and do.

Democracy versus discretionary power

This section ought to be superfluous. The fact that it is not reflects badly on a world that seems to have forgotten the minimum requirements for a functioning liberal democracy. So here we are, stating what once upon a time everyone knew well, namely that the chief purpose of law is to create a level playing field between the weak and the powerful. While a level playing field does not preclude exploitation and serious violations of freedom, it is the very least the rule of law must provide. To reduce all human interaction to power relations is the opposite of the rule of law and a gateway to despotism. To prevent the reduction of human interaction to power relations and to keep despotism at bay, the executive's discretionary power must be minimized by a sovereign body politic with the means to minimize it.

From this perspective, Dr Schäuble's proposals make bleak reading. The fiscal overlord he proposes is a type of leviathan whose remit is binary: to say either yes or no to a budget submitted to its office by a member state. It will thus have the right to scrap and return to sender government budgets that violate the eurozone's (Maastricht) rules. But how would this work in practice?

Let's go back in time a little. To 2009. When Ireland's twin bubbles of property and banking burst, the government was forced by the European Central Bank to tack on to the state's books private debt and then demand of taxpayers that they borrow mountains of money to repay it.[35] The result was that the budget deficit, and public debt, skyrocketed, violating the eurozone's rules in the process. Similarly in Spain – where the government had nurtured a pre-crisis debt-to-income ratio lower than Germany's – the 2008 crisis caused the government budget deficit and debt to rise above the Maastricht limits. What would Schäuble's leviathan have done at that point – send the Spanish and Irish government's budgets back to Madrid and Dublin? For what purpose?

The fact is that there was no level of austerity that could have driven Dublin or Madrid's deficits under 3 per cent of GDP without demolishing their national economies and leading the countries to a hard default on their public debt a year later. Similarly with France in 2015: there exists no level of austerity that can push its deficit within the rules without, in the process, wrecking the eurozone in the medium term and immediately bringing to power the ultra-right National Front.

In other words, if the fiscal leviathan is to play any substantive role, it must be able to say a great deal more than *nein*. It cannot be binary – respond with 1 or 0, yes or no. It must be at liberty to propose to national governments alternative budgets that nonetheless still break the rules. Of the rule-breaking budgets, some favoured by national governments and one by the leviathan, it must be the leviathan's that prevails. If not, what is the point of its existence?

But then what happens if the national government resists implementing the leviathan's preferred budget and turns down its overtures for reasons that the leviathan deems inappropriate or unconvincing? Surely Wolgang Schäuble believes that the leviathan must be equipped with the power to steer a national budget in particular ways that cannot flow uniquely and naturally from the existing agreed-upon rules. Massive discretionary power will therefore be created at Europe's centre – de facto even if denied *de jure*.

Returning once again to 2008, suppose Dr Schäuble's scheme had been in place. Our fiscal leviathan would have stayed inactive before the euro crisis (at least in the case of the Irish and Spanish budgets, which were well within the rules year in, year out) but then would have swung furiously into action once the crisis hit, exercising maximal discretionary power across the continent. Would it have displayed the same penchant for intervention in the case of Ireland as it would have in the case of the German government, which also flouted both the deficit and debt limits prescribed by Maastricht? Whatever the answer, it is clear that the enactment of the German finance minister's blueprint for improving the eurozone's governance would have propelled the eurozone after 2008 into the realm of naked power relations between the leviathan and Europe's crisis-hit societies, violated the rule of law at a European level and denied Europe's weaker citizens and states any constitutional protection from arbitrary, discretionary power.

Granted that any leviathan would need to have the authority not only to reject but also to fashion member-state government budgets, could a euro chamber within, or complementary to, the European Parliament provide the missing body politic to protect Europeans from their own executive and maintain the rule of law at the heart of Europe? The minimum conditions for this protection to be effective are that the euro chamber (a) is uniquely empowered to hire or fire the leviathan; (b) is the source of final authority regarding the contents of each member state's budget; and (c) has powers that are clearly demarcated by a constitution.

It is crystal clear that at least two of these conditions will not be met. Neither the German government nor the Parisian elites would countenance allowing the euro chamber to hire or fire the leviathan. Nor would they dare embark upon the writing of a euro constitution.

It turns out that grafting a federal democracy onto a Brussels-based technocracy is not a simple matter, especially when said technocracy represents a holy alliance between apparatchiks, a powerful Central European cartel of heavy industry, national politicians who have their own cosy relationship with bankrupt local bankers, and large international banks. And so all talk of gradual moves towards a political union and 'more Europe' are not first steps towards a European democratic federation but rather a leap into an iron cage that prolongs the crisis and wrecks any prospect of a genuine federal European democracy in the future. Throwing the peoples of Europe into that iron cage in the name of progress towards a promised United States of Europe will complete the business of delegitimizing 'Europe' in the eyes of Europeans. In a never-ending loop of frightful reinforcement, authoritarianism and economic malaise will continue to feed off each other until Europe is brought to its breaking point.

Decentralized Europeanization. Or how to replace TINA with TATIANA

Iron cages do not evolve naturally into democratic federations. It would be foolhardy to expect a democratic political union to emerge after locking the eurozone's countries together into a system of arbitrary, discretionary power without the political surplus recycling necessary to harmonize the union. A dark state of permanent austerity-driven low-investment high-unemployment equilibrium is the only natural outcome, something which does not augur well for a democratic federation.

Empire builders are impatient with checks and balances on the executive, especially when in a hurry and under duress. Even when their intended actions are good and proper, they are bound to turn nasty without limits on the executive. Once the EU executives' austerity policies pushed Europe into deflation, proposals like those of Wolfgang Schäuble and Karl Lamers reflected the understandable craving for a parliamentary fig leaf of officials seeking even more arbitrary power to achieve their impossible goals. My brief ministerial experience in 2015 allowed me a front seat at meetings in which the German finance minister presented his vision for Europe. What Schäuble had to say was ample confirmation of the above assessment: Europe was to salvage its foundering monetary union by means of a disciplinarian political union the polar opposite of a democratic federation. And Greece was to be the sacrificial goat that would put the fear of God in France's elites, eliciting their consent to Dr Schäuble's version of political union.

But enough lamentations about official Europe's natural tendency towards crisis-fed despotism. Is there a modest, realistic counter-proposal? Can we balance deep criticism of the European Union with an appreciation of the tremendous costs that its fragmentation would bring? Can the existing far-from-perfect institutions be utilized to arrest the crisis and revive democracy in Europe? Even before the eurozone was officially engulfed in crisis, these questions preoccupied me. Together with two great friends and fellow economists, Stuart Holland, a former British parliamentarian, and Jamie Galbraith, the renowned American economist, I set out to create a blueprint for addressing Europe's peculiar crisis.

We were not naive enough to think that our blueprint would be implemented on the strength of its rationality. No, its purpose was simpler: to be able to counter official Europe's doctrine with our own. To respond to Eurocrats insisting, 'There is no alternative' (TINA) that respects the treaties and the current rules with, 'That, astonishingly, there is an alternative' (TATIANA). Our TATIANA, entitled 'A Modest Proposal for Resolving the Eurozone Crisis', is a blueprint for addressing the crisis through Europeanizing its four components – the crises of public debt, banks, underinvestment and the poverty explosion – while decentralizing political power through a reduction in the discretionary power exercised illicitly by the Brussels–Frankfurt–Berlin triangle. Seen from another less politically charged perspective, the proposal's greatest merit is that it offers a way to abandon the eurozone's problematic principle of perfectly separable debts and banking sectors and to introduce the missing political surplus recycling mechanism without creating autocratic discretionary power at Europe's centre and without any immediate need to rewrite the European Union's existing rules and treaties.

How can this seemingly contradictory set of aims be achieved at once? How can we Europeanize the solution to the crisis without centralization? Our answer is that the Europeanization of the four sub-crises (debt, banks, underinvestment and poverty) can be achieved through redeploying existing European institutions – the European Central Bank, the European Stability Mechanism and the European Investment Bank – in a manner that

> keeps the discretionary power of its management at a minimum by stating clear rules that they must follow under their new redesigned roles; addresses systematically the eurozone's systemic problems with public debt, banks that are undercapitalized, aggregate investment that is woefully

low and poverty that is on the rampage; and makes it feasible for national governments to stick to the existing rules of the eurozone.

The reason why no moves towards a political union are necessary under this proposal, and thus no discretionary power is needed for some new fiscal leviathan, is that the redeployment we propose

> does not require the German, Austrian or Finnish governments to pay for the Greeks' or the Italians' debts or investment needs; can be effected within existing treaties; and is to be handled on the basis of fully rule-bound management of existing institutions.

While this is not the place to explain in full the 'Modest Proposal' (which is included instead as an appendix), its intention was to find a way to simulate a federation, a United States of Europe, by means of automated rules that, unlike those of the Maastricht Treaty and its successors, actually work. Our mission was to devise additional rules that are consistent with the letter of existing rules and require no new discretionary power for Brussels or Frankfurt. Using them, the four sub-crises could be dealt with at the European level – be Europeanized – while real power is returned to national parliaments. Hence my term 'Europeanized decentralization'.

None of our suggested policies violates the eurozone's existing rules. In fact, they could be implemented fully through the creation of supplementary rules for the European Central Bank, European Stability Mechanism and European Investment Bank, which, unlike the current ones, throw up no contradictions and, therefore, require no discretionary power for the administrators attempting to implement them. In the process, relieved of major headaches, national governments can respect existing rules more easily and have more room to implement their parliaments' priorities.

Alexis de Tocqueville once wrote that those who praise freedom only for the material benefits it offers have never kept it long. In today's

Europe those who wax lyrical about the sanctity of its existing rules are their own worst enemy and the handmaidens of discretionary, autocratic power. Europe's democrats must, for this reason, beware of those speaking of moves towards political union and 'more Europe' when their real objective is to preserve an unsustainable monetary architecture. Continuing to impose impossible rules opens the door to the ugly ghosts of our common past.

Given the European Union's history and the current state of the eurozone, political union, fiscal union and various other ideas for further centralization are neither viable nor desirable. The institutions of the European Union were designed back in the 1950s and 1960s in order to bleach politics out of them. And since nothing is as political nor as toxic as an attempt to depoliticize a political process, the result was institutions at odds with the concept and practices of a democracy.

Europeans understand this better now that the euro crisis has brought to the surface the consequences of their union's institutional design. Especially after the crushing in July 2015 of the Greek government in which I served, Europeans increasingly see the Brussels and Frankfurt technocracies as forces of occupation, a little like the French looked at the Vichy administrators. They do not want Brussels as it is structured today to evolve into their central government in response to a crisis of the European Union's own making. And with good reason.

The German philosopher Jürgen Habermas long ago recognized that capitalism has the tendency to develop a 'legitimacy deficit' – a situation in which citizens, independently of their political beliefs or ideology, lose confidence in the right of political and administrative authorities to act as they do.[36] As Europeans lose their trust in Europe's institutions, they face a dreadful Faustian bargain: accept less democracy now and more centralization tomorrow, and some time in the future you may get something akin to a federal state. Alas, accepting this deal will not bring federation any closer. Instead, it will

> bolster the economic crisis and ensure the debt mountains grow taller, while further suppressing investment into a decent future; delegitimize the European Union even more in the eyes of Europeans; replace whatever democracy we have left

at the national level with consultative processes that Brussels uses in order to cement a permanent commitment to deflationary, highly redistributive policies (in favour primarily of banks and reliably of the strong and already powerful); reduce political debates on economic policy to pseudo-technocratic discussions among unelected managers whose allegiance lies with a technocracy created to service the interests of the ubiquitous Central European cartel and an all-devouring financial sector; ascribe pretend-accountability to a European parliament, or a euro chamber, which in reality acts nothing like a parliament but rather uses the semblance of a parliament in order to conceal the fact that European law is passed in the radical absence of a genuine parliamentary process; and entrench in European law the dangerous idea that sovereignty is passé in the era of globalization.

None of these developments is consistent with a sustainable European Union. At some point Europeans will shake this monstrosity off their backs and escape from the iron cage under construction around them. Unfortunately, the resulting European disintegration will come at a horrendous socioeconomic cost, today's equivalent of the generalized depression of the 1930s. The trick is to escape the cage without destroying our common home.

The paradox of a continent divided by a common currency must be replaced by another paradox: that of decentralized Europeanization – a rule-based redeployment of key European institutions (the ECB, the ESM and the EIB) to attack Europe's four sub-crises while reinvigorating Europe's national democracies. Then and only then, once democracy has been revived at the level of the member states, can we begin the conversation that we must have about what future we want for Europe.

Meanwhile, my first-hand experience of the manner in which Europe is ruled brings to mind with renewed resonance the figure of Kapnias, the man whose story I recounted at the beginning of this chapter. His particular form of evil taught me how our loathing of democracy's worst enemies can reinforce their commitment and renew their spirit. It taught me that only steady, unwavering, dispassionate, hate-free resistance can overcome their determination. It taught me that a Greek who had never encountered a Jew – nowadays a Pakistani – could be programmed to believe that therein lay the cause of all his suffering. It also taught me that the serpent dies hard. That once its DNA is implanted into societies through the humiliation of enforced and unconditional surrender,[37] it lurks for a long, long time, waiting for a systemic crisis to spawn again.

'When I return home tonight, I shall find myself in a parliament in which the third-largest party is a Nazi one,' I told Wolfgang Schäuble in front of the gathered press during my first visit to the German Ministry of Finance back in February 2015.[38] It was a plea for joint action. He, and the German press, took it as posturing.

Seven months later, in September 2015, after Dr Schäuble and the Eurogroup had succeeded in overthrowing our government by asphyxiating us enough for Prime Minister Tsipras to surrender, Golden Dawn increased its parliamentary representation in Athens,[39] Greece's debt reached greater heights, our society lost its will to reform itself and, most seriously, European democracy was wounded deeply. The refugee emergency that same summer, with tens of thousands of wretched souls arriving on Greece's shores, and with Europe and America's leaders bickering about how not to receive them, confirmed that Europe's integrity and soul are in disrepair.

New borders, new divisions and greater divergence is the harvest European monetary union has reaped in a continent the world had wanted so much to look up to. A continent that once produced so much light now exports bleakness and recession to the rest of the world. But it does not have to be this way. Innovative policies can combine the decentralization of power that Europeans crave with the Europeanization of basic, common problems, which they need. But it will take a radical idea to pull this happy paradox off and stop the slithering serpent. It is indeed a preposterous idea, which – you guessed it – also comes from my problematic, insufferable, brilliant neck of the woods: the idea of democracy.

To put the figure of Kapnias to rest once and for all across Europe, Europeans must regain control of their politics and their money from unaccountable technocrats. We need to take a leaf from the Americans' ideological book so as to move from a Europe of 'We the governments . . .' and 'We the technocrats . . .' to a Europe of 'We the European people . . .'

During this process it would help to extend to our continent's every corner the French triptych of liberty, fraternity and equality, amended to accommodate three fresh principles:

1. No European nation can be free as long as another's democracy is violated.
2. No European nation can live in dignity as long as another is denied it.
3. No European nation can hope for prosperity if another is pushed into permanent insolvency and depression.

Only when these principles are respected throughout Europe will the foul smirk be wiped off the faces of Kapnias's successors.

8

Europe's Crisis, America's Future

Global finance imploded once in 1929 and again in 2008. In 1929, after Wall Street's banks fell into a black hole of their own making, the common currency of that era began to unravel. This was the gold standard. Soon after, in Europe we ended up with Nazis and assorted fascists in power. In 2008, after Wall Street's banks caved in under the weight of their derivative trades, the common currency of our era began to unravel. This was the euro, a revival of the gold standard in the heart of Europe.

By February 2010 the 2008 blast had reached Europe, bringing to breaking point its weakest link, Greece. The euro started to buckle, with potentially frightful consequences for Europe's banks, business, people and politics. But instead of fretting over the appalling prospect of a postmodern 1930s, Europe's leaders had different priorities. Timothy Geithner, the US treasury secretary who had spent the previous twelve months fighting the crisis on the other side of the Atlantic, could not believe his ears in a meeting with his European counterparts. 'We're going to teach the Greeks a lesson,' they told him. '[W]e're going to crush them.'[1]

Geithner is not known for his tenderness. He would have lost very little sleep if it had been only a matter of the Greeks being destroyed by angry Northern Europeans. Indeed, he told his interlocutors to go ahead if that was their wish: 'You can put your foot on the neck of those guys if that's what you want to do. But you've got to make sure that you send a countervailing signal of reassurance to Europe and the world that you're going to hold the thing together and not let it go. [That you're] going to protect the rest of the place.'[2] Surrounded by morally outraged Europeans, Geithner was the only one in the room to keep his eye on the proverbial ball – the terrible effect that 'crushing' the Greeks would have on the Germans, the French, indeed the Americans.

Around the same time, quite independently and in ignorance of Geithner's conversation with Europe's finance ministers, I was voicing my fears of what was about to hit Europe in an article entitled 'A New Versailles Haunts Europe'.[3] 'Turning countries like Greece into sundrenched wastelands,' I wrote, 'and forcing the rest of the eurozone into an even faster debt-deflationary downward spiral, is a most efficient way of undermining Germany's own economy.' My fear, and I think Geithner's too, was that history was about to repeat itself. In 1929 all the burden of adjustment was forced upon the weakest debtors. Such a policy cannot succeed since the resulting deflation poisons debt dynamics and mass joblessness poisons democracy. Inevitably it did not succeed. In 2010 once again the greatest burden fell on the weakest of shoulders. Within a couple of years Europe was losing its integrity and is now at an advanced stage of surrendering its soul.

The ghost of Versailles

Le Figaro's 1992 headline celebrating the Maastricht Treaty as a new Treaty of Versailles – one that would make Germany pay again for France, and without a single shot being fired – was undoubtedly an egregious affront to European history.[4] The French conservative newspaper was clearly blind to the folly of Versailles. The essence of that sorry treaty was not so much that it crushed Germany economically and caused Germans untold collective pain, but that, in the end, it was an own goal: a terrible deal even for the victors – a self-defeating punitive act that John Maynard Keynes understood early on[5] and the rest of the world came to recognize as such in the 1930s, when it was too late.

While it was offensive for the French conservative newspaper to portray Maastricht as a new Versailles, it is perfectly accurate to draw parallels between Versailles and the eurozone's bailouts, Greece's in particular. In 2010, quoting from Keynes's Dr Melchior: A Defeated Enemy, his autobiographical reflection on the terms of that treaty, but simply changing the names of the protagonists, I wrote[6] of the Greek government's 'insincere acceptance . . . of impossible conditions which it was not intended to carry out – an acceptance which made Greece [Germany] almost as guilty to accept what she could not fulfil as the troika [Allies] to impose what they were not entitled to exact'.

Amused by the extent to which Keynes's criticism of the Versailles Treaty fitted the Greek drama, I went on, quoting this time from his book *The Economic Consequences of the Peace*:

> Moved by insane delusion and reckless self-regard, the Greek [German] people overturned the foundations on which we all lived and built. But the spokesmen of the European Union [Great War's victorious Allies] have run the risk of completing the ruin, which Greece [Germany] began, by a bailout agreement [Versailles Treaty] which, if it is carried into effect, must impair yet further, when it might have restored, the delicate, complicated organization, already shaken and broken by the 2008 crisis [the war], through which alone the European peoples can employ themselves and live.

To many readers it may seem a terrible exaggeration to suggest that the Greek bailout posed a threat to Europe and indeed to the global economy. But it is not.

European officials were wrong to hope that in order to save Northern Europe's banks it would be enough to lend huge irretrievable sums to Greece and then let my country wallow in permanent depression as a cautionary tale. This strategy, which was then used as the template for the rest of the European periphery, turning the majority of European states into what I jokingly refer to as Bailoutistan, was always going to backfire on the European economy. Tim Geithner and Jack Lew, his successor at the US Treasury, understood this well. They shared the view that what started in Greece in 2010 with an absurd bailout and a hideous level of austerity has put Europe into a position that undermines America's recovery and threatens the prospects of China, Latin America, even India and Africa.

America's future imperilled

The United States provided the stabilizers that global capitalism relied upon after the Second World War. Bretton Woods, the broader global plan in which it was embedded, and the brave new post-1971 world of Paul Volcker[7] stood behind capitalism's postwar planetary-scale triumph.

What did America bring to global capitalism with such success? Washington's rejection of deficit phobia. Deficit phobia goes hand in hand with a penchant for mercantilist surplus fetishism. When deficit-phobic politicians rule the most powerful economies, a 1930s-like beggar-thy-neighbour economic war of all against all eventually rears its ugly head. Countries then compete for the world's reserves and are led, as if by an invisible hand, to a terrible economic equilibrium out of which all sorts of political and moral evils spring. After 1944 the world was blessed with New Dealers in Washington who understood all this perfectly well and who were committed to never allowing the tragedy of the 1930s to revisit the planet. Here is how LBJ's deputy national security adviser Francis Bator described their thinking and their policies in 1968:

> Through most of the postwar period the problem of inconsistency has been masked – and the world spared the damaging effect – because the United States, with the cooperation of the rest of the world, has been prepared not merely to stay out of the competition for reserves, but to play the role of world central bank, pumping out liquidity, letting others satisfy their desires for surpluses and reserves, while at the same time running down its gross reserves and increasing the nation's liquid liabilities. The system worked precisely because the United States was so long immune to deficit phobia.

Both before and after the Nixon Shock, America created a terrain on which the German, Japanese and later Chinese companies and economies could accumulate reserves and surpluses. Washington's readiness to go into the red was a prerequisite for the rest to succeed.

There was no philanthropy in this, just enlightened self-interest by American officials who understood capitalism's weird ways.

America's capacity to bear the weight of global capitalism on its shoulders diminished perilously in 2008. Wall Street's collapse was contained by the actions of people like Timothy Geithner and Ben Bernanke,[8] but America's global surplus recycling capacities did not recover. From 2009 onwards, America's lack of deficit phobia helped draw a line under the recession; the US trade deficit grew again, helping Chinese and German factories somewhat revive their damaged fortunes, and the US federal government's budget deficit continued to offer global investors the refuge they craved.[9] Nevertheless, the US deficit is no longer capable of maintaining the mechanism that kept the global flow of goods and profits balanced prior to 2008. The American Minotaur is wounded and incapable of performing the duties Paul Volcker and others assigned to it back in the late 1970s.

China's government tried valiantly to stabilize its economy – and indeed the global order – by deliberately creating an investment bubble built upon a property bubble inflated by regional government land sales.[10] While Beijing's ploy succeeded for a while in keeping Chinese, and to a large extent German, factories busy by providing them with demand for their products, the bubbles it created are now deflating. Germany exploited this made-in-China bubble to soak up the products that it had previously sent to Europe's deficit countries, such as Spain, Greece and Portugal, whose imports had collapsed in the meantime. But unlike Berlin, whose deficit phobia prevents it from realizing its duty to help recycle global surpluses, Beijing understood well both its duty and its own limitations. It comprehended that its capacity to inflate the Chinese economy out of trouble and in so doing stabilize the surplus European countries was not going to last long. That unless Europe joined America, Japan and China in helping stabilize the global flows of goods and money, China's bubbles would deflate and the world would sink into deeper trouble.[11]

Washington officials were aware this would happen and have been keeping an anxious eye out for any sign of a return to rationality by the Europeans. Alas, the deficit phobia of Europe's surplus nations, their commitment to what I labelled 'the principle of perfectly separable public debts and banking sectors' (see Chapter 7, 'Back to the

USA') and their complete subjugation of the rest of the eurozone member states have ensured that Washington, Tokyo and Beijing have received no assistance from an inward-looking macroeconomically naive eurozone.

Greece, once again, was the litmus test, a test that the Brussels–Frankfurt–Berlin triangle consistently fails. Washington has every reason to be furious with the Europeans for its deficit phobia and the detrimental effect this has. Despite the mountains of money that the Fed has printed to stimulate the domestic economy, US-based corporations refuse to invest sufficiently in quality jobs and productive machinery, fearing another chill wind from Europe that will, in a feedback loop with China's slowdown, reduce economic activity worldwide. If today the US job market is replete with American workers who would like to work longer hours but cannot, if wages are stuck in a rut, if companies prefer to use spare cash to buy back their own shares rather than invest, Europe's failings are a large part of the reason.

In short, with America's capacity to stabilize the globe gone, the greatest past beneficiaries of that now-gone capacity, the Europeans, are now abrogating their duties to America and to the rest of the world.

From Geithner's apoplexy to Lew's angst

When Timothy Geithner encountered the Europeans' gross failure to comprehend the true nature of the eurozone crisis[12] and Greece's symptomatic significance, he was brought to the verge of apoplexy.[13] His successor at the US Treasury, Jack Lew, came into the fray when things had calmed down considerably but was still struck by Europe's incomprehension of its negative impact on the global economy.

On 30 October 2013 Lew presented to Congress the Treasury Department's 'Report to Congress on Economic and Exchange Rate Policies'.[14] In it he took a swipe at Germany, accusing it of exporting economic depression to the rest of the eurozone and indeed to the global economy. Wolfgang Schäuble's ministry responded the next day with: 'There are no imbalances in Germany that need correction. On the contrary, the innovative German economy contributes significantly to global growth through exports and the import of components for finished products.'[15] It is rare in any argument for one side to be completely right and the other comprehensively wrong. This is one of them. Jack Lew was spot on and the German response utterly ludicrous. The US Treasury's underlying analysis was founded on basic macroeconomics that Berlin and the Eurogroup (as I have personally witnessed), refuses to acknowledge. The rationale is straightforward.

Berlin's plan for eurozone member states to overcome the crisis relies on a combination of net exports and balanced budgets. Given the great excess of savings over investment in both the surplus and the deficit eurozone member states, the only way Berlin's plan can work is if the eurozone turns into a mercantilist fiend. What this means in simple numbers is that to escape its crisis in this manner the eurozone must reach a current account surplus[16] in relation to the rest of the world of no less than 9 per cent of total European income.

Lest we forget, China was deemed a great destabilizing force on the global order when its trade surplus was at those levels back in 2008. Since one economy's trade surplus is another's deficit, increasing the net exports of a large economy like China or Europe means also exporting deflation to the rest of the world. A 9 per cent eurozone trade surplus would destroy the hopes of America, China, Latin America, India, Africa and South East Asia for stability and growth.[17] It would mean massive unemployment in the rest of the world, political instability and calls to erect protectionist barriers that would reduce incomes everywhere, including in Germany.

This is why the US Treasury looks at Berlin and Brussels's plans with a mixture of incomprehension and revulsion. Washington knows that if the deficit-phobic policies Berlin has been trying to foist on the rest of the eurozone (beginning with the Greek guinea pig) succeed, they will destroy whatever balance is left in the global economy. But given that ultimately these policies cannot succeed,[18] they are bound to accomplish two other tasks at once: further wreck Europe's periphery[19] and deliver continuing deflationary shocks to the global economy.

American officials have been watching all this from across the Atlantic, fretting at the sight and sound of the forces of deflation that an inane Europe, oblivious to its policies' self-defeating nature, is sending Washington's way. Personal encounters with American officials have led me to the following realizations.

1. They know America no longer has the power to stabilize the world economy by itself.
2. They understand that Europe's policies are detrimental to America's future.
3. They are frustrated that their European interlocutors are not only ignorant of simple macroeconomic laws but, curiously, not even ashamed of their ignorance.

Epilogue: religious rules ripening

When economies founder, religious inventions are never far behind. The eurozone's rules and their staying power despite their abject failure cannot be understood fully without some grasp of the manner in which religion-sourced thinking gains the upper hand at times of prolonged crisis.

During a debate in September 2015[20] Emmanuel Macron, France's minister of the economy, warned that the continuing euro crisis was ensnaring Europe in a new religious war between Catholics and Calvinists. At that point I interjected, in jest, to say that this left Orthodox Greeks out of the picture, possibly as we are a people forced to implement orthodox economic policies whose abject failure forces us to become catholic in our protestations. Less humorously, Macron and I were alluding to the lack of serious economic analysis permeating Brussels and Frankfurt and its substitution with a quasi-religious commitment to defending the eurozone's original faith. The eurozone's defenders, I would add, have taken a leaf out of the book of almost every established church: they are interdenominational when it comes to manufacturing logically impaired doctrines that politicians then parrot across the continent as truths.

Economic 'analyses' (dogmas is a better name) are endorsed only to the extent that they confirm the European Commission or the

European Central Bank's orthodox prophecies. When the facts disagree with the dogmas, it is too bad for the facts. Empirical evidence damning Ponzi austerity is, for example, met with the Jesuit-like strategy of arguing in favour of the austerity dogma and at the same time in favour of the facts that contradict the dogma. Meanwhile, the bureaucrats' rituals tighten the circle of true believers to the extent that those excluded – such as those who dare challenge the troika's pronouncements – can only be 'saved' through ceaseless repetition of incantations in praise of redemptive austerity.

The American institutionalist Clarence Ayres (1891–1972) once wrote of bureaucrats, in an uncannily prescient portrait of the Eurogroup, the European Commission, the European Central Bank, the European Stability Mechanism and the rest:

> they pay reality the compliment of imputing belief to cere-
> monial status, but they do so for the purpose of validating
> status, not for the purpose of achieving efficiency.

In important ways, Europe is being run by a web of Belief that has been separated from Reason and from Evidence. Its ways resemble less the method Descartes, Hume, Newton or Leibniz made famous and more the network of mythological convictions that anthropologist Evans-Pritchard discovered in the 1930s to be the ideological mechanism supporting the power structures of an African tribe known as the Azande:

> Azande see as well as we that the failure of their oracle to
> prophesy truly calls for explanation, but so entangled are
> they in mystical notions that they must make use of them
> to account for failure. The contradiction between experi-
> ence and one mystical notion is explained by reference to
> other mystical notions.[21]

Expediency turns 'modern' people too to ritual belief, especially so in the absence of rational debate within a functioning democracy. In times of crisis and stress modern societies caught up in ritual beliefs quickly descend into self-flagellation.

In a 2013 article entitled 'We Germans do not want a German Europe'[22] Wolfgang Schäuble argued that the majority of Europeans supported his recipe for ending the eurozone crisis (ignoring most macroeconomists, the US Treasury and the rest of the world). '[A] clear majority of people,' wrote the German finance minister 'not just in Northern Europe, but also in the south, [are] in favour of combating the crisis through reforms, public spending cuts and debt reduction.' This may well be so. But it is beside the point. Bewildered Europeans caught in a permanent downward spiral and devoid of democratic control over those whose decisions determine their lives are turning inward and blaming themselves. Back in the Middle Ages, when the Black Death hit Europe, most Europeans genuinely believed that the plague was caused by sinful living and could be exorcized through self-flagellation. They were of course wrong, but something similar is happening today.

Today the dominant text is not the Bible or its interpretations by those claiming to have a hotline to the divine. It is, rather, the rulebook created by the treaties and the bailout agreements: contractual arrangements that those who have entered the circle of the Euro-faithful must abide by or else. I know this because I experienced it personally. You have a choice, I was told in no uncertain terms, between the existing terms of your country's bailout agreement (as signed by previous Greek governments) and the highway. Fascinatingly, when I tried to start a conversation on the appropriateness and realism of these terms and the rules they relied upon, the answer was not 'The rules are fine, proper and implementable because . . .' but rather 'The rules are the rules are the rules . . .'[23]

It was a little like encountering Henry Ford all over again, only this time not in the context of selling his Model T, which a customer could order in any colour he liked as long as it was black, but at the level of international economic decision-making, where our newly elected government could choose any policy mix it liked as long as it was virtually identical to the calamitous one imposed by the troika on previous Greek governments.[24]

Religious dedication to contradictory rules that economic forces have no respect for has brought powerful empires down in the past – the Soviet Union most recently. Now the European Union seems hell-bent on treading this path to nowhere. The no-bailout rule is a good case in point. It reflected a solemn commitment when it was penned in 1993 but was impossible to observe in the face of the inevitable euro crisis that hit in 2010. Tragically, this paradox guided everything the eurozone did subsequently.

Instead of asking 'How should we deal with this crisis?' the powers that be asked an almost religious question: 'How should we bail out Greece, Ireland and the others without seeming to violate the no-bailout dogma?' It takes only a second's thought to realize that by posing the second question rather than the first Europe was bound to go astray.

A myriad of sins followed from that wrong turn. While it would have been straightforward and perfectly legal to allow Irish banks or the Greek state to default to their private creditors so as to respect the 'no bailout' clause, the authorities' guilty desire to bail out the German and French banks without telling taxpayers that this was what they were doing led to the need to violate the no-bailout rule by concocting another axiom: the no-default rule, which was never part of Europe's original set of rules. Both the freshly minted no-default rule and the original 'no bailout' clause were political whims of the strong disguised as legal constraints upon the weak. The strong break their rules at will and concoct new rules whenever they think it suits them. The most splendid example of this is Dr Schäuble's most recent ruling, which is that Greece cannot default within the eurozone but could do so if it was forced to leave the euro. This is extraordinary because, first, no such rule was ever agreed to and, second, the rules do not permit any member state to be thrown out of the eurozone.

In brief, Europe's religious dedication to rules is nothing but a veil behind which the strong make up the rules as they go along to suit their own political agenda. Perhaps that would not be so bad if the said agenda was not quick-marching Europe and the global economy into an economic, political and moral morass.

Afterword:
From Dissonance to Harmony

During the five months of 2015 in which I took a front-row crash course in Europe's political feuds I confirmed one thing: a titanic battle is being waged for Europe's integrity and soul, with the forces of reason and humanism losing out, so far, to growing irrationality, authoritarianism and malice. The rest of the world, America in particular, is concerned but not as much as it ought to be. Europe has twice in the past hundred years dragged the planet down into an appalling quagmire. It can do so again. Europe, as the New Dealers understood in the 1940s, is too important to leave to us Europeans. The whole world has a stake in the victory of rationality, liberty, democracy and humanism in the birthplace of those ideas.

Leonard Schapiro, writing on Stalinism,[1] warned us that 'the true object of propaganda is neither to convince nor even to persuade. But to produce a uniform pattern of public utterances in which the first trace of unorthodox thought reveals itself as a jarring dissonance.'[2] During five months of negotiating with the Eurogroup on behalf of Greece I bore the brunt of precisely this type of propaganda. My attempts to infuse some rational humanism into the negotiations on my country's fiscal and reform agenda were met with a concerted effort to turn our sensible proposals into such a jarring dissonance. It is quite remarkable, but somewhat disheartening, that an insightful statement once written about Stalinism has so much resonance today in the corridors of power in Brussels, Frankfurt and Berlin.

But dissidents should take heart. False dogmas are condemned to be found out eventually, in Europe as they were in the Soviet Union and elsewhere. What matters here and now is that they should be found out quickly. For the human toll of this crisis in Europe is too high and has the capacity to reach parts of the planet that do not deserve to suffer as a result of yet another European debacle. When Gandhi was asked what he thought of Western civilization, he famously replied, 'It would be a very good idea.' If asked what we think of the European Union today, we could do worse than answer, 'What a splendid idea! If only we could pull it off!'

I think we can pull it off. But not without a break from Europe's past and a large democratic stimulus that the fathers of the European Union might have disapproved of.

Acknowledgements

I began writing *And the Weak Suffer What They Must?* in 2012 after my wife Danae and I moved to Austin, where I had taken up a post at the University of Texas's Lyndon B. Johnson School of Public Affairs. My writing benefited from interaction with students at the LBJ School as well as the encouragement offered in Austin by two very special people: Danae and my great friend and colleague Jamie Galbraith.

Soon after I started researching the book, Wendy Strothman became my literary agent, Nation Books agreed to publish it and the book began to take shape. Alas, I failed to finish the first draft before January 2015. This proved a significant failure in view of the unexpected dissolution of Greece's parliament and the sudden calling of the 25 January general election, the result of which was my election to parliament and subsequent appointment as Greece's finance minister. The book's place on the back burner was thus immediately guaranteed.

Six months later I was minister no longer. Indeed, by September 2015 the parliament to which I had been elected had also been dissolved. And so during the summer of 2015 I found the time to return to my manuscript. With my head full of new facts and images from a front-row seat looking into the heart of Europe's crisis I amended the already written chapters and added new material. I was careful not to incorporate into the book my experiences from the negotiations I was involved in during the first half of 2015 and also to leave out the thriller that led our government to clash with official Europe and with the International Monetary Fund – a clash that ended with the *coup d'état* by which the government was effectively brought down.[1] Only insights pertinent to my account of what led to the euro crisis of 2010 and to Europe's inability to handle it efficiently ever since made it into the text. The thriller will have to wait for another book – to be told, as it deserves to be, from a greater distance.

Will Hammond and Alessandra Bastagli, among the other good people at Penguin Random House and Nation Books, deserve heartfelt thanks for their splendid editing, as does my brother-in-arms Nicholas Theocarakis for his usual meticulous critical comments. Lastly, I want to thank the countless people who shared ideas, facts, gossip and analyses with me, in particular Lord (Norman) Lamont for his gracious guidance regarding the events of 1990–3, as related in Chapter 5.

Appendix: A Modest Proposal

Extracts from 'A Modest Proposal for Resolving the eurozone Crisis' by Yanis Varoufakis, Stuart Holland and J. K. Galbraith, July 2013

The eurozone crisis is unfolding on four interrelated domains.

Banking crisis: There is a common global banking crisis, which was sparked off mainly by the catastrophe in American finance. But the eurozone has proved uniquely unable to cope with it, and this is a problem of structure and governance. The eurozone features a central bank with no government, and national governments with no supportive central bank, arrayed against a global network of megabanks they cannot possibly supervise. Europe's response has been to propose a full Banking Union – a bold measure in principle which is left permanently in abeyance in practice.

Debt crisis: The credit crunch of 2008 revealed the eurozone's Principle of Perfectly Separable Public Debts to be unworkable. Forced to create a bailout fund that did not violate the 'no bailout' clauses of the ECB charter and Lisbon Treaty, Europe created the temporary European Financial Stability Facility (EFSF) and then the permanent European Stability Mechanism (ESM). The creation of these new institutions met the immediate funding needs of several member-states, but retained the flawed principle of separable public debts and so could not contain the crisis. Thus, beginning in the summer of 2012, the ECB came up with another approach: monetizing public debt first through a policy that was announced but was never activated (the Outright Monetary Transactions' Program – OMT) and, in 2014, actual quantitative easing based on the odd principle of buying public debt in proportion to each national economy's size (and not in proportion to its deflationary spiral). While these measures have ameliorated the credit crunch, they have overcome neither the debt crisis nor the deflationary process afflicting the whole of the eurozone.

Investment crisis: Lack of investment in Europe threatens its living standards and its international competitiveness. As Germany alone ran large surpluses after 2000, the resulting trade imbalances ensured that, when crisis hit in 2008, demand and investment in the deficit regions collapsed. With the burden of adjustment falling on the deficit economies in the deficit zones, which could not bear it, and no mechanism for offsetting by reflation in the surplus nations, the scene was set for disinvestment in the regions that needed investment the most. Thus Europe ended up with both low total investment and an uneven distribution of that investment between its surplus and deficit regions.

Social crisis: Years of harsh austerity have taken their toll on Europe's peoples. From Athens to Dublin and from Lisbon to Eastern Germany, millions of Europeans have lost access to basic goods and dignity. Unemployment is rampant. Homelessness and hunger are rising. Pensions have been cut; taxes on necessities meanwhile continue to rise. For the first time in two generations, Europeans are questioning the European project, while nationalism, and even Nazi parties, are gaining strength.

Political constraints for any solution

Any solution to the crisis must respect realistic constraints on political action . . . . Four constraints facing Europe presently are:

(a) The ECB will not be allowed to monetize sovereigns directly in a manner that helps reduce heavy legacy debts in the countries weighed down by them. There will be no ECB purchases of government bonds in the primary market and no ECB leveraging of the EFSF-ESM to buy sovereign debt from either the primary or secondary markets.

(b) The ECB's OMT and quantitative easing programme does not match stability with growth and, sooner or later, will be found wanting.

(c) Surplus countries will not consent to 'jointly and severally' guarantee Eurobonds to mutualize debt and deficit countries. France, mainly, will resist the loss of sovereignty that would be demanded of it without a properly functioning federal transfer union which Germany, understandably, rejects.

(d) Europe cannot wait for federation. If crisis resolution is made to depend on federation, the eurozone will fail first. The treaty changes necessary to create a proper European Treasury, with the powers to tax, spend and borrow, cannot, and must not, be held to precede resolution of this crisis.

The next section presents four policies that recognize these constraints.

The Modest Proposal – Four crises, four policies

The Modest Proposal introduces no new EU institutions and violates no existing treaty. Instead, we propose that existing institutions be used in ways that remain within the letter of European legislation but allow for new functions and policies.

These institutions are:

> The European Central Bank – ECB
> The European Investment Bank – EIB
> The European Investment Fund – EIF
> The European Stability Mechanism – ESM

POLICY I – CASE-BY-CASE BANK PROGRAM (CCBP)

For the time being, we propose that banks in need of recapitalization from the ESM be turned over to the ESM directly – instead of having the national government borrow on the bank's behalf. The ESM, and not the national government, would then restructure, recapitalize and resolve the failing banks, dedicating the bulk of its funding capacity to this purpose.

The eurozone must eventually become a single banking area with a single banking authority, a single deposit insurance scheme and a common fiscal backstop. But this final goal has become the enemy of good current policy . . . Our proposal is that a failing bank should be removed from its national jurisdiction and moved to a new, dedicated eurozone jurisdiction. The ECB appoints a new board of directors with a view to resolving or recapitalizing the bank. In the latter case, the ESM provides the capital, and shares equivalent to the needed capital injection will pass to the ESM. Restructuring of the bank may entail a merger, downsizing, even a full resolution of the bank, with the understanding that steps will be taken to avoid, above all, a haircut of deposits. Once the bank has been restructured and recapitalized, the ESM will sell its shares and recoups its costs.

POLICY 2 – LIMITED DEBT CONVERSION PROGRAM (LDCP)

The Maastricht Treaty permits each European member-state to issue sovereign debt up to 60 per cent of its national income. Since the crisis of 2008, most eurozone member-states have exceeded this limit. We propose that the ECB offer member-states the opportunity of a debt conversion for their Maastricht Compliant Debt (MCD), while the national shares of the converted debt would continue to be serviced separately by each member-state.

The ECB, faithful to the non-monetization clause in its charter, would not seek to buy or guarantee sovereign MCD directly or indirectly. Instead it would act as a go-between, mediating between investors and member-states. In effect, the ECB would orchestrate a conversion servicing loan for the MCD, for the purposes of redeeming those bonds upon maturity.[1]

The conversion loan works as follows. Refinancing of the Maastricht compliant share of the debt, now held in ECB-bonds, would be by member-states but at interest rates set by the ECB just above its (ultra low) own bond yields. The shares of national debt converted to ECB-bonds are to be held by it in debit accounts. These cannot be used as collateral for credit or derivatives creation.[2] Member-states will undertake to redeem bonds in full on maturity if the holders opt for this rather than to extend them at lower, more secure rates offered by the ECB.

Governments that wish to participate in the scheme can do so on the basis of Enhanced Cooperation, which needs at least nine member-states.[3] Those not opting in can keep their own bonds even for their MCD. To safeguard the credibility of this conversion, and to provide a backstop for the ECB-bonds that requires no ECB monetization, member-states agree to afford their ECB debit accounts super-seniority status, and the ECB's conversion servicing loan mechanism may be insured by the ESM, utilizing only a small portion of the latter's borrowing capacity. If a member-state goes into a disorderly default before an ECB-bond issued on its behalf matures, then that ECB-bond payment will be covered by insurance purchased or provided by the ESM.

POLICY 3 – AN INVESTMENT-LED RECOVERY AND CONVERGENCE PROGRAM (IRCP)

The IRCP we propose is supported by the following facts.

Europe desperately needs growth-inducing, large-scale investment. Europe is replete with idle cash whose owners are too scared to invest in productive activities, fearing lack of aggregate demand once the products roll off the production line. The ECB wants to buy high quality paper assets in order to stem the deflationary expectations that are the result of the above. The ECB does not want to have to buy German or Italian or Spanish assets lest it be accused of violating its charter or favouring Germany, Italy, Spain etc.

Here is what the ECB could do to achieve its complex objectives.

The European Investment Bank (EIB) [and its smaller offshoot the European Investment Fund (EIF)] should be given the green light to embark upon a pan-eurozone Investment-led Recovery Program to the tune of 8 per cent of the eurozone's GDP, with the EIB concentrating on large-scale infrastructural projects and the EIF on start-ups, SMEs, technologically innovative firms, green energy research, etc.

The EIB/EIF has been issuing bonds for decades to fund investments, covering thus 50 per cent of the projects' funding costs. They should now issue bonds to cover the funding of the pan-eurozone Investment-led

Recovery Program in its totality; that is, by waiving the convention that 50 per cent of the funds come from national sources.

To ensure that the EIB/EIF bonds do not suffer rising yields, as a result of these large issues, the ECB can be on standby, ready to step into the secondary market to purchase as many of these EIB/EIF bonds as are necessary to keep the EIB/EIF bond yields at their present, low levels. To stay consistent with its current assessment, the level of this type of QE could be set to €1 trillion over the next few years.

In this scenario, the ECB enacts QE by purchasing solid eurobonds, as the bonds issued by the EIB/EIF are issued on behalf of all European Union states (lacking the CDO-like structure of ESM bonds). In this manner, the operational concern about which nation's bonds to buy is alleviated. Moreover, the proposed form of QE backs productive investments directly, as opposed to inflating risky financial instruments, and has no implications in terms of European fiscal rules (as EIB funding need not count against member-states' deficits or debt).

POLICY 4 – AN EMERGENCY SOCIAL SOLIDARITY PROGRAM TO FIGHT AGAINST THE RISE OF POVERTY (ESSP)

We recommend that Europe embark immediately on an Emergency Social Solidarity Program that will guarantee access to nutrition and to basic energy needs for all Europeans, by means of a European Food Stamp Program modelled on its US equivalent and a European Minimum Energy Program.

These programmes would be funded by the European Commission using the interest accumulated within the European system of central banks, from TARGET2 imbalances, profits made from government bond transactions and, in the future, other financial transactions or balance sheet stamp duties that the EU is currently considering.

Rationale

Europe now faces the worst human and social crisis since the late 1940s. In member-states like Greece, Ireland, Portugal, but also elsewhere in the eurozone, including core countries, basic needs are not being met. This is true especially for the elderly, the unemployed, for young children, for children in schools, for the disabled, and for the homeless. There is a plain moral imperative to act to satisfy these needs. In addition, Europe faces a clear and present danger from extremism, racism, xenophobia and even outright Nazism – notably in countries like Greece that have borne the brunt of the crisis. Never before have so many Europeans held the European Union and its institutions in such low esteem. The human and social crisis is turning quickly into a question of legitimacy for the European Union.

Reason for TARGET2 funding

TARGET2 is a technical name for the system of internal accounting of monetary flows between the central banks that make up the European System of Central Banks. In a well-balanced eurozone, where the trade deficit of a member-state is financed by a net flow of capital to that same member-state, the liabilities of that state's central bank to the central banks of other states would just equal its assets. Such a balanced flow of trade and capital would yield a TARGET2 figure near zero for all member-states. And that was, more or less, the case throughout the eurozone before the crisis.

However, the crisis caused major imbalances that were soon reflected in huge TARGET2 imbalances. As inflows of capital to the periphery dried up, and capital began to flow in the opposite direction, the central banks of the peripheral countries began to amass large net liabilities and the central banks of the surplus countries equally large net assets.

The eurozone's designers had attempted to build a disincentive within the intra-Eurosystem real-time payments' system, so as to prevent the build-up of huge liabilities on one side and corresponding assets on the other. This took the form of charging interest on the net liabilities of each national central bank at an interest rate equal to the ECB's main refinancing level. These payments are distributed to the central banks of the surplus member-states, which then pass them on to their government treasury.

Thus the eurozone was built on the assumption that TARGET2 imbalances would be isolated, idiosyncratic events, to be corrected by national policy action.

The system did not take account of the possibility that there could be fundamental structural asymmetries and a systemic crisis.

Today, the vast TARGET2 imbalances are the monetary tracks of the crisis. They trace the path of the consequent human and social disaster hitting mainly the deficit regions. The increased TARGET2 interest would never have accrued if the crises had not occurred. They accrue only because, for instance, risk-averse Spanish and Greek depositors, reasonably enough, transfer their savings to a Frankfurt bank. As a result, under the rules of the TARGET2 system, the central banks of Spain and of Greece have to pay interest to the Bundesbank – to be passed along to the Federal Government in Berlin. This indirect fiscal boost to the surplus country has no rational or moral basis. Yet the funds are there, and could be used to deflect the social and political danger facing Europe.

There is a strong case to be made that the interest collected from the deficit member-states' central banks should be channelled to an account that would fund our proposed Emergency Social Solidarity Programme (ESSP). Additionally, if the EU introduces a financial transactions' tax, or stamp duty proportional to the size of corporate balance sheets, a similar case can be made as to why these receipts should fund the ESSP. With this proposal, the ESSP is not funded by fiscal transfers or national taxes.

CONCLUSION: Four realistic policies to replace five false choices

Years of crisis have culminated in a Europe that has lost legitimacy with its own citizens and credibility with the rest of the world. Europe is unnecessarily still on a low-investment, negligible growth path. While the bond markets were placated by the ECB's actions, the eurozone remains on the road towards disintegration.

While this process eats away at Europe's potential for shared prosperity, European governments are imprisoned by false choices:

between stability and growth
between austerity and stimulus
between the deadly embrace of insolvent banks by insolvent
    governments, and an admirable but undefined and indefi-
    nitely delayed Banking Union

between the principle of perfectly separable country debts and
the supposed need to persuade the surplus countries to
bankroll the rest

between national sovereignty and federalism.

These falsely dyadic choices imprison thinking and immobilize govern-ments. They are responsible for a legitimation crisis for the European project. And they risk a catastrophic human, social and democratic crisis in Europe.

By contrast the Modest Proposal counters that:

The real choice is between beggar-my-neighbour deflation and an investment-led recovery combined with social stabilization. The invest-ment recovery will be funded by global capital, supplied principally by sovereign wealth funds and by pension funds which are seeking long-term investment outlets. Social stabilization can be funded, initially, through the TARGET2 payments scheme.

Taxpayers in Germany and the other surplus nations do not need to bankroll the 2020 European Economic Recovery Programme, the restructuring of sovereign debt, resolution of the banking crisis, or the emergency humanitarian programme so urgently needed in the European periphery.

Neither an expansionary monetary policy nor a fiscal stimulus in Germany and other surplus countries, though welcome, would be sufficient to bring recovery to Europe.

Treaty changes for a federal union may be aspired to by some, but will take too long, are opposed by many, and are not needed to resolve the crisis now.

On this basis the Modest Proposal's four policies are feasible steps by which to deal decisively with Europe's banking crisis, the debt crisis, underinvestment, unemployment as well as the human, social and political emergency.

While broad in scope, the Modest Proposal suggests no new insti-tutions and does not aim at redesigning the eurozone. It needs no new rules, fiscal compacts or troikas. It requires no prior agreement to move in a federal direction while allowing for consent through enhanced cooperation rather than imposition of austerity.

It is in this sense that this proposal is, indeed, modest.

References

Allin, D. (2011), 'De Gaulle and American Power' in B. M. Rowland (ed.), *Charles de Gaulle's Legacy of Ideas*, New York: Lexington Books

Ambrose, S. E. (1989), *Nixon, Vol. 2: The Triumph of a Politician 1962–1972*, New York: Simon and Schuster

Ball, G. (1982), *The Past Has Another Pattern*, New York: Norton

Bator, F. (1968), 'The Political Economics of International Money', *Foreign Affairs* 47(1)

Bator, F. (2001), 'Lyndon Johnson and Foreign Policy: The Case of Western Europe and the Soviet Union' in A. Lobel (ed.), *Presidential Judgement: Foreign Policy Decision Making in the White House*, Washington: Hollis

Becker, A. (2013), 'German Economic Miracle: Thanks to Debt Relief', *Deutsche Welle* website, http://www.dw.de/german-economic-miracle-thanks-to-debt-relief/a-16630511, last accessed December 20, 2014.

Brecht, B. (1989), *The Threepenny Opera*, trans. C. I. Isherwood and D. I. Vessey, London: Penguin

Condorcet, M. de (1795), *Outlines of an historical view of the progress of the human mind: being a posthumous work of the late M. de Condorcet*, London: Johnson

Connolly, B. (1995), *The Rotten Heart of Europe*, London and Boston: Faber & Faber

Coudenhove-Kalergi, R. N. (Graf von) (1923), *Pan-Europa*, Vienna: A. A. Knopf, second edn 1926

Crawford, A. F. and Keever, J. (1973), *John B. Connally: Portrait in Power*, Austin: Jenkins

Dallek, R. (1995), *Franklin D. Roosevelt and American Foreign Policy: 1932–1945*, Oxford: Oxford University Press

Eichengreen, B. (2011), *Exorbitant Privilege: The Rise and Fall of the Dollar*, Oxford: Oxford University Press

Evans-Pritchard, E. E. (1937, 1976), *Witchcraft, Oracles and Magic among the Azande*, Oxford: Clarendon

Ferrell, R. H. (ed.) (2010), *Inside the Nixon Administration: The Secret Diary of Arthur Burns, 1969–1979*, Lawrence: University Press of Kansas

Funk, W. (1942), 'Das wirtschaftliche Gesicht des neuen Europa', *Europäische Wirtschaftsgemeinschaft*, Berlin: Verein Berliner Kaufleute und Industrieller & Wirtschafts-Hochschule Berlin

Galbraith, J. K. (2012), *Inequality and Instability: A Study of the World Economy Just Before the Great Crisis*, Oxford: Oxford University Press

Galbraith, J. K. and Varoufakis, Y. (2014), 'Wither Europe? The Modest Camp versus the Federalist Austerians', openDemocracy.org, 11 June 2014, https://opendemocracy.net/can-europe-make-it/james-galbraith-yanis-varoufakis/whither-europe-modest-camp-vs-federalist-austeri

Geithner, T. (2014), *Stress Test: Reflections on Financial Crises*, New York: Broadway Books

Gilbert, M. (2003), *Surpassing Realism: The Politics of European Integration Since 1945*, Oxford: Rowman and Littlefield

Godley, W. (1992), 'Maastricht and All That', *London Review of Books* 4(19), 8 October 1992, 3–4

Gray, W. G. (2007), 'Floating the System: Germany, the United States, and the Breakdown of Bretton Woods, 1969–1973', *Diplomatic History* 31(2), 295–323

Gros, D. and Thygesen, N. (1992), *European Monetary Integration: From the European Monetary System to the European Monetary Union*, London: Longman

Habermas, J. (1975) *Legitimation Crisis*, trans. T. Macarthy, Boston: Beacon Press, German original published 1973

Halevi, J. and Varoufakis, Y. (2003), 'The Global Minotaur,' *Monthly Review* 55 (July–August), 56–74

Hersh, S. (1983), *The Price of Power: Kissinger in the Nixon White House*, New York: Simon and Schuster

Kaldor, N. (1980), *Collected Economic Essays of Nicholas Kaldor*, London: Wiley, published on behalf of the Royal Economic Society; see Chapter 12, 'Further Essays on Applied Economics', 187–220

Keynes, J. M. (1920), *The Economic Consequences of the Peace*, New York: Harcourt Brace

Keynes, J. M. (1924), *A Tract on Monetary Reform*, London: Macmillan

Keynes, J. M. (1925), *The Economic Consequences of Mr Churchill*, London: Hogarth Press

Keynes, J. M. (1932), 'The World's Economic Outlook', *Atlantic Monthly* 149 (May), 521–6

Keynes, J. M. (1936), *The General Theory of Employment, Interest and Money*, London: Macmillan

Keynes, J. M. (1949), *Two Memoirs: Dr Melchior, a Defeated Enemy, and My Early Beliefs*, New York: A. M. Kelley

Keynes, J. M. (1980), 'Closing Speech, Bretton Woods Conferences, July 22, 1944' in D. E. Moggridge (ed.), *Collected Writings of John Maynard Keynes, Vol. XXVI, Activities 1941–1946; Shaping the Post-War World, Bretton Woods and Reparations*, London: Macmillan for the Royal Economic Society

Kissinger H. (1994), *Diplomacy*, New York: Simon and Schuster

Kissinger, H. (1979), *The White House Years*, New York: Simon and Schuster

Klinkowstroem, A. de (1880), *Mémoires, documents et écrits divers laissés par la prince de Metternich chancelier de cour et d'état*, Paris: Plon

Krotz, U. and Schild, J. (2012), *Shaping Europe: France, Germany and Embedded Bilateralism from the Elysée Treaty to 21st Century Politics*, Oxford: Oxford University Press.

Laughland, J. (1997), *The Tainted Source*, London: Little, Brown and Co.

Lipgens, W. (ed.) (1984), *Documents on the History of European Integration, Vol. 1: Continental Plans for European Union 1939–1945*, New York: Walter de Gruyter

Lipgens, W. and Loth, W. (eds) (1988), *Documents on the History of European Integration, Vol. 3: The Struggle for European Union by Political Parties and Pressure Groups in Western European Countries 1945–1950*, New York: Walter de Gruyter

Ludlow, P. (1982), *The Making of the European Monetary System*, London: Butterworth

Marshall, M. (2012), *The Bank: The Birth of Europe's Central Bank and Rebirth of Europe's Power*, New York: Random House Business

Mirowski, P. and Plehwe, D. (2009), *The Road from Mont Pelerin: The Making of the Neoliberal Thought Collective*, Cambridge, MA: Harvard University Press

Mitchell, B. (2015) *Eurozone Dystopia: Groupthink and Denial on a Grand Scale*, Cheltenham: Edward Elgar

Naumann, F. (1915, 2012), *Mitteleuropa*, trans. C. M. Meredith from the original classic edition, London: Forgotten Books

Piketty, T. (2014), *Capital in the Twenty-First Century*, Cambridge, MA: Belknap Press

Reinert, E. S. (2004), *Globalization, Economic Development, and Inequality: An Alternative Perspective*, Aldershot: Edward Elgar

Rosamond, B. (2000), *Theories of European Integration*, Basingstoke: Palgrave Macmillan.

Rowland, B. M. (ed.) (2011), *Charles de Gaulle's Legacy of Ideas*, New York: Lexington Books

Rueff, J. (1971), *The Monetary Sin of the West*, New York: Macmillan

Schaller, M. (1996), *The Nixon 'Shocks' and the United States–Japan Strategic Relations'*, Woodrow Wilson Center, Washington, DC

Schaller, M. (1997), *Altered States: The United States–Japan Relations since the Occupation*, New York: Oxford University Press

Schoenborn, B. (2014), 'Chancellor Erhard's silent rejection of de Gaulle's Plans: the Example of Monetary Union', *Cold War History* 14(3), 377–402

Silber, W. L. (2012), *Volcker*, New York: Bloomsbury Press

Stephey, M. J. (2008), 'A Brief History of the Bretton Woods System', *TIME*, 21 October; see http://content.time.com/time/business/article/0,8599,1852254,00.html, last accessed on 9 December 2014

Stiglitz, J. (2013), *The Price of Inequality: How Today's Divided Society Endangers Our Future*, New York: W.W. Norton

Stuermer, M. (2011), 'The General and the Germans' in B. M. Rowland (ed.), *Charles de Gaulle's Legacy of Ideas*, New York: Lexington Books

Triepel, H. (1906), *Unitarismus und Föderalismus im Deutschen Reich*, Tübingen: J. C. B. Mohr (Paul Siebeck)

Varoufakis, Y. (2011), *The Global Minotaur: America, Europe and the Future of the World Economy*, London: Zed Books; second edn 2013, third edn 2015

Varoufakis, Y., Halevi, J. and Theocarakis, N. (2011) *Modern Political Economics: Making Sense of the Post-2008 World*, London and New York: Routledge

Varoufakis, Y., Holland, S. and Galbraith, J. K. (2013), 'A Modest Proposal for Resolving the eurozone Crisis', https://varoufakis.files.wordpress.com/2013/07/a-modest-proposal-for-resolving-the-eurozone-crisis-version-4-0-final1.pdf. Available in book form in German (published by Kunstman) and in French (published by the Veblen Institute), with a foreword from former French prime minister Michel Rocard

Varoufakis, Y. (2015), 'Dr Schäuble's Plan for Europe: Do Europeans Approve?' *Die Zeit* (29), 15 July 2015. English version available at http://www.zeit.de/2015/29/schuldenkrise-europa-wolfgang-schaeuble-yanis-varoufakis.

Volcker, P. A. (1978–9), 'The Political Economy of the Dollar', *FRBNY Quarterly Review*, Winter, 1–12 (Fred Hirsch lecture at Warwick University, Coventry, England, 9 November 1978)

Notes

Preface: The Red Blanket

1. Glezos, whose political activism began in May 1941 when he climbed, with Apostolos Santas, the walls of the Acropolis to remove, unseen by German sentries, the swastika flag, has been leading the campaign for German war reparations to Greece and, more poignantly, for the repayment by the German state of an enforced 'loan' extracted by the German high command from the Bank of Greece during the occupation.

2. Karl Marx and Friedrich Engels, *The Manifesto of the Communist Party*.

1 And The Weak Suffer What They Must

1. John Connally's lewd metaphor is quoted in Schaller (1996, 1997). So impressed was Nixon with Connally's no-nonsense perspective on what needed to be done with Europe (and, to a lesser extent, Japan) that, according to Kissinger (1979), Ambrose (1989) and Hersh (1983), the president asked his closest confidants to 'figure out how the hell we can get [Vice President] Agnew to resign early' with a view to replacing him with Connally – his 'logical successor' as Nixon called him.

2. The swoop in question was the delinking of the value of the dollar from gold. Of course, President Nixon dressed up this awful announcement as a domestic US measure: 'a New Economic Program complete with tax cuts and a 90-day wage and price freeze' (Eichengreen, 2011, p. 60).

3. See Silber (2012), Chapter 5.

4. For ten months after the Nixon Shock Washington humoured the Europeans with negotiations on how to re-establish the fixed exchange rates between the dollar and European currencies. An agreement was indeed reached, called the Smithsonian Agreement or Accord. Alas, it was too late, and in America neither

Connally nor Volcker, nor indeed anyone else, truly believed that the vase, once broken, could be repaired.

5. These are not Connally's exact words (which have not been taken down for posterity) but they do capture quite accurately the spirit of his message. Upon exiting these meetings, he diplomatically, and misleadingly, put on a face of American neediness when addressing reporters covering his tour of European capitals. His precise words were: 'We told them that we were here as a nation that had given much of our resources and our material resources and otherwise to the world to the point where frankly we were now running a deficit and have been for twenty years, and it had drained our reserves and drained our resources to the point where we could no longer do it and frankly we were in trouble and we were coming to our friends to ask for help, as they have so many times in the past come to us to ask for help when they were in trouble. That is in essence what we told them.' Transcript of archival material from BBC Radio 4's *Analysis: Dollars and Dominance*, broadcast at 20.30 BST on Thursday, 23 October 2008.

6. Connally used this precise phrase in November 1971 at a meeting of finance ministers in Rome, in the context of a regular G10 meeting. He was widely reported to have used the same phrase, behind closed doors, during his tour of European capitals in the previous August. See Crawford and Keever (1973).

7. Paul Volcker, who was later to become president of the New York Federal Reserve, before President Carter appointed him chairman of the Federal Reserve in 1978, was instrumental in persuading John Connally to convince President Nixon to 'jettison' Europe. Not everyone in the administration was happy. Indeed, Arthur Burns, who in 1970 had been appointed chairman of the Federal Reserve by Richard Nixon (and whom Volcker replaced in 1978) had these pointed words to say: 'Poor and wretched Volcker – never knowing where he stood on any issue – had succeeded in instilling an irrational fear of gold on his tyrannical master [John Connally], whom he tried constantly to please by catering to his fear of foreigners (particularly the French) instead of his capacity (not inconsiderable) for straight reasoning.' See Ferrell (2010), p. 65.

8. Interestingly, both John Connally and Paul Volcker were lifelong Democrats drafted by Nixon into his Republican administration. This put them at odds with a number of Republicans in the administration who opposed their combined drive to persuade President Nixon to make his shocking announcement in 1971.

9. See Bator (2001).

10. Francis Bator, who worked closely with President Johnson on what to do with Bretton Woods, published an article in *Foreign Affairs* at the time (see Bator, 1968) outlining in detail the administration's plans to effect a gradual transformation of Bretton Woods. The idea was to introduce far greater flexibility into the system without, however, destroying it, as its sudden disintegration would cause enormous social damage both within and outside the United States.

11. This characterization of Volcker is Richard Nixon's. He called him that when he heard that Volcker might have been responsible for a story leaked to the *Wall Street Journal*, to the effect that America was facing a 'tremendous crisis on the international monetary front'. Nixon feared that Volcker had leaked the story to put pressure on Connally to do that which, in the end, Nixon himself did on 15 August 1971: end the Bretton Woods system.

12. White had earned his economics PhD at Harvard and had served in the US Treasury Department as assistant to Secretary Henry Morgenthau Junior. A convinced internationalist, he not only helped create the International Monetary Fund but also became the IMF's first managing director. The IMF and the World Bank had been designed in Bretton Woods as the system's twin institutional pillars. In 1947 he resigned abruptly under a cloud of innuendo that he had acted as a Soviet spy. He died the following year of a heart attack.

13. War undoubtedly makes for odd bedfellows. In 1925 John Maynard Keynes had authored a pamphlet entitled 'The Economic Consequences of Mr Churchill'. This lambasted Churchill, who would in 1943 send him to Bretton Woods to represent his government, for having dragged Britain back into the gold standard. In the pamphlet Keynes argued that the pound had been fixed at too high a value vis-à-vis gold and prognosticated, accurately, that the gold standard would prove a ball and chain for the British economy, causing an unnecessary, never-ending recession. Keynes's pamphlet can be credited for having depleted support for the gold standard among UK opinion makers to such an extent that, following the crash of 1929, Britain was among the first countries to exit it; which it did in 1931 to ameliorate the Great Depression, two years before President Roosevelt pulled the United States out. Perhaps it is worth noting also that the pamphlet's title was a wordplay on the earlier book that had made Keynes famous: *The Economic Consequences of the Peace*, published in 1919, which presciently warned that the harsh reparations imposed by the Versailles Treaty upon a defeated Germany would inflict as much pain on the vengeful victors as it would on Germany.

14. In 1936 Keynes's views on capitalism were captured in his tour de force, *The General Theory of Employment, Interest and Money* (Keynes, 1936). By September 1941 Keynes had distilled these thoughts into a 'plan' for the future of global capitalism which he presented at Bretton Woods in 1944 (Keynes, 1980). His take on the task he and his fellow negotiators had undertaken at the Bretton Woods conference is summed up in this sentence: 'We have had to perform at one and the same time the tasks appropriate to the economist, to the financier, to the politician, to the journalist, to the propagandist, to the lawyer, to the statesman – even, I think, to the prophet and to the soothsayer' (Keynes, 1980, p. 101).

15. Thucydides, *The History of the Peloponnesian War*, Book 5, s. 89: 'δυνατὰ δὲ οἱ προύχοντες πράσσουσι καὶ οἱ ἀσθενεῖς ξυγχωροῦσιν.'

16. Ibid. s. 90, my translation and emphasis.

17. Keynes's warning came in the form of his book *The Economic Consequences of the Peace* (1919).

18. The decoupling of the dollar from the yen, the franc and the Deutsche Mark caused European and Japanese manufacturers to lose much of their advantage vis-à-vis American multinationals as the dollar plummeted. Meanwhile, the dollar price of oil skyrocketed, further jeopardizing German and Japanese manufacturers, whose exposure to foreign oil imports was always greater than that of American companies.

19. Perhaps the most stunning epitaph to Keynes's proposal came in 2011, in the midst of the euro crisis. Here is how I described it in the epilogue to my book *The Global Minotaur: America, Europe and the Future of the World Economy* (Varoufakis, 2013).

> I was ever so surprised, the other day, listening to a radio interview by Dominique Strauss Kahn, the IMF's managing director, responding to a journalist's question about how the global economy ought to be reconfigured in the aftermath of the 2008 Crisis. His astonishing answer was, 'Never in the past has an institution like the IMF been as necessary as it has been today . . . Keynes, sixty years ago, already foresaw what was needed; but it was too early. Now is the time to do it. And I think we are ready to do it!' The date was 21 January 2011. Four months later, Strauss Kahn was forced to resign his stewardship of the IMF, following his arrest in a New York hotel on sexual assault charges that were, subsequently, dropped.

20. See George Krimpas's 'The Recycling Problem in a Currency Union', which appears as an addendum to Chapter 12 of Varoufakis et al. (2011).

21. See Keynes (1932).

22. In Keynes's 1941 words, under fixed exchange rates 'the burden of adjustment [will be thrown] on the country which is in the *debtor* position on the international balance of payments, – that is on the country which is (in this context) by hypothesis the *weaker* and above all the *smaller* in comparison with the other side of the scales which (for this purpose) is the rest of the world.' Keynes (1980), p. 27.

23. When President Roosevelt suggested that the only thing Americans had 'to fear is fear itself' he was alluding to the self-fulfilling terror that prevents private surplus funds from being invested when most needed, and to the need for political intervention that overcomes this fear through directing investments to states and regions where the greatest debts, unemployment and deficits are concentrated. Roosevelt's vision was to be later reinforced, after Pearl Harbor, by his administration's eye-opening experience of running the war economy, gathering decisive evidence, if any was needed, that there is nothing natural about high unemployment and that depression is a failure of policy, not an act of God that we ought to submit to.

24. It is worthwhile comparing Nevada's fate with that of Ireland – a member of that other currency union, the eurozone. Just like Nevada, in 2008 Ireland faced a massive collapse of its real estate and banking sectors. But unlike Nevada, Ireland had to fend for itself when it came to propping up its banks and paying its unemployment benefits. Lacking a printing press, it had to go cap in hand to the money markets to borrow huge quantities of money that, in Nevada's case, had been paid for at the federal level. Naturally, the money markets, caught up in their credit-crunch mentality, would not cough up the money at anything below usurious interest rates. Thus, Ireland ended up accepting a massive loan from European governments, the European Central Bank and the International Monetary Fund, which rendered the Irish state insolvent and pushed its society into long-term negative equity. Nevada, in the meantime, exited the crisis quickly and with very little debt in comparison.

25. Similarly with America's military budget, which from the early phases of the Second World War was mobilized not only in order to win the war against Japan and Germany but also the war against unemployment and poverty, which had persisted in the wake of the Great Depression. To this day, when Boeing or Lockheed are awarded defence contracts, these come with conditions requiring them to build production facilities in deficit states like Tennessee or Missouri. Such surplus recycling, ushered in for the first time by the New Dealers in the 1930s and 1940s, allowed the dollar zone – also known as the United States of America – a degree of protection from recessions, which begin in the deficit regions and spread out like menacing bushfires into the surplus states.

26. Besides the IMF, which is still with us (performing, post-1971, a very different role to that envisaged for it at Bretton Woods), a second institution was designed at the 1944 conference. This was the International Bank for Reconstruction and Development (IBRD), today known simply as the World Bank. Whereas the IMF was proposed by Keynes as the world's central bank, to issue and manage the world currency, the IBRD's purpose was to mobilize idle savings and turn them into productive investments in relatively underdeveloped deficit nations. And just as the IMF ended up functioning very differently, so did the World Bank. Nevertheless, of these two Bretton Woods institutions, it is the World Bank that remains more faithful to Keynes's initial intentions.

27. In this context, the IMF had an additional role: it would provide short-term loans to nations that needed to defend their exchange rates due to some unexpected trade deficit or while the IMF was in the process of approving a devaluation.

28. If we add to this the speculator's cost of borrowing from the French banks, which they would now have to fork out themselves, it is easy to see why a Bundesbank intervention was a scary prospect for the speculators.

29. German surpluses are only recycled to the rest of Europe by means of what I earlier referred to as fair-weather recycling; that is, the kind of recycling effected by Frankfurt's commercial banks. This type of recycling, as explained above, inflated bubbles during the good times and did nothing to aid recovery once the bubbles burst. In contrast, American surpluses during the Bretton Woods era were directed by means of a political recycling mechanism that smoothed out credit shortages in the deficit countries at times of crisis and prevented the build-up of bubbles during periods of growth.

30. A development partly due to the increased productivity and better technology of German and Japanese industries, improvements unlikely to have materialized without the consistent support of American policymakers.

31. Computed at the Bretton Woods fixed rate of $35 per ounce.

32. Prior to the Nixon Shock, there were two markets for gold: the official market, in which large banks and governments traded their stocks of gold at $35 per ounce, and the unofficial or shadow market, for example informal transactions between jewellers and private individuals who traded gold on a smaller scale but at prices considerably higher than the official level. By the late 1960s the unofficial price had risen to $55 per ounce, revealing the Bretton Woods system's high stress levels. However, for speculators to make big profits from their bet that gold would rise further, it was essential that the big players (banks and governments) were also released from the official price.

33. Exactly as the French authorities relied on the Bundesbank to keep the Deutsche Mark price of the French franc stable.

34. In 1968 a desperate situation called for desperate measures. Central banks agreed to stick to the $35 per ounce price when trading gold among themselves but allowed the commercial price to rise at will, even when it came to large-scale trades between banks. These twin prices – one official, one unofficial – were a major defeat for global capitalism. The West could no longer berate the Soviets for lying about the true value of the rouble, quoting an official exchange rate that bore no relation to the rouble's black-market value. Now the dollar also had two values in terms of gold: one official, one unofficial. Furthermore, this 'solution' did not solve anything much. The greater the divergence of the unofficial price of gold from its official $35 value the greater the confidence of speculators that they would, in the end, force Washington to devalue the dollar relative to gold and other currencies.

35. The 'special relationship' with the United States that Britain was proclaiming as a replacement for its imperial reach was interpreted by de Gaulle as evidence that, if Britain were to be admitted to the European Union, it would act as Washington's Trojan horse.

36. In 1965 President de Gaulle ordered the removal of 25,900 bars of gold, weighing more than 350 tons, from the basement under the New York Federal Reserve and their transportation to Paris. It was a logistical nightmare whose symbolism was made more poignant because it involved the French navy's unfriendly return to the shores of the United States. (See the *New York Times*, 2 March 1965, p. 45.) The trigger, however, for the Nixon Shock was the British government's demand that $3 billion held by the Bank of England be swapped for American-held gold at the official $35 per ounce, which trailed the unofficial price by at least $18. That announcement was made on Wednesday, 11 August 1971. It was the straw that John Connally and Paul Volcker ensured would break Bretton Woods's back, which is what they convinced President Nixon to do the following weekend in their Camp David meetings.

37. See Stephey (2008).

38. After the Nixon Shock, the French government changed its tune instantly. From open hostility to the idea of a dollar-backed global financial system (see Chapter 2), President Pompidou began demanding that the United States reconstitute Bretton Woods, even if that meant a lower dollar value in relation to gold and other currencies. When Washington rebuffed the French president's demands, Pompidou pleaded. President Nixon indulged him in December 1971 with an agreement at the Smithsonian Institution in Washington, in the context of a G10 meeting. The idea was to give Bretton Woods another chance with new, more 'realistic' exchange rates. Except that it was too late. The genie was out of the bottle and it refused to get back in. Within eighteen months major currencies were floating and Europe was in deep trouble.

2 An Indecent Proposal

1. Kurt Schmücker was not atypical of the Christian Democrats who ruled West Germany uninterruptedly from 1949 until 1969. At the tender age of eighteen, in 1937, he joined the Nazi Party and three years later went to war, serving in the *Wehrmacht* till the bitter end. A year after the war ended, he joined the Christian Democrats and became the party's youngest member of the federal parliament in the 1949 elections. In 1963, after Ludwig Erhard (an accomplished economist who had been minister of finance since 1949 and overseen Germany's impressive economic reconstruction 1949–63) became Germany's chancellor, Schmücker took over the Ministry of the Economy. Having only completed a typography course, Schmücker nursed much anxiety about his capacity to take over Erhard's role. As it turned out, both Erhard and Schmücker were booted out of government in 1966 as a result of Germany's first postwar recession, which was arguably engineered for political purposes by the Bundesbank.

2. The EEC was renamed the European Union by the Treaty of Maastricht, 1 November 1993, at the same time as the rules governing the euro were agreed. In this book I shall refer to the EEC as the European Union for purposes of continuity.

3. Their conversation began with Schmücker addressing Giscard's concerns that free trade within the European Union would create trade imbalances that would destabilize the exchange rate between the franc and the Deutsche Mark. He suggested that EU members should sign a formal contract and abide by agreed rules of contact regarding government fiscal and monetary policies so the system would be stable. Giscard had other thoughts. The dialogue below is quoted in Schoenborn (2014).

GISCARD: This is too little! We have not yet talked about it in the government, but de Gaulle has told me that dangerous developments as we are now experiencing cannot be avoided or overcome without a common currency of the EEC countries. We need a single currency for the EEC!

SCHMÜCKER: In order to achieve the same effect, the currencies can also be maintained nominally while the monetary policies of the individual Member States are put under strict discipline through contractual rules.

GISCARD: Why choose this system, which works only as long as everybody goes along?

SCHMÜCKER: I am just looking for a successful method without obliging France to renounce her sovereignty. A single EEC currency would be a supranational matter. So far France has been speaking out against any kind of supranational arrangement.

GISCARD: De Gaulle has told me explicitly that he deems a single EEC currency necessary. He takes the view that no other way remains. If one state repeatedly pushes another into inflation, the only ones to benefit are the Socialists.

SCHMÜCKER: What do we do, if the other four will not join in? The creation of a monetary union is a decisive political step forward. Once the monetary union is accomplished, further political consequences will automatically ensue. Erhard's attempts to advance the political union have not produced the desired response from all governments. Hence we can expect that the proposal will be sceptically received. Or do you imagine that France and Germany should forge ahead?

GISCARD: An agreement between France and Germany should be considered only if the others do not participate. In this case the agreement must be drafted in such a way that others will have the option, both legally and practically, to join in at any time.

4. See Gray (2007).

5. *Planification* refers to the penchant French administrators have had since the time of Napoleon for grand, large-scale planning. Examples of *planification* span urban development, energy policy (especially the plan that resulted in the extraordinary production of more than 95 per cent of French electricity by state-owned and -designed nuclear power stations), the creation of an advanced military-industrial complex, the superfast railways crisscrossing France and spilling into Britain and Belgium, even projects like Concorde and Airbus Industrie – the successful competitor to Boeing.

6. A full account of the designs that Erhard frustrated to become Germany's chancellor follows.

7. See Schoenborn (2014).

8. Giscard was a committed Keynesian who had little time for de Gaulle's conservative views on how an economy should be managed. In particular, he harboured considerable contempt for Jacques Rueff, an economist who believed strongly in the gold standard and whom de Gaulle considered his economic guru. As a result, Giscard's tenure as finance minister in de Gaulle's cabinet was precarious.

9. To give one such example, in 1962 General Motors fired French workers without consulting the French government. A year later, in 1963, it purchased French car maker Simca and immediately proceeded to sack a portion of its workforce. Meanwhile, General Electric was eyeing a number of plants that Paris viewed as of strategic importance for France.

10. The phrase is frequently, and mistakenly, attributed to de Gaulle. Its rightful procreator was Giscard. Here is how Jacques Rueff, the French economist whose theories Giscard rejected (but with whom he had to work) explained what Giscard meant by exorbitant privilege:

> [W]hen a country with a key currency runs a balance-of-payment deficit – that is to say, the United States, for example – it pays the creditor country dollars, which end up with the latter's central bank. But the dollars are of no use in Bonn or in Tokyo or in Paris. The very same day, they are re-loaned to the New York money market, so that they return to the place of origin. Thus the debtor country does not lose what the creditor country has gained. So the key-currency country never feels the effect of a deficit in its balance of payments. And the main consequence is that there is no reason whatever for the deficit to disappear, because it does not appear. (Rueff, 1971, p. 78)

11. See Ball (1982), p. 271.

12. Konrad Adenauer made his mark in German politics well before the Second World War, serving as Cologne's mayor from 1917 to 1933. A devout Catholic and a committed opponent of Prussia's dominance of Germany, he used his office to argue for a new Rhenish state within the Weimar Republic, liberated from Berlin's iron rule. When his efforts led nowhere, he initiated talks with French officials with a view to establishing an autonomous Rhineland within the context of a grand Central European design that would bring German–French reconciliation. While he was later acquiescent in the rise of the Nazi Party, which he tried to accommodate within the Cologne city administration, the Nazis considered Adenauer an unsafe patriot for having come so close to the French in the 1920s. At war's end, the bombed-out Cologne found itself in the British zone and Adenauer was asked to serve again as the city's mayor. He agreed but in December 1945 suffered the humiliation of being dismissed by a British army general for 'incompetence' when in reality his dismissal was due to his public statements condemning the city's unrestrained wartime bombing by the RAF. Adenauer never forgave the British for this humiliation.

13. John Wills Tuthill, at the time US ambassador to the European Economic Community.

14. In 1953 the United States famously convened a conference in London to cajole Germany's creditors into accepting a huge reduction of the defeated country's debts to them.

15. See Schoenborn (2014).

16. See NSC Meeting Memo, 5 February 1963, 4.30 p.m., FRUS, 1961–3, vol. 13, 175–9; Memorandum of Conversation, Carstens and Rusk, 5 February 1963, 6 p.m., ibid., 186; NSC Meeting, 31 January 1963, ibid., 162, Kennedy Library.

17. The preamble emphasized 'the supreme importance of transatlantic cooperation' and was devised as a 'solution' to the Elysée Treaty 'problem' by American officials, who lost no time in letting Erhard's office know that it should be considered. The preamble in essence annulled the treaty's spirit of creating a Franco-German alliance independent of the United States. According to Erhard's presentation of the preamble to Bonn parliamentarians, the preamble was essential in order 'to liberate the Elysée Treaty from any wrong interpretation of German policy'.

18. See Schoenborn (2014).

19. From 1945 to 1958.

20. So fierce was de Gaulle's opposition to the idea of an American-designed European economic community (which emerged formally in 1950 as the European Coal and Steel Community) that he went into the political wilderness until 1958, when the Fourth Republic's collapse gave him the opportunity to refashion the French constitution, and France's politics, in his image.

21. American readers ought to take note that de Gaulle's sharp criticism of the US postwar global plan was one that significant American policymakers shared. For example, George F. Kennan (a diplomat whose Long Telegram from Moscow begat the logic of 'containing' the USSR) and Robert Taft (the Senate Republican leader who opposed President's Roosevelt's New Deal) also deplored the prospect of a world divided into American and Soviet spheres in opposition to each other. Their difference with de Gaulle was that the French president had the means and the determination to make the American bloc unmanageable.

22. See Connolly (1995), p. 7.

23. Their thinking was simple: if the French state forfeited the right to print money, either by reverting to the gold standard or by adopting the Deutsche Mark, prices would stop rising and the trade unions would lose all bargaining power over employers; with the government unable to boost overall demand, especially during a slump, the trade unions would have a choice between accepting high unemployment – which would destroy their power base – and accepting low wages. In short, by forfeiting its printing presses the French state would ensure that organized labour became less militant, more 'German'. And if this also meant a greater propensity to recession, it was considered a small price to pay. Today, with France in permanent stagnation under the euro, France's elite is simultaneously unapologetic regarding that choice and concerned about the rising tide of discontent and anti-European racist ultranationalism.

24. 'By war!' See Connolly (1995), p. 7.

25. Erhard's rebellion against Adenauer should be placed in the context of many Germans' fear of an American withdrawal. Paul Volcker is quoted by his official biographer as saying that he 'recalled JFK's threat . . . to cut off military aid to Europe unless Europeans promised not to attack the dollar as the world's currency.' See Silber (2012), p. 55.

26. In a fascinating, and exceedingly rare, coincidence of opinions both the *Wall Street Journal* and *Pravda* (the Soviet Communist Party's official newspaper) hailed de Gaulle's call for a return to the gold standard as 'inspired'. The *Wall Street Journal* did so because, following the way the Roosevelt administration dealt with Wall Street, it never had liked the New Dealers, while the Soviets, one of the planet's primary gold producers, had every reason to see demand for gold rise.

27. Quoted in Laughland (1997), p. 231.

28. Jacques Rueff was an influential economist whom de Gaulle had known for years before, in 1958, turning to him to disinflate the French economy just as the general was making his political comeback (which saw him found the Fifth Republic before becoming its first president). De Gaulle was nursing painful memories of how he had lost power shortly after the war because of runaway inflation. So when Rueff succeeded in killing inflation off in 1958, which involved erasing a number of zeros from the currency, tying the franc's new value firmly to the dollar and keeping state spending under strict control, de Gaulle was impressed. Rueff was a 'goldbug', a believer in tying the quantity of paper money to the quantity of gold in the state's possession to prevent politicians from messing with the currency's value. This helps explain why de Gaulle, in his attempt to discredit America's dollar-backed global financial system, turned to the gold standard as an alternative. However, it is my considered opinion that de Gaulle was an opportunistic adopter of the gold fetish, unlike Rueff, who was a true believer. Perhaps it is important also to note that Rueff was a member of the libertarian Mont Pelerin Society, alongside economists like Friedrich von Hayek and Milton Friedman. For the significance of this society see Mirowski and Plehwe (2009). De Gaulle, who was wedded to the French tradition of a state-planned economy, tolerated Rueff's libertarian economic views only because, unlike Hayek, Rueff accepted the state's leading ethical, cultural and social role in society.

29. According to Allin (2011), de Gaulle felt that just as the USSR was overstretched logistically and militarily across Eurasia, the United States was overstretched financially across the breadth and width of the Bretton Woods system.

30. See Dallek (1995). Germany's return to a pastoral economy was the express intention of the Morgenthau Plan, named after Henry Morgenthau Junior, US treasury secretary, and co-signed by the United States and Britain on 16 September 1944. In the spring of 1945, after Germany had surrendered to the Allies, General Eisenhower issued a directive to US commanders in Germany, coded JCS1067, ordering them to desist from 'taking steps towards the rehabilitation of Germany [or] designed to maintain or strengthen the German economy'. JCS1067 clearly stated that deindustrialization and a reduction in German living standards were the intention. On 1 August 1945, at the Potsdam Conference, the United States, the USSR and Britain agreed on the 'reduction or destruction of all civilian heavy-industry with war potential' and on 'restructuring the German economy towards agriculture and light industry'. In 1946 the Allies reduced Germany's steel production to less than six million tons annually, around 75 per cent of Germany's prewar steel output. As for car production, it was decided that output should dwindle to around 10 per cent of what it was before Germany invaded Poland.

31. See Dallek (1995).

32. See Reinert (2004), p. 158.

33. For a longer exposition of the historical events in this section, see Varoufakis (2013), Chapter 3.

34. Even though, it must be said, the United States had a track record on this: after the Versailles Treaty of 1919, which imposed intolerable reparations upon

Germany after the Great War, America was unique among the victors in supporting the German economy with credit and bilateral deals that lessened the burden the treaty placed upon the defeated country.

35. Secretary of defense and previously secretary of the navy.

36. James Byrnes's successor as secretary of state and deliverer of the infamous Marshall Plan.

37. George Marshall's successor in the State Department.

38. Recall Chapter 1.

39. Heavy industry centres are typified by large, networked, powerful corporations. To cover their overheads these entities must have large outputs and contain their labour costs. This means that local people (mostly wage earners) cannot consume all that the factories are producing. This is why powerhouse economies require a hinterland to generate the necessary demand for their surplus goods. If the exchange rate between the powerhouse economy and the hinterland is fixed, the hinterland will remain in permanent trade deficit in relation to the powerhouse economy. To keep financing these permanent deficits, surplus recycling is necessary. In good times banks play that role, which Chapter 1 described as fair-weather recycling.

40. De Gaulle briefly came out of retirement in 1954 to shoot down in the French national assembly the idea of a European defence community, confirming his rejection of a German–French alliance under the Pax Americana umbrella. Then, in 1958, when France was deeply embroiled in the hideous Algerian colonial war, he was appointed prime minister to sort out the mess. Only he, as the nation's war hero, had the authority to pull French troops out of France's own Vietnam. After that, and with Jacques Rueff's successful monetary reforms which killed off inflation, the road was clear for the general to rewrite the constitution to create the Fifth Republic and move into the presidency. It was at that stage that he very reluctantly accepted the notion of a united Europe revolving on a Franco-German axis, in which France would play the dominant administrative role.

41. Kennan was working in the US embassy in Moscow, from where in February 1946 he sent the Long Telegram analysing the reasons why the United States ought to consider the task of containing the USSR its top priority. At that same time, Greek left-wing partisans, who had led the glorious resistance to the Nazis, were being persecuted by the British-backed government and Nazi sympathizers. In March 1946 a regiment of these partisans opened hostilities against the government and thus Greece's second, and most lethal, civil war began.

42. The Truman Doctrine was America's declaration that what begins in Greece ends up as a major confrontation with the USSR. It committed funds and resources to supporting the Greek national army against the partisans, who received next to no support from a Soviet Union bound by its Yalta Agreement

commitments to concede to Greece remaining in Britain's sphere of influence. When Britain withdrew from the Greek civil war, exhausted by its own economic crisis in 1946, it passed the baton to President Truman.

43. Harry Truman had moved into the White House after President Roosevelt's death in 1945.

44. He made a comeback in 1957 as chairman of Deutsche Bank, a post that he kept until 1967.

45. See Becker (2013).

46. On 28 October 1940, as German forces wiped the floor with the Allies everywhere else, Mussolini gave the Greek government an ultimatum: surrender or be invaded. Greece rejected it; Italy invaded from already occupied Albania and a ramshackle Greek army defeated the invaders, scoring the first Allied victory of the Second World War. Hitler was forced to delay his invasion of the Soviet Union and divert forces to the Balkans in order to subdue the 'annoying' Greeks. This five-month delay helped the Soviets immensely as the German troops, by the time they reached Russia's steppes, had to reckon with . . . General Winter. Moreover, from 1942 to 1944 Greek partisans constantly engaged the Nazi occupiers, causing considerable damage and confining them to the urban centres. The price the Greek population suffered was immense, in terms of murders, persecution, destruction of the country's infrastructure and famine.

47. See Preface.

48. Naumann (1915, 2012).

49. Coudenhove-Kalergi (1923).

50. His words in a letter dated September 7, 1914, quoted in Laughland (1997), p. 115.

51. During the first year of the Marshall Plan the total sum involved was of the order of $5.3 billion, a little more than 2 per cent of the United States' GDP. By 31 December 1951, when the Marshall Plan came to an end, $12.5 billion had been spent. The result was a sharp rise in European industrial output (about 35 per cent) and, more importantly, political stabilization and the creation of sustainable demand for both European and American manufactured products.

52. See Rosamond (2000), pp. 20–21.

53. Technically speaking, the European Union was formed in 1993, with the Maastricht Treaty. Before that it was known as the European Economic Community or European Common Market. For simplicity, throughout this book I use the term European Union to refer to the continuum of institutions and treaties which began in 1950 and, in the process, yielded today's European Union.

54. See the *New York Times*, 2 March 1965, p. 45.

55. Lyndon B. Johnson had to restrain his own administration officials from lashing out at the French. Prompted by them to respond belligerently, he turned them down flat, saying, 'When someone asks us to leave their house, we leave.' See Bator (2001).

56. As explained previously, no politician likes headlines announcing devaluation. Equally, politicians in surplus countries, whose exchange rates need to go up, know that such a revaluation will anger exporters, whose goods and services will cost foreigners more, leading to a fall in sales.

57. Recall that under the Bretton Woods arrangements finance ministers met regularly at the IMF's Washington offices to discuss any necessary changes in the official exchange rate between their currencies. At those meetings, and while the dollar and the franc were under pressure from speculators, American officials routinely told their German counterparts something simple: 'Either the Bundesbank must print more Deutsche Marks or you must agree to an increase in the value of the mark here and now.' German politicians were in a difficult position. They could not fully control what the Bundesbank did. Moreover, if they agreed to increase the value of the Deutsche Mark, they would incur the wrath of the Bundesbank and of German exporters – a supremely powerful alliance that shared an interest in low German inflation (the Bundesbank's main concern, and the reason it was reluctant to print more and more Deutsche Marks) and a stable (non-rising) exchange rate consistent with export growth.

58. See Connolly (1995), p. 7.

59. Willy Brandt, the Social Democrats' progressive leader, was vice chancellor. He emerged from that role with his reputation and image strengthened to the extent that, at the 1969 general election, he succeeded in winning sufficient votes to form the first Social Democratic administration (in alliance with the small Free Democratic Party), pushing the Christian Democrats into opposition for the first time. Karl Schicker of the Social Democrats and Franz Josef Strauss, leader of the ultra-conservative Bavarian Christian Social Union, shared the economic ministries during the years of the grand coalition: Strauss was minister of finance and Schiller minister of the economy. Later, in 1971, Schiller moved to the Ministry of Finance.

60. Cut to 1997. Europe was preparing for its common currency and Germany was dictating to the rest of Europe its terms for abandoning its cherished Deutsche Mark and turning the Bundesbank into a franchise of the jointly owned European Central Bank. One of these conditions was that the whole of Europe submit to a stability and growth pact brimming with the philosophy of 1967.

61. Monetary tightening usually involves boosting interest rates. By increasing the cost of borrowing francs, or equivalently increasing the interest paid to those who save them, Paris aimed to attract more money to French bank accounts from abroad. If investors indeed responded by converting their dollars and Deutsche Marks to francs in order to take advantage of higher franc bank account interest rates, the international demand for francs would increase, thus boosting the French currency's value – as de Gaulle intended. The downside of an interest rate rise was that the cost of investing in France rose and, all other things being equal, economic activity and jobs would suffer. Which is precisely what happened on this occasion.

62. See Stuermer (2011).

63. See Gray (2007).

64. See Gray (2007).

65. These were the events and developments that take us, full circle, to the beginning of Chapter 1 and John Connally's brash invocation to his president to 'screw the foreigners'.

66. I owe this quotation to Klaus Kastner.

67. Four years after *Le Figaro*'s outrageous article, Lucas Delattre wrote in the pro-European *Le Monde*, 'At bottom, Chancellor Kohl has succeeded in obtaining peacefully what others have attempted to obtain by conquest since Bismarck: a zone of peace and of prosperity all around Germany' (1 January 1996). What had changed? How had we gone from the euro operating like another Versailles Treaty that made Germany 'pay' to a German triumph that Bismarck would applaud? The answer is that in 1993 the Bundesbank ensured that France's monetary ambitions were crushed. The fact that millions of Europeans suffered unemployment and hardship in the process was nothing more than collateral damage. But more of this in later chapters.

3 Troubled Pilgrims

1. The European Monetary System was meant as a European version of Bretton Woods, following the latter's unravelling after the 1971 Nixon Shock (see Chapter 2). See Ludlow (1982).

2. *Corriere Della Sera*, 16 September, 1978, mentioned in Ludlow (1982), p. 182.

3. Schmidt was also a former finance minister (1972–4). He replaced the popular chancellor Willy Brandt in 1974 after a spy scandal implicating a Brandt aide forced the latter's resignation. Like Brandt, Schmidt ruled in coalition with the small Free Democratic Party (FDP), but in 1982 the FDP swapped sides, voted Schmidt out of office and went into a new coalition with the Christian Democrats under Chancellor Helmut Kohl – the man who would, together with Giscard's successor, President François Mitterrand, inaugurate the euro in 1992 (signing the Maastricht Treaty, which replaced the EMS with the common currency known as the euro).

4. See, for instance, Connolly (1995).

5. Marshall (2012) reports that Giscard and Schmidt later suggested that the idea for a European central bank came to them in Aachen cathedral when paying their respects to Charlemagne.

6. Recall the explanation in Chapter 1 of why a common currency or fixed exchange rates squeeze the deficit nations into the ground in times of crisis in the absence of political surplus recycling, which the gold standard certainly lacked. See section 'Political surplus recycling, or barbarism'.

7. Which, under finance minister and head of the Reichsbank (as the German central bank was known during and before the war) Hjalmar Schacht, was unrestrained by the gold standard and free to adjust the quantity of money in a manner that enabled the Nazi regime to boost output and employment from 1933 to 1938.

8. See Chapter 2, section entitled 'Tumult across the Rhine', for a reminder of how the president of the Bundesbank admitted to having taken strong action to topple Erhard's government.

9. Countries that were meant to join the union the following year. In the end only Britain, Ireland and Denmark joined in 1973, Norway refusing to do so to this day.

10. The constraints were even tighter than at Bretton Woods. Whereas under Bretton Woods currencies were allowed to fluctuate by plus or minus 1 per cent in relation to the dollar, in Europe's snake the permitted oscillations were limited to plus or minus 0.75 per cent in relation to the Deutsche Mark. This meant that, for instance, the Belgian franc was meant to stay within the extremely tight range of 19.85–20.15 francs to one Deutsche Mark. To confine the Belgian franc to such a narrow tunnel, Belgium and Germany's central banks had to intervene constantly, with the former using up its stock of marks and dollars to buy Belgian francs, and the latter printing Deutsche Marks also to buy Belgian francs.

11. '[O]nce the sequence of bankruptcies has begun, incomes are destined to fall while the private and public debts to the foreign banks remain the same. The price of a fixed exchange rate is a bankrupt state in a death embrace with impecunious citizens and an insolvent private sector.' See Chapter 1, section entitled 'Political surplus recycling, or barbarism'.

12. For example, the European Exchange Rate Mechanism (ERM) in the early 1990s. See Chapter 4, section entitled 'Frankfurt's long shadow'.

13. On 28 February 1978, to be precise.

14. See Gilbert (2003), p. 143. Schmidt's preference for a right-wing victory in France is less puzzling than it seems at first. Even though he was on the centre left, he feared that a centre-left French government would embark on a spending spree that the Bundesbank would see as a *casus belli*, making it impossible for Schmidt to convince Germany's elites to accept monetary union with France.

15. Recall Chapter 2, section entitled 'Tumult across the Rhine'.

16. Located in Coventry, England.

17. See Volcker (1978–9).

18. It is also full of clues as to Chancellor Schmidt's thinking regarding the necessity of the European Monetary System. But more on this later.

19. 'Unearned income' refers to rents, income from the ownership of paper assets including bonds and stocks, property rights over a piece of land that happens to contain gas or oil, etc. In contrast, 'earned income' refers to wages for labour services provided and profits from entrepreneurial activity.

20. Paradoxically, during the Great Depression real wages did not fall. Indeed, they increased a little. Money wages, that is wages measured in dollars, fell steeply, but prices fell even faster, ensuring that those with jobs saw their purchasing power rise. The problem which made that depression 'great' was that very few workers managed to keep their jobs so as to benefit from increased real wages.

21. This is a common theme in all serious studies of inequality. See Galbraith (2012), Stiglitz (2013) and Piketty (2014).

22. In the first two decades of the twentieth century financialization occurred in conjunction with the creation of the first networked corporations. As the construction of electricity power stations and grids required massive capital investment, smaller banks combined forces to form megabanks, which then financed new megacorporations such as Edison, General Electric and Ford. The rise of the megabanks created a surge of newly minted private money (as the bankers had the capacity to lend much larger sums), which boosted the stock exchange, creating the roaring 1920s, which of course crashed and burned in 1929.

23. Recall the exchange in Thucydides's *Peloponnesian War* between the Athenian generals and the Melians, whom they enslaved after having razed their city to the ground. Also see Chapter 1, section entitled 'The Melians' reply'.

24. See Marquis de Condorcet (1795).

25. That the Soviet sphere of influence would also be severely damaged added considerable impetus to his project.

26. The same attitude resurfaced in Berlin in the early 2000s, when US-sourced private money minting was making it possible for the rest of Europe to boost its purchases of German exports while the German state was keeping a lid on German wages and state expenditure.

27. Recall the explanation in Chapter 1 of why capitalism faces a stark choice between political surplus recycling and 'fair-weather' recycling which leads, eventually, to barbarism.

28. I first used the allegory of a global Minotaur to describe the second postwar phase of American economic dominance in an article jointly authored with Joseph Halevi; see Halevi and Varoufakis (2003). Later it became the inspiration for the title of my book on the global crisis; see Varoufakis (2011).

29. *Le Monde*, 16 November 2011. 'La décision de faire participer la Grèce à la monnaie unique était une grave erreur.' Interview by Jérôme Gautheret.

30. *Les Echos*, 18 February 2015. 'Valéry Giscard d'Estaing: "La Grèce doit sortir de l'euro."' Interview by Nicolas Barré.

31. Eurexit is my neologism for the expulsion of Europe from the dollar zone, following the 1971 Nixon Shock. Regarding Grexit, Giscard is not the only eurozone pioneer to contemplate it seriously. Germany's finance minister Wolfgang Schäuble is another.

32. This dialogue, between Mitterrand and Delors, was related to me by former British parliamentarian and economics professor Stuart Holland, a colleague and a friend of mine who worked at that time, in the early 1990s, as Delors's adviser. Stuart was privy to these conversations and his account will be appearing in his autobiography, when it is finished.

33. Recall the previous chapter's account of how the European Union was constructed as the political administration of a Central European heavy industry cartel, unlike the United States, which was always a political mechanism to mediate between belligerent social classes and antagonistic vested interests.

34. The Werner Report was commissioned in 1968, as the European Commission was beginning to fear that the Bretton Woods system was on its last legs. It was written in 1969 and submitted to the European Commission in 1970, foreshadowing Europe's monetary union.

35. See the article that appeared in the *New Statesman* on 12 March 1971, entitled 'The Dynamic Effects of the Common Market'. Also reprinted in Kaldor (1980).

36. See previous note.

4 *Trojan Horse*

1. My emphasis. Readers can watch this speech online. Just visit YouTube and type into the search box 'Margaret Thatcher's last speech as prime minister' or 'in Parliament'.

2. The Eurogroup is, in effect, the body that makes all the important decisions concerning the running of the eurozone, one of the world's largest economies. It consists of the finance ministers of the eurozone member states, the president of the European Central Bank, the economics and finance commissioner of the European Commission and, interestingly, a representative from the International Monetary Fund, usually the head of the IMF's European desk but on occasion the managing director herself. Remarkably, the Eurogroup is an informal body. While its power is immense, it does not exist in European law and is accountable to no properly instituted body including the European

Parliament. Europe's democratic deficit is nowhere as pronounced as in the Eurogroup.

3. See previous note.

4. Quoted in Connolly (1995), p. 121.

5. Recall Chapter 2, section entitled 'War by other means'.

6. When the financial crisis hit the United States in 2008, the state of Nevada did not have to borrow from international investors in order to bail out the banks operating in Nevada or to pay the unemployment benefits of laid-off construction workers. The federal government did that through the FDIC (Federal Deposit Insurance Corporation) and its federal social security and unemployment insurance funds. This is why Nevada bounced back instead of falling into a black hole of state insolvency that would have led to huge austerity, which in turn would have shrunk further the Nevadan economy. Federal institutions capable of stabilizing both banks and state governments were clearly what the eurozone needed; for example, a proper banking union that would include FDIC-like powers to resolve and recapitalize at the level of the union.

7. Such examples included the European Financial Stability Facility, its successor the European Stability Mechanism and the so-called Banking Union, instituted in 2014, which sounds very much like a US federal system for supervising and dealing with bank failures (the FDIC-Fed) but which in reality is a pseudo-union whose true nature is confirmed in the breach of federal principles rather than in their observance. See Chapter 6.

8. European Union law was traditionally initiated, debated and passed at the European Council, which comprises heads of European governments as well as the councils of ministers representing member states on particular issues. European legislation is determined at an intergovernmental level, with national parliaments signing off after the event and without any opportunity to introduce amendments to the laws that heads of governments have already agreed. This process of law-making preceded the creation of the European Parliament. Courtesy of its late arrival on the political landscape, the European Parliament has always played second fiddle to the European Council. Even today, after decades of struggling to acquire more legislative powers for itself, the European Parliament has no right or capacity to initiate legislation but is confined to a rubber-stamping role.

9. Which is, of course, the claim of the Scottish National Party and its campaign for Scottish national independence.

10. Under the pretext of the 'emergency' their monetary union had amplified.

11. Recall Volcker's University of Warwick speech (see section entitled 'That "goddamn Volcker", again' in Chapter 3) in which he advocated a 'controlled disintegration in the world economy' as 'a legitimate objective for the 1980s'.

12. Once again encounter the awful dilemma of a deficit country's government, which must either abandon its ambition to keep its currency pegged to that of a surplus country or introduce policies that reduce the nation's deficits (trade and government budget) by means of austerity, which diminishes incomes, destroys jobs and lowers the state's capacity to come to the aid of its weaker citizens.

13. A German carmaker who manufactures gearboxes in Portugal, engines in Slovakia and car electronics in Germany, and who plans to sell these cars in Europe, is happier when these countries use the same currency. Prior to the euro, the expectation of exchange rate fluctuations between, say, Portugal's escudo and the Deutsche Mark introduced a despised element of uncertainty. Oligopolists prefer to worry about fluctuations in demand for their wares, which they can handle through discounts or intra-European trading, than to have their cost accounting messed up by the vagaries of the foreign exchange markets.

14. Schmidt was instrumental in organizing the failure and eventual overthrow of the radical leftist government that took over in Portugal after the 1975 revolution, which ended a long right-wing dictatorship. He also played a key role in preventing the Left from making gains during the transition of Spain from Franco's fascist regime to parliamentary democracy.

15. Greek pensions had already declined by approximately 40 per cent between 2011 and 2014. The majority of Greece's poor were low-pension over-sixty-year-olds for whom life had become nasty, brutish and increasingly short. (Life expectancy began to fall for the first time in seventy years.) Against this background, Greece's creditors were demanding of me acquiescence in a further cut in pensions amounting to more than 1 per cent of national income; they also proposed the elimination of a small sum (around 100 euros monthly, known as the 'social solidarity payment') paid to those on ridiculously low pensions (e.g. on 200 euros per month).

16. A deficit country (like France) operating within a monetary union with a surplus country (like Germany) cannot avoid capital flight the moment the monetary union is hit by a crisis. At the slightest hint that the monetary union may dissolve and the two countries will re-create their national currencies, anticipating a devaluation of the deficit country's money, savers prefer to take their cash out of the banks of the deficit country and transfer it to a bank in the surplus country. Thus money emigrates en masse from the deficit to the surplus country; economic activity in the deficit country wanes, and, as a result, the deficit country's tax revenues fall and its national budget goes increasingly into the red. This is the reason why the euro crisis put France's national budget under increasing strain.

17. As a crisis within a monetary union builds, capital flight from deficit countries into surplus countries benefits not only the surplus countries' banks but also

their governments. The reason Germany's government budget benefited from the euro crisis was that much of the foreign money coming into Germany was used to buy government bonds – German public debt. As demand for these bonds increased, the German government could issue new bonds offering lower interest rates (think of these interest rates as the price Germany had to pay to borrow: the greater the demand for its debt, the lower the price Berlin had to pay) Indeed, the flow of money from the deficit countries to Germany's public debt helped Germany's government save more than €80 billion between 2011 and 2014 in the form of the reduced cost of debt servicing.

18. A sequence of such U-turns was to follow over the years. That of the Greek socialist party (PASOK) government in 2010 is a case in point, followed a few months later by the Spanish and Portuguese socialist parties, and the Irish Labour Party, which implemented a full-on austerity government following the collapse of Ireland's banks. President François Hollande also reversed course immediately after his election in 2012. However, the most spectacular conversion of an anti-austerity European government to one pursuing such an agenda was that of the Syriza government in Greece. A stand-off between Greece and the Eurogroup led in July 2015 to our utter capitulation and, of course, to my resignation from the Ministry of Finance. The exact process by which our government was defeated is another story, which cannot be covered here.

19. Trichet would inherit the presidency of the European Central Bank in 2003. Perhaps the most lamentable central banker ever, he increased interest rates a couple of months before the world of finance imploded in the autumn of 2008. As if that were not enough, a year after the euro crisis commenced, in 2011, he increased interest rates once more just as Europe's monetary union was falling off a cliff.

20. See Connolly (1995), p. 97.

21. As always, any increase in the Bundesbank's interest rates made it that much harder for the franc to keep up with the Deutsche Mark's value, forcing the French authorities into even more austerity and the political and social costs that this entailed in order to maintain the semblance of a strong franc.

22. In the end the process took three years longer (the euro was inaugurated in 2000) but, more importantly, the process was nothing like as smooth as planned.

23. See Gros and Thygesen (1992), p. 166. Years later I came across Daniel Gros in Brussels while serving as Greece's finance minister. He had the same faith in the superior logic of the monetary union's design, and the perpetual clashes between that faith and reality had dented neither his belief nor his professional standing.

24. Total public debt could not exceed 60 per cent of national income, and government budget deficits had to stay below 3 per cent of national income.

Puzzlingly, no limits were placed on private debts and deficits, the result being Ireland's and Spain's crises in 2009–11.

25. See Connolly (1995), p. 121.

26. The rejection was unexpected because all the mainstream parties had recommended acceptance. This was not the only such event. In Ireland and in France 'no' campaigns in similar votes did exceedingly well despite mainstream parties being in favour of the Brussels line.

5 The One That Got Away

1. Recall from the previous chapter how Margaret Thatcher's downfall was triggered by her intransigent opposition to Europe's monetary union. Tony Benn (1925–2014) was a giant of Britain's Left. A member of Parliament for almost fifty years and cabinet minister in Harold Wilson's government, Benn was an exemplar of Britain's democratic socialist tradition. During the 1975 referendum that brought the United Kingdom into the European Union, Benn opposed entry. His position resonated powerfully with that of many British Conservatives, who also feared the diminution of Parliament's authority, albeit for different reasons; namely, the imperative to hold to the principle of one nation, one parliament, one currency (see Chapter 4, section entitled 'Not in its nature'). Today a new Labour leader, Jeremy Corbyn, who has been influenced greatly by Tony Benn, is trying to work out his strategy over the European Union while the current Tory prime minister, David Cameron, is preparing for a referendum that will decide whether Britain leaves the European Union altogether or stays to continue whining from within, confined to the increasingly lonely space reserved for countries that are in the union but not in the eurozone.

2. Except when one nation state imposes upon all the rest its own standards, rules and regulations, as the United States has been attempting to do with the transatlantic and trans-Pacific trade deals known as TTP and TTIP.

3. All developments spearheaded by the shift towards financialization that came after the Nixon Shock and Paul Volcker's Minotaur-related exploits. See Chapter 3 especially the section entitled 'A timeless beast', and Varoufakis (2011, 2013).

4. Take for example the housing market. When prospective buyers have more money, in aggregate, to spend on a fixed number of houses, more money is chasing each house, thus pushing house prices up – a typical case of inflation.

5. That is, increasing interest rates every time the Bank of England estimated that the total amount of money (a measure called M3, which included banknotes and liquid deposits, for example current account deposits) was rising at a faster rate than the quantity of goods and services produced.

6. The European Monetary System-European Exchange Rate Mechanism inaugurated in 1978 (recall Chapter 3).

7. As the pound–mark exchange rate weakened, and each pound bought fewer Deutsche Marks, the sterling price of German imports into Britain rose. At a time when the dollar was also rising vis-à-vis the pound, pushing transport and energy costs up, and Britain's post-1983 growth sucked into the UK more imports, prices rose across the board. The weaker the pound, the higher the rate of inflation. This is why by 1990 German inflation was so much lower than Britain's.

8. In practical terms that meant setting a target exchange rate between the Deutsche Mark and pound sterling of 2.95 to 1 with a plus or minus 6 per cent margin of fluctuation. This meant that if the pound fell below 2.775 Deutsche Marks, Britain's authorities were committed to intervening by buying Deutsche Marks or pushing British interest rates up in order to keep the pound within the agreed band.

9. In a private communication he told me, 'We needed to lower our inflation rate urgently, and actually the ERM did achieve that spectacularly. The effect was felt via inflationary expectations for a long time afterwards, and that helped create the boom that benefited Blair and Brown. I don't think we would have got inflation down so far so quickly without being in the ERM. The mistake was in not withdrawing from the ERM, as I urged Major in summer 1992, when inflation had fallen and was in a further downward trajectory.'

10. The pound always rises when the Labour Party loses an election, especially when opinion polls are pointing to a Labour victory. Nothing enthuses the money markets more than an unanticipated Tory victory.

11. The Bundesbank was ultra-worried that the federal government's largesse towards East Germans would boost inflation. To contain it, it increased interest rates.

12. See Connolly (1995), p. 142.

13. See Connolly (1995), p. 148.

14. Lamont's recommendation was motivated by true-blue Tory instincts. EMS-ERM membership translated into terribly tight money. Monetarists like Lamont believe that reducing the quantity of money during recessionary times makes a recession much worse. So the EMS-ERM forced Lamont to borrow and spend more as a fiscal counterbalance to tight money. But this went against Lamont's ideological revulsion at deficit spending. By exiting the EMS-ERM, Lamont was able to let interest rates slide, increase the money supply and thus unhook himself from the necessity to follow what he considered to be a Keynesian fiscal policy.

15. Lamont's own account, as he related it to me, is: 'What happened was that I was in Washington on September 18 and I was asked by a reporter why I was so cheerful. I replied, "It's a beautiful sunny day. But it's funny you say that, as my wife said she heard me singing in the bath this morning." So the story is not quite as the myth has become. But the press rightly perceived that I did not regard our exit from the ERM as an unmitigated disaster. My view is that the ERM performed a task as an anti-inflation tool and that it disintegrated in my hands when it had fulfilled its usefulness. We benefited from being in and we benefited from getting out.'

16. After the Labour Party came to office in 1997, the new prime minister, Tony Blair, was keen to join the political project that was the euro. Just as in the case of John Major, Blair's chancellor Gordon Brown slammed the brakes on entry into the eurozone long enough to give the euro a chance to demonstrate its unsuitability. Lamont and Brown, whatever their failures, proved pivotal in keeping Britain out of the eurozone, the result being that the errors made during their reigns had mild effects on the British economy when compared to the calamity unfolding in continental Europe. The reason of course was that the British finance ministry, the treasury, benefited from the constant support of the Bank of England, which was willing and able immediately to counter recession with looser money. This capacity was sadly designed out of the European Central Bank at the behest of the Bundesbank, whose condition for not strangling the euro at birth was precisely that: the ECB should not have either the capacity or the institutional tendency to come to the aid of recessionary economies under its purview.

17. Sweden and Finland experienced a large influx of foreign money while the EMS-ERM illusion lasted. Speculators were attracted to high profit rates and, once they believed that their currencies' value (when measured in Deutsche Marks) was stable, licked their lips in anticipation of high returns from sending their money to Stockholm and Helsinki. Swedish and Finnish banks lent the inflowing capital as if there was no tomorrow, helping create bubbles in various sectors. When the EMS-ERM broke down, and the Nordic currencies devalued, a mountain of debt in foreign currency became unpayable; the debtors went bust, and so did Sweden's and Finland's banks. In 1992 the governments of Sweden and Finland were forced to step in, bail out the banks, nationalize them and sell them back to the private sector after they had been cleansed of bad loans. While the resulting recession was sharp, the manner in which the banking disaster was dealt with should go down in history as a success story. If only the eurozone had dealt with its 2008–12 banking crisis in a similar manner.

18. France has a unique constitution that allows for the 'cohabitation' of a socialist president and a conservative prime minister if the latter secures a majority in parliament in midterm elections.

19. The 'yes' campaign won with 50.8 per cent, with just below 540,000 votes separating it from the 'no' vote out of 26,381,000 cast.

20. By 'looser money' economists refer to the readiness to set lower interest rates. Lower interest rates in Germany were always good news in deficit countries like Britain and France, as they lessened the flow of capital from them to Germany.

21. The first being that Berlin wanted a single currency for political reasons and to liberate German exporters from the constant fear of devaluation of their foreign clients' currencies.

22. That had to wait for the euro crisis to hit in 2010, setting off a chain reaction that led to Paris losing control of . . . Paris.

23. Allowing a British trade unionist who had opposed the privatization of Britain's electricity industry to tell me triumphantly that the sector had been renationalized – except by the wrong nation!

24. The friend shall remain anonymous as he is currently in a European Union post that might be jeopardized by such a revelation.

25. Recall the section entitled 'France's slow-motion defeat' in Chapter 4.

26. Recall the section entitled 'Aspirational riff-raff' in Chapter 4.

27. On the day the European Central Bank was inaugurated in Frankfurt a number of officials likened its establishment to the coronation of Charlemagne and the creation of a Christian European empire. It may not be not too indelicate at this point to add a further footnote: that it took the hideous murder of thousands of Muslim men in Srebrenica a year later, in 1995, and the spectacular failure of European United Nations' peacekeepers to protect them for Europe to discover that there were home-grown Muslim European citizens for whom a revival of Charlemagne's legacy offered no attraction.

28. A political surplus recycling mechanism steps in when the fair-weather recyclers, the banks, exit in a hurry, leaving behind them ruins and unpayable debts. A political mechanism for investing into these regions during a depression is the only way a fixed exchange rate can be maintained without emptying the deficit country of people and turning it into a giant golf course for visiting bankers. Recall Chapter 1's section entitled 'Political surplus recycling, or barbarism'.

29. A shorter version of this was told to me by Lord (Norman) Lamont as we were preparing for a head-to-head debate; I believe it was in Melbourne. Our friendship began more or less at that point.

30. *Le Figaro*, 18 September 1992.

31. In this context Italy and Spain should suffer worse recessions by keeping the lira and the peseta higher than optimal for their labour markets, while Germany should revalue its currency at the expense of its exporters to accommodate the *franc fort* fantasy.

32. Connolly (1995), p. 170, quotes Keynes (1924): 'Each time the franc loses value, the Minister of Finance is convinced that the fact arises from everything but economic causes. He attributes it to the presence of foreigners in the corridors of the Bourse, to unwholesome and malign forces of speculation. The attitude is rather close to that of the witch doctor who attributes the illness of cattle to the "evil eye", and the storm to an insufficient quantity of sacrifices made before some idol.'

33. This being the only way that the depressed country's exports could become competitive without further reductions in wages and domestically produced prices.

34. I did not believe that the threat of enforced exit was credible. It is mainly for this reason that I resigned when my prime minister told me he was about to capitulate. I shall have much more to say on this in a full account dedicated to the Athens Spring and its crushing.

6 *The Reverse Alchemists*

1. This is banker-speak for securing an interest rate somewhat above the bank's own borrowing rate and, hopefully, above interest rates charged to the bank's average client.

2. After the 2008 financial sector implosion, the banks with the most risk managers ended up in the deepest of black holes. The Royal Bank of Scotland, to give one example, employed *four thousand* risk managers and ended up needing a £50 billion bailout from the British taxpayer.

3. During 1998–2007 interest rates fell everywhere as credit was turbocharged by the shenanigans of the West's financiers. However, Germany's increasing trade surplus in relation to Europe's south and the resulting flow of money to Germany meant that the price of money (the rate of interest) in Germany was always lower than in Southern Europe.

4. The greater the supply of loans to a debtor like the Greek state, the lower the interest rate the bank had to charge to convince the debtor to take on even more loans. Thus the difference, or spread, between the interest rates paid by the Greek and the German governments shrank, giving even more incentive to the bankers to lend even more money to such debtors.

5. One way to help a stressed debtor is to reduce the interest rate charged or to prolong the repayment period without charging additional interest. Such interest rate relief naturally reduces the value that the creditor will recoup.

6. If I write on a piece of paper 'I, Yanis Varoufakis, confirm that I shall pay the bearer of this piece of paper a sum of X euros by such-and-such a date. This piece of paper is freely transferable' to the extent that I am considered credit-worthy, such an IOU has market value and could be sold by a bearer who prefers a sum less than X now than to wait until the specified date to collect X euros.

7. And when these IOUs expired, the whole process was repeated, with the banks issuing new IOUs that the government guaranteed again so they could be swapped with the IOUs about to expire.

8. The only difference between us was that I was not sufficiently motivated to keep quiet about it. But that's another story.

9. Peter Hartz, who designed these reforms, was Volkswagen's personnel director. There is a nice irony here in view of Volkswagen's implication in the major emissions scandal, which has cast a long shadow over German manufacturing.

10. Mini-jobs restricted workers to sixteen hours per week, at a standard monthly salary of 400 to 450 euros.

11. Poorer Greeks' money wages and pensions were increasing by something like 3.5 per cent, a large rise by European standards of the time, and the official inflation rate, they were told, was only 3 per cent. So their purchasing power must have been rising too. But it was not. The reason is that the inflation rate for poorer Greeks was much higher, around 9 per cent, but inflation for richer Greeks was . . . negative. Negative? Yes. If you had a mortgage on a mansion in Athens's northern suburbs, the large drop in interest rates caused by the practices of my fellow-traveller Franz and his colleagues meant that your living costs fell! So, during the first few years of the euro, the 'good times', the Greek grasshoppers were prospering while the ants struggled. By 2010 the grasshoppers had taken their loot out of the country without paying their taxes, and it was the ants who were called upon to bail out the bankrupt state and the bankrupt banks through pension cuts, wage cuts, cuts in their health services, etc.

12. Unnecessarily. A recession that Europeans did not have to have. Allowing Greece to default and restoring German and French banks to health the way that the Swedes and the Finns had done in 1992 (see Chapter 5, note 17) would have avoided this recession. See Chapter 7, section entitled 'Decentralized Europeanization. Or how to replace TINA with TATIANA' for examples of alternative policies to mindless austerity.

13. Data made available by the Bank of International Settlements.

14. The IMF had already developed the reputation of a ruthless bailiff, following the Third World debt crisis, the Latin American crisis and the South East Asian crisis. Ironically, at a time, in 2010, when its managing director, the infamous Dominique Strauss-Kahn, was trying to soften the IMF's image, Chancellor Merkel insisted it should be part of the troika. She needed it in order to convince her own members of parliament that the bailout's austerity conditions would be brutally imposed. Thus the IMF's makeover failed as it became embroiled in another sequence of 'rescues' that forced the weak to suffer that which they did not deserve.

15. Which was of course necessary given that the first bailout was always going to fail, being nothing more than the original Ponzi austerity scheme.

16. In the end Syriza did not win that election but came in a strong second. Its victory eventually came on 25 January 2015 in an election that I contested successfully and which resulted in my becoming Greece's minister of finance.

17. Seeing that the ECB was buying Greek bonds, the theory went, investors might have been encouraged to do so too.

18. This ploy might have worked except that M. Trichet, in a move of baffling folly, pre-announced the amount the ECB would spend on these purchases to counter the speculators. It was an open invitation to speculators to make money, as long as they could spend more money than the ECB was willing to. In Wild West terms, it was the equivalent of Clint Eastwood rolling up to the site of the showdown announcing to his opponent how many bullets he had left in his revolver. Then again, there is a simpler explanation as to why M. Trichet and the ECB did this: they only cared about making the French and German banks whole (by buying for them at full price the Greek government bonds whose value had crashed), with the story about striving to keep Greece in the money markets being only a poor excuse.

19. In the first Greek bailout, in May 2010, Europe's ridiculously hard line towards Greece was no to a haircut, no to debt relief, yes to a huge loan (€110 billion) with high interest rates. The only beneficiaries were of course the beneficiaries that the bailout had been designed to benefit: French and German banks. Once their losses were averted, Brussels and Frankfurt began to plan for the inevitable haircut, which would hit small Greek bondholders and tragically the Greek pension funds whose charters obliged them to hold their capital in Greek government bonds. So a second bailout, which included a haircut for the weak, was ratified fully by the spring of 2012. To contain the skyrocketing debt, bonds held in private hands were haircut substantially and twice – once in the spring of 2012 and once again in December 2012 – that time under the guise of a 'debt buyback'. In short, in 2012 Greece's private debt was cut in real value terms by 85 per cent. Except that the bankers and the ECB, which under Trichet had purchased more than €50 billion of Greece's public debt, were fully protected. The Greek state borrowed another €130 billion from which to infuse €50 billion into Greek banks and up to another €50 billion to pay back the ECB, which behaved like a hedge fund holdout. The only victims of the haircut were the small holders of Greek debt and pensioners, whose pension funds were effectively robbed of their capital base.

20. The first countries to violate the Maastricht Treaty rules were Germany and France, almost immediately after the euro was established. In particular, following the 2001 dot-com recession, Berlin had a choice between breaking the 3 per cent budget deficit limit, which was part of the Maastricht rules, or imposing harsh austerity upon the German economy. It opted for the former. Similarly with France a few months later.

21. Which were already issuing their own worthless IOUs with guarantees from the insolvent Greek state.

22. Through the so called Emergency Liquidity Assistance (ELA) programme of the ECB.

23. Between 2008 and 2010, when the banks' immediate needs were taken care of by the ever-generous taxpayers, the eurozone's debt-to-income ratio rose from 66.2 to 80 per cent. Then, between 2010 and 2014, austerity pushed the zone's debt above 91 per cent of GDP. However, in the countries where the greatest austerity was imposed, debt exploded. The following table tells the sad tale of Ponzi austerity.

Year	eurozone	Greece	Ireland	Portugal	Spain	Italy
2008	66.2%	105.4%	25%	68.3%	36.1%	103.6%
2010	80%	129.7%	64.4%	83.7%	54%	116.4%
2014	91%	175%	123%	129.7%	92.1%	130%

24. This is the 'moral hazard' argument, according to which the possibility of common debt would give each an incentive to indulge in loose living.

25. So Germany would bear around a quarter of the liability as its national income was a quarter of the eurozone's.

26. See Geithner (2014). In addition to his account of this incident in his book, Geithner had a lot more to say in a recorded interview with the *Financial Times*'s Peter Spiegel (published on Spiegel's blog: http://blogs.ft.com/brussels-blog/2014/11/11/draghis-ecb-management-the-leaked-geithner-files/) The former US treasury secretary is quoted as saying, referring to the said meeting, 'They turn to me in their meeting, they ask me for my views, my normal views which you'll find boringly familiar at this point, and a bunch of their ministers go walk out afterwards and say: "Who's Geithner to tell us what to do?" . . . That wasn't so great.'

27. Central banks do not literally print money on such occasions. Instead, every commercial bank has an account with its central bank (the Bank of America has such an account at the Federal Reserve, Deutsche Bank has one at the European Central Bank, and so on). Instead of printing cash and handing it over to them, the central bank allows the commercial bank to draw money from its accounts with the central bank that the commercial bank never deposited there – something akin to an overdraft facility. In exchange, the commercial bank hands over to the central bank as collateral some asset – for example, a stack of mortgages or personal loans that the central bank can collect on if the commercial bank defaults or goes bankrupt. The central bank's hope is that the commercial bank will then lend this money to its customers (such as companies or families wishing to buy a house or a car) with the effect of stimulating the real economy.

28. Monti had an impressive record both as an economics professor and especially as the European Commission's commissioner for competition policy. In that role he famously clashed with behemoths like Microsoft and was acknowledged as a skilled and honest operator. However, his image was tainted once he came to be seen as Mrs Merkel's appointee to Italy's highest office despite the fact that, once in office, he acted in the interests of Italy and put up a major struggle at the European Council to bring about a proper banking union (see below, section entitled 'Monti's mutiny'). On a personal note, Mario Monti and I have since discovered a great deal of common ground and a mutual appreciation of our perspectives on what Europe must do to overcome its crisis.

29. Ireland was felled by its banks and property developers. The tsunami of capital from Germany's banks was flowing straight into Ireland's commercial banks, which were then lending it on to developers. White elephants in Dublin's financial district, row upon row of new blocks of flats in the middle of nowhere, and second and third mortgages were the outcome. With prices racing ahead creating a semblance of homeowner wealth, credit card use multiplied and a generalized consumer spending spree occurred. When the credit crunch spread from Wall Street and London, land prices collapsed, construction workers were laid off, mountainous debts went bad and the banks themselves, the Anglo-Irish Bank in particular, imploded. In a move that will remain in Irish annals as a stigma comparable to the potato famine, the Dublin government succumbed to ECB blackmail: make the German creditors of Ireland's commercial banks whole – even a bank that was closed down and thus is no longer systemically important for Ireland's financial sector – or else!

30. See Brecht, *The Threepenny Novel* (1989), in which the following exchange appears between two characters named McHeath and Peachum. McHeath says, 'Brute force is out of date – why send out murderers when one can employ bailiffs?' To which Peachum replies, 'Admittedly, murder is a last resort, the very last – but it is still useful.'

31. The differences between Greece and Ireland are instructive. Ireland had a tiny debt before 2008. Greece had a large one. The reason is simple: capital flow from the surplus countries was directed into the Greek state, which in turn passed it on to developers – those who built highways, 2004 Olympic sites, etc. In Ireland the same capital flow went directly into the banks, which then passed it on to the developers, bypassing the state. Thus, Irish public debt was tiny while private debt was gargantuan – the opposite case to that of Greece – but when the crisis hit, the result was the same: the Irish state took on the burden of private debt and collapsed. The Greek state just collapsed.

32. Of course, a few months later, on the last day of June 2015, the ECB shut down the entire Greek banking system to force our government into accepting the troika's bailout logic. It was the price we had to pay for refusing to let our central bank be blackmailed.

33. By purchasing its treasury bills and bonds.

34. Imagine what would have happened in 2008 in the United States if it were structured along the lines of the eurozone. The Nevadan banks would have had to be recapitalized by the state government of Nevada without help from the Fed and at a time when the state government would also be borrowing to fund increased unemployment and social security payments. The state government would have immediately lost access to money markets, become insolvent and thus caused the world's banking community to cut off all banks domiciled in Nevada from international markets. State and banks would have been in free fall. If, further, the state had been forced by Washington to accept a huge bailout loan from the federal government on condition of extreme austerity that would have shrunk Nevadans' incomes significantly, there would have been two outcomes: Nevada would have been well and truly finished, and Missouri or Mississippi or New Mexico would have been the next states to fall as jittery investors thought twice before lending to other weak state governments. This is precisely what happened to the eurozone, beginning of course with Greece.

35. In contrast to institutions like the EFSF, which, as we saw above, amplified financial shocks rather than absorbed them.

36. Which was later beefed up in an article entitled 'Banking union must be built on firm foundations', *Financial Times*, 12 May 2013.

37. The banking union that was agreed to in the end specified that when a bank needs capital injections, the first thing to happen is that the national government provides the capital needed to raise the bank's minimum capital ratio (T1) to 4.5 per cent of its assets. After that a series of haircuts must follow. First to have their hair cut are the shareholders and bond holders, followed by depositors with more than €100,000 in the bank. Only if these haircuts are not enough to render the bank solvent does the European Stability Mechanism (ESM) chip in with 80 per cent of the remaining funds needed, with the national government picking up the remaining 20 per cent of the tab.

38. As happened in Cyprus in 2013.

39. Noyer's point was simple. The ECB had lost control of interest rates. A profitable, creditworthy Italian or Spanish business had to borrow at huge interest rates, reflecting the Italian or Spanish state's woes. It was an admission that Europe's central bank had lost control of Europe's money and that Italian and Spanish businesses were facing an uphill struggle. See *'Verbindung zwischen Banken und Staaten muss durchtrennt werden,'* *Handelsblatt*, 18 July 2012, http://www.

handelsblatt.com/politik/konjunktur/christian-noyer-im-interview-verbindung-zwischen-banken-und-staaten-muss-durchtrennt-werden/6886472.html.

40. Speech by Mario Draghi, president of the European Central Bank, at the Global Investment Conference in London, 26 July 2012. See https://www.ecb.europa.eu/press/key/date/2012/html/sp120726.en.html.

41. Additionally, to placate Berlin, Mario Draghi pledged that the OMT would not be activated for countries that had not submitted to the strictures of the . . . troika. This was more draconian a stipulation than it first seems. No Italian or Spanish government would survive long if it surrendered to the invasive troika. Which meant that the OMT would only be activated if Italy or Spain were so far down the black hole of insolvency that their governing parties acquiesced in their loss of power.

42. As the interest rates of government bonds (the rates at which a government borrows) fall, commercial banks make less money from lending to the government. So, at least in theory, they have a greater incentive to lend to business instead. As commercial banks redirect money from lending to government to lending to business, the supply of money to the private sector increases, the price of that money falls – commercial interest rates decline – and, hey presto, business enjoys lower interest rates.

43. That is the creation of central bank money to be lent indirectly to member state governments – the absolution of what the Maastricht Treaty deemed the greatest of sins.

44. The fact that a few weeks earlier Syriza had been defeated in Greece's general election, allowing for another coalition government, which would remain in the troika's pocket, to be formed, gave further cause for optimism in Frankfurt and Brussels that the worst was over.

45. In the case of the Irish banks, the private bonds that they had purchased were uninsured. In the case of Greek state bonds, their buyers knew that these were Greek law contracts, meaning that they could be given a haircut by a future stressed Greek government. This is precisely why the interest rates were higher than in Germany. Higher risk, higher rewards. As long as the gamble paid off, the German bankers reaped benefits that they shared with no one. But when the gambles turned bad, as Irish banks and the Greek state failed, they demanded that the taxpayers of Greece and Ireland pay up as if they had bought insurance from them.

46. No government can legally impose a liability on Jill in order to bail out Jack without passing a suitable piece of legislation through parliament. In this case, the illegitimacy of the transfer was heightened by the fact that Jack was a foreign unsecured bond holder and Jill an Irish citizen who had never authorized her government to saddle her with a new debt (with associated cuts to benefits, wages and pensions, plus tax hikes) for his benefit.

47. The government tore up – 'retired' – the promissory notes once it took them back from the central bank.

48. As were of course Greek pension funds, except that no one really cared about the pensioners.

49. There is strong suspicion that Greek bankers lent the 10 per cent to one another.

50. See Germany's financial daily *Handelsblatt*, http://www.handelsblatt.com/downloads/8124832/1/stellungnahme-bundesbank_handelsblatt-online.pdf.

51. The OMT constituted an open invitation to bond dealers to test the ECB's resolve at a time of their choosing. It was a temporary fix bound to stop working when circumstances emboldened the bond dealers.

52. From an economic viewpoint, very low interest rates are only partly due to the OMT announcement and Mr Draghi's 'whatever it takes' statement. The latter pushed the interest rates on Italy's and Spain's debt down, but it was generalized austerity and the very low level of investment that pushed profit and growth rates down. An economy featuring low investment and no growth also results in low average profit rates. Recession, low profits and low returns to money – low interest rates – go together. So while OMT 'worked' to subdue the cost of servicing Italy's and Spain's public debt, it worked too well in an austere environment in that it caused a generalized deflation that kept the eurozone permanently stuck in recession.

53. See Keynes (1936), p. 183.

54. Except when QE pushed the yen or the dollar down, thus helping Japanese and American exporters mop up foreign demand, adding a beggar-thy-neighbour dimension to its effects.

55. This is why in its never-enacted OMT programme Mr Draghi had to introduce, as a condition, that the country whose bonds the ECB purchases must first be put into the straitjacket of a troika programme.

56. Directed and produced by Carol Reed and based on a Graham Greene novel, *The Third Man* was released in 1949.

57. 'But to my mind, though I am native here / And to the manner born, it is a custom / More honour'd in the breach than the observance.' *Hamlet*, William Shakespeare, 1602.

7 Back to the Future

1. The Golden Dawn Party, whose deputies sat in Greece's parliament immediately opposite the ministerial box, is often referred to as a neo-Nazi party. This is wrong. There is arguably nothing 'neo' in their Nazi ideology. They

worship Hitler, their symbol is a variant of the swastika, they dress like Nazis, they salute like Nazis. In short, they are fully fledged Nazis bereft of any pretence to a twenty-first-century makeover.

2. Georgia Xenou was the great-grandmother of my daughter, my first wife Margarita's grandmother.

3. By 1947, under the Truman Doctrine, the prosecution of the civil war by the West had been passed on from Britain to the United States. British troops were withdrawn and replaced by US military advisers. The injured Xenos's torture and murder are described in an eyewitness account published in Greek. The book is entitled *The Dead Brigade*, and its author was Constantine Papakonstantinou, whose *nom de guerre* was Captain Belas. See pp. 623–4 of volume 1 (1986, third edition 2002).

4. As mentioned in the Preface, I made this point in the press conference at the Federal Ministry of Finance in Berlin in February 2015, as part of a plea to the German finance minister and the German public to support the new Greek government's efforts to stem recession and root out the emergent Greek Nazi party.

5. After the end of the Great War, Eleftherios Venizelos, a pro-British anti-royalist republican, secured on behalf of Greece the right to administer the Anatolian coastal city of Smyrna (today's Ismir). However, soon after the Greek army took control of Smyrna, Venizelos's government collapsed and the new royalist government ordered the army to march on Ankara. Countless incensed patriotic Turks joined Kemal's army, and eventually he managed to push the Greek army into the sea. The Turks then proceed to 'cleanse' from the region millions of ethnic Greeks who had been living there since the time of Homer. In Greece that defeat, in 1922, is to this day known as the Catastrophe.

6. My references to Nazism as a serpent are due to the impression left upon a younger version of me by Ingmar Bergman's 1977 film *The Serpent's Egg* – a story highlighting the distorted pseudo-scientific imperatives behind the Nazi experiment. The title itself was borrowed from a line spoken by Brutus in Shakespeare's *Julius Caesar*: 'And therefore think him as a serpent's egg / Which hatch'd, would, as his kind grow mischievous / And kill him in the shell' (Act 2, Scene 1).

7. By the time the Red Army entered Berlin's outskirts, only seven hundred men of the Charlemagne SS survived, fighting tooth and nail in defence of Hitler. In the last two days no more than thirty were still fighting in the centre of Berlin.

8. See Lipgens (1984), p. 72.

9. Ibid. p. 73. Try your luck with the rest of these quotes, also taken from Lipgens's book.

i. The solution to economic problems . . . with the eventual object of a European customs union and a free European market, a European clearing system and stable exchange rates in Europe, looking towards a European currency union.

ii. The results of excessive nationalism and territorial dismemberment are within the experience of all. There is only hope for peace by means of a process which on the one hand respects the inalienable fundamental patrimony of every nation but, on the other, moderates these and subordinates them to a continental policy . . . A European Union could not be subject to the variations of internal policy that are characteristic of liberal regimes.

iii. A new Europe: that is the point, and that is the task before us. It does not mean that Italians and Germans and all other nations of the European family are to change their spots and become unrecognizable to themselves or to one another from one day or one year to the next. It will be a new Europe because of the new inspiration and determining principle that will spring up among all these peoples . . . The problem of the hierarchy of states will no longer arise. At least in its usual form, once we have cut off the dragon's head; that is, the notion of state sovereignty. Moreover, this does not have to be done outright, but can be achieved indirectly, e.g. by creating interstate European bodies to look after certain common interests (exchange rates, communications, foreign trade, etc.).

iv. [To see this federation process through], all that is required of European states is that they be loyal, pro-European members of the community and cooperate willingly in its tasks . . . The object of European cooperation being to promote peace, security and welfare for all its peoples. (This comes from a well-received, at the time, policy document that recommended the need to 'put forward a European con-federal solution based on free cooperation among independent nations [culminating in uniting Europe] on a federal basis'.)

v. We must create a Europe that does not squander its blood and strength on internecine conflict, but forms a compact unity. In this way it will become richer, stronger and more civilized, and will recover its old place in the world . . . National tensions and petty jealousies will lose their meaning in a Europe freely organized on a federal basis. World political development consists inevitably in the formation of larger political and economic spheres.

vi. It is not very intelligent to imagine that in such a crowded house like that of Europe, a community of peoples can maintain different legal systems and different concepts of law for long.

vii. In my view a nation's conception of its own freedom must be harmonized with present-day facts and simple questions of efficiency and purpose . . . Our only requirement of European states is that they be sincere and enthusiastic members of Europe.

The authors are:

i. From a report submitted by Hans Frohwein in June 1943 to the Nazi Foreign Ministry's 'Europe Committee', entitled 'Basic Elements of a Plan for a New Europe'.

ii. Alberto De Stefani, Mussolini's first finance minister. De Stefani was dismissed two years after his appointment but remained a full member of the Grand Council of Fascism until the regime's collapse. This statement comes from 1941.

iii. Camillo Pellizzi, editor of *Civiltà Fascista*. The first paragraph is from an article entitled 'The Idea of Europe', the second from a letter by him to Ugoberto Alfassio-Grimaldi, 4 September 1943. Pellizzi was an academic who propagandized fascism and was elected to university chairs in the dubious fields of the history and doctrine of fascism (University of Messina, 1938) and the doctrines of the state (University of Florence, 1939) He survived the war's end to live the drab life of an academic sociologist.

iv. Cécile von Renthe-Fink, Nazi diplomat holding the rank of minister of state. In 1943, when the quoted statement was issued, together with Joachim von Ribbentrop, Hitler's foreign minister 1938–45, Renthe-Fink proposed the creation of a European confederacy. Under this scheme, Europe would use a single currency managed by a central bank based in Berlin. The proposed European economic and monetary union would be subject to common legislation on labour market policies and a free trade agreement. Interestingly, the greatest supporter of the von Ribbentrop–Renthe-Fink idea was Frenchman Pierre Laval. Laval was prime minister of Vichy, the Nazi vassal French state that Hitler created in the parts of France that he did not care to occupy. Pierre Laval was so keen to see France as part of a single-currency union with Germany that in a letter to Hitler he suggested including in it France's colonies so as to bring about an 'atmosphere of confidence' in the new, uniting Europe.

v. Vidkun Quisling, the notorious Norwegian Nazi prime minister of occupied Norway, whose name has become synonymous with 'collaborator'. After the war a Norwegian court convicted him of treason, war crimes and embezzlement. He was executed by firing squad in Oslo on 24 October 1945. He made this statement in 1942.

vi. Adolf Hitler, addressing the Reichstag, 1936.

vii. Joseph Goebbels, 1940.

10. This murder was the theme of Costa Gavras's film Z.

11. Leading to the red blanket of my childhood; see Preface.

12. The reason for this is simple: eliminate local competitors to the imported goods, using the local distribution networks in the process.

13. The official rate of inflation reflects the average price increases in a 'representative' citizen's goods and services 'basket'. But the representative citizen does not exist. Put differently, she is a figment of the statistician's imagination – a creature consuming parts of each good or service in proportion to the total expenditure on these goods or services in the economy. Meanwhile, the rich get richer, and the more they spend the more the official rate of inflation reflects the price inflation of the rich. For example, in an economy of falling interest rates and increasing rents, with the rich occupying increasingly opulent houses, housing costs appear to be falling in the official statistics. The pain poorer families face from increasing rents is bleached out of the statistics as the falling mortgage repayments of the rich grossly outweigh the rising rents of the poor.

14. The standard joke that 'when Bill Gates walks into a pub everyone becomes a millionaire *on average*' suffices to make the point that there is no such thing as an average or representative person and, moreover, when the average improves this may very well mean nothing good for the majority.

15. See Varoufakis (2013) 'The Serpent's Greek Lair' in the *Witte de Wit Review*, November, http://wdwreview.org/desks/the-serpents-greek-lair/.

16. The race card was thus added to misogyny: the vast majority of prostitutes in Greece were either native Greek or migrants from Eastern Europe.

17. In the end most of the women apprehended, tested and put on display were native Greek and drug dependent. See *RUINS*, a splendid documentary available with English subtitles at: https://www.youtube.com/watch?v=9zyEegBtC1Q.

18. Sweden's social democratic prime minister, in office between 1969 and 1976.

19. See the Chapter 3 section entitled 'That "goddamn Volcker", again'.

20. See the Chapter 3 section entitled 'A timeless beast' and, for a longer treatise, Varoufakis (2011).

21. See the Chapter 6 section entitled 'Frenzy.'

22. Whatever happened to 'mutual advantage'? I suppose the same people who diminished industry and devalued labour through their financialization exploits felt the need to diminish the English language too.

23. In Homer's *Odyssey* (Book IX), the lotus was one of the many impediments that the vengeful gods put in Odysseus' path to prevent him and his men from returning home to Ithaca. It was, together with the Sirens' song, perhaps the most dastardly. Unlike the Cyclops or the menacing seas, enemies that brought out the best in the men, the lotus fruit made them soft and happy, unwilling to go back to sea to struggle towards their eventual homecoming. Odysseus had to resort to brute force to make his men return to the boats. He had to 'force them to be free', anticipating a famous expression coined by Jean-Jacques Rousseau.

24. See Klinkowstroem (1880).

25. On an aside, Metternich has an important Greek connection, one that resonates with various themes in this book. He was the greatest opponent of Greece's national liberation struggle, which began in 1821 and ended up with the establishment of the modern Greek nation state. His concern was that the creation of a Greek state would undermine the Ottoman empire – which it did – thus disturbing the balance of power between the Ottoman, Russian, Austro-Hungarian and British empires. Metternich persuaded the Russian tsar not to support the Greeks and even promised the British full repayment of Austrian debts if London were to support his policy of strangling the Greek revolution at birth. Lord Byron and other philhellenes directed many of their slings and arrows at Metternich. One wonders what Europe would be like today if Britain, Russia and France had not, in the end, altered their position by coming to the Greeks' aid in the decisive naval battle of Navarino in 1827.

26. See Triepel (1906), as quoted in Laughland (1997).

27. Henry Kissinger once wrote this about the effect of the way Germany was unified on its world outlook: 'The reason German statesmen were obsessed with naked power was that, in contrast to other nation-states, Germany did not possess any integrating philosophical framework. Bismarck's Reich was not a nation-state, it was an artifice, being foremost a greater Prussia whose principal purpose was to increase its own power . . . It was as if Germany had expended so much energy achieving nationhood that it had not had the time to develop a concept of its own national interest . . . The Kaiser wanted to conduct Weltpolitik without even defining the term or its relationship to the German national interest' (Kissinger, 1994, p. 137).

28. See Chapter 6, section entitled 'Whatever it takes?'

29. See 'More integration is still the right goal for Europe', by Karl Lamers and Wolfgang Schäuble, *Financial Times*, 31 August 2014. Note that the German finance minister chose to publish this piece as the debate on the eurozone's failure to shake off the euro crisis was flaring up again following a speech delivered at Jackson Hole by Mario Draghi, the ECB's president, in which he acknowledged the deflationary pressures upon Europe's common currency area and the role of universal austerity in fomenting them.

30. The Christian Democratic Union is the party of Chancellor Angela Merkel, previously led by Helmut Kohl, the pro-European leader who presided over German reunification and forged an alliance with President Mitterrand around the idea of creating a single currency: the euro.

31. See also another highly influential 1994 paper (again with Karl Lamers) entitled 'Überlegungen zur europäischen Politik'; visit https://www.cducsu.de/upload/schaeublelamers94.pdf.

32. Speech to the House of Commons, 16 November 1998 (Hansard, vol. 319, col. 685, from 7.20 p.m., debate topic: European Parliamentary Elections Bill).

33. Drs Schäuble and Lamers, in their previously quoted 2014 *Financial Times* article, suggest a euro congress or chamber comprising members of the European Parliament solely from the eurozone member states, so excluding British, Swedish and Hungarian members, whose countries do not share the euro. Other proponents of 'more Europe' have suggested that the euro chamber should consist of members of national parliaments in proportion to the countries' population size, so as to extend the existing sovereignty of national parliaments over fiscal matters and ultimately to legitimize the eurozone's fiscal overlord.

34. This is also the view of the so-called Glienicker Gruppe of German economists comprising Armin von Bogdandy, Christian Calliess, Henrik Enderlein, Marcel Fratzscher, Clemens Fuest, Franz C. Mayer, Daniela Schwarzer, Maximilian Steinbeis, Constanze Stelzenmüller, Jakob von Weizsäcker and Guntram Wolff. Another group, this time comprising French economists, also holds similar views. The Piketty Group consists of Thomas Piketty, Florence Autret, Antoine Bozio, Julia Cagé, Daniel Cohen, Anne-Laure Delatte, Brigitte Dormont, Guillaume Duval, Philippe Frémeaux, Bruno Palier, Thierry Pech, Jean Quatremer, Pierre Rosanvallon, Xavier Timbeau and Laurence Tubiana. For a critical comparative account of these two groups' views see Galbraith and Varoufakis (2014).

35. Recall Chapter 6's section entitled 'Despotism'.

36. See Habermas (1975).

37. As Germany was in 1919 with the Versailles Treaty; France, Greece and many others after 1939, or Europe's periphery currently under the troika's watchful eyes.

38. Recall the Preface.

39. Golden Dawn increased its seats from seventeen to eighteen in the three-hundred-member chamber, retained its status of third-largest party in parliament and tragically became the largest party to oppose the troika's failed economic programme, thus becoming the leading opponent of a programme that 80 per cent of Greeks disdain.

8 *Europe's Crisis, America's Future*

1. Geithner is now on public record (see the transcripts of the Geithner tapes released by Peter Spiegel in his *Financial Times* blog, http://blogs.ft.com

/brusselsblog/author/peterspiegel/). These are his exact words reporting what Europe's leaders told him: '"We're going to teach the Greeks a lesson. They are really terrible. They lied to us. They suck and they were profligate and took advantage of the whole basic thing and we're going to crush them." [That] was their basic attitude, all of them.' See also Geithner (2015).

2. Ibid.

3. Which can be now be found on my blog, yanisvaroufakis.eu or at the URL http://yanisvaroufakis.eu/2010/11/21/a-new-versailles-treaty-haunts-europe-and-this-time-it-is-not-just-me-thinking-so/.

4. See Chapter 5, section entitled 'Europhilia, Germanophobia and the French elites'.

5. See Keynes (1920).

6. See Note 3.

7. A period that I have labelled the era of the Global Minotaur (1971–2008); see Chapter 4 and Varoufakis (2011).

8. Interventions that were despicable in many ways, the manner in which they rewarded Wall Street bankers in particular. Nonetheless, they were interventions that succeeded in arresting the global free fall. See Varoufakis (2011) as well as the last chapter of the later editions (2013, 2015).

9. When the crisis hit America in 2008, investors found themselves in the paradoxical position of rushing to buy US treasury bills in large numbers. The economy that caused the crash benefited from the investors' rush to buy bonds issued by the country that also issues the world's reserve currency. A reminder of what Giscard d'Estaing described as America's exorbitant privilege (see Chapter 2).

10. For the complete argument, see Varoufakis (2011), and Chapter 9 of either the 2013 or 2015 edition.

11. Indeed, this process began in August 2015, as Chinese share and land prices lost a large portion of their value.

12. Recall Chapter 6, section entitled 'Ignorance'.

13. Geithner's apoplexy is writ large in his taped discussion published in Peter Spiegel's *Financial Times* blog; see http://blogs.ft.com/brusselsblog/2014/11/11/draghis-ecb-management-the-leaked-geithner-files/.

14. See http://www.treasury.gov/resource-centre/international/exchange-rate-policies/Documents/2013-10-30_FULL FX REPORT_FINAL.pdf.

15. See http://www.ft.com/intl/cms/s/0/821fbcba-41b1-11e3-b064-00144feabdc0.html?siteedition=uk&siteedition=intl#axzz2j5g4LpZX.

16. Defined as the difference between total receipts from exporting goods and services and total expenditure on imported goods and services.

17. Recall that the eurozone's income is much greater in 2015 than China's was in 2008. So a 9 per cent eurozone current account surplus now would be three times as great as China's was in 2008. Looking at actual percentages, China and the eurozone's current account surpluses are today about the same, at 2.1 per cent of income. In contrast, in 2008 China enjoyed a 10 per cent surplus whereas the eurozone registered a small deficit.

18. For example, success in pushing Europe's current account surplus to such heights will also boost the euro's exchange rate, causing exports to drop.

19. The reader will, I hope, understand my appreciation of American pragmatism on these matters. US officials and commentators have the capacity to agree with 'lefties' like this author when the issues boil down to simple matters of logic. Recently I have noticed Democrats and Republicans alike agreeing with me on these issues without much hesitation. So far I have been quoting New Dealers and Democrats like Geithner and Lew. Here is what Professor Martin Feldstein, a Republican, had to say about the construction of the eurozone back in 1992: 'If a country or region has no power to devalue, and if it is not the beneficiary of a system of fiscal equalization, then there is nothing to stop it suffering a process of cumulative and terminal decline leading, in the end, to emigration as the only alternative to poverty or starvation.' Quoted in Godley (1992).

20. At the 41st Forum of the European House – Ambrosetti, 5 September 2015, Lake Como.

21. See Evans-Pritchard (1937).

22. *Guardian*, 19 July 2013; see http://www.theguardian.com/commentis-free/2013/jul/19/we-germans-dont-want-german-europe?INTCMP=SRCH.

23. John Maynard Keynes argued that blind commitment to rules and contracts is the real parent of revolution. In his *Tract on Monetary Reform* (p. 68) he had this to say: 'When . . . we enter the realm of State action, *everything* is to be considered and weighed on its merits. Changes in Death Duties, Income Tax, Land Tenure, Licensing, Slavery, and so on through all ages, have received the same denunciations from the absolutists of contract, who are the real parents of Revolution.'

24. I was told that the basic parameters of the 'programme' were non-negotiable but that we could implement them with 'maximum flexibility'. Which sounded almost OK, until I realized that 'maximum flexibility' boiled down to a choice between cutting child benefits and reducing the minimum pension. Or having enough leeway to regulate how much yoghurt goes into an ounce of tzatziki.

Afterword: From Dissonance to Harmony

1. Leonard Schapiro (1900–83) was an eminent student of Soviet communism and professor at the London School of Economics.

2. Quoted in Connolly (1995), p. xvi.

Acknowledgements

1. Strictly speaking, the Syriza government survived, with Prime Minister Tsipras and the majority of ministers still in place. However, the government was forced to overthrow itself – to abandon its most cherished principles – as the price of staying in office. It was a price I was not prepared to pay.

Appendix: A Modest Proposal

1. For a member state whose debt-to-GDP ratio is 90 per cent of GDP, the ratio of its debt that qualifies as MCD is two-thirds. Thus, when a bond with a face value of say €1 billion matures, two-thirds of this (€667 million) will be paid (redeemed) by the ECB with money raised by the ECB itself from money markets through the issue of ECB bonds.

2. Any more than a personal debit card can be used for credit.

3. Article 20 (TEU) and Articles 326–334 (TFEU) provide that: 'Enhanced cooperation should aim to further the objectives of the Union, protect its interests and reinforce its integration process. Such cooperation should be open at any time to all Member States. The decision authorizing enhanced cooperation should be adopted by the Council as a last resort, when it has established that the objectives of such cooperation cannot be attained within a reasonable period by the Union as a whole, and provided that at least nine Member States participate in it.' Council approval of an enhanced cooperation procedure may be unanimous or by qualified majority.

Index

penguin.co.uk/vintage